D0712527

SOCIALISM
and the LITERARY ARTISTRY
of WILLIAM MORRIS

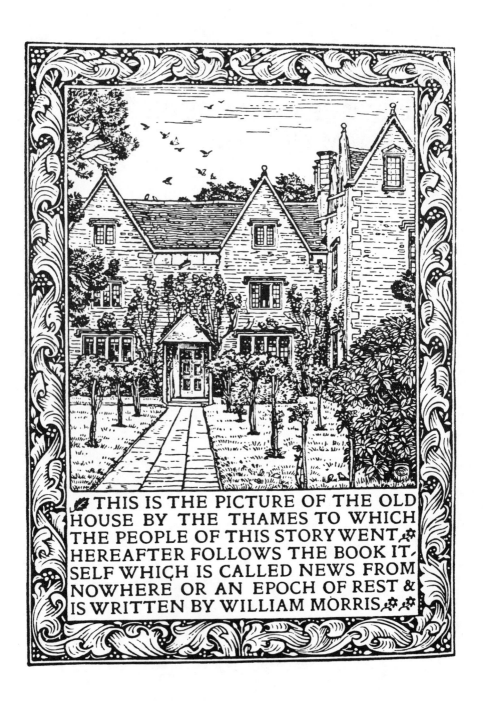

THIS IS THE PICTURE OF THE OLD
HOUSE BY THE THAMES TO WHICH
THE PEOPLE OF THIS STORY WENT.
HEREAFTER FOLLOWS THE BOOK IT-
SELF WHICH IS CALLED NEWS FROM
NOWHERE OR AN EPOCH OF REST &
IS WRITTEN BY WILLIAM MORRIS.

SOCIALISM
and the LITERARY ARTISTRY
of WILLIAM MORRIS───────

Edited by FLORENCE S. BOOS
and CAROLE G. SILVER

UNIVERSITY of MISSOURI PRESS
COLUMBIA and LONDON

Library of Congress Cataloging-in-Publication Data

Socialism and the literary artistry of William Morris / edited by
    Carole G. Silver and Florence S. Boos
        p.   cm.
    ISBN 0–8262–0725–1 (alk. paper)
    1. Morris, William, 1834–1896—Criticism and interpretation.
2. Socialism and literature. I. Silver, Carole G. II. Boos,
Florence Saunders, 1943–.
PR5087.S6S63   1989
821'.8—dc19   89–4834
                                                     CIP

∞™ This paper meets the requirements of the
American National Standard for Permanence of Paper
for Printed Library Materials, Z39.48, 1984.

Designer: Kimberly Kramer
Typesetter: Connell-Zeko Type & Graphics
Printer: Thomson-Shore, Inc.
Binder: Thomson-Shore, Inc.
Type face: Times Roman

5 4 3 2 1   94 93 92 91 90

For JOSEPH RIGGS DUNLAP

CONTENTS

SOCIALISM
and the LITERARY ARTISTRY
of WILLIAM MORRIS

FLORENCE S. BOOS

Introduction

A Dream of John Ball and *News from Nowhere* are only the best known of William Morris's many efforts to realize an ideal of humane and genuinely "popular" socialist art. As a restless liberal in 1878, he had written that "art so sickens under selfishness and luxury, that she will not live thus isolated and exclusive."[1] As a disaffected member of Hyndman's Social Democratic Federation, he published the first version of *Chants for Socialists* in 1884, the year he joined with Andreas Scheu, Friedrich Engels, Eleanor Marx, and other SDF dissidents to found the new Socialist League. During his time as editor of *Commonweal,* the League's newspaper from 1885 through 1889, he also published the following works in its pages:

"The Pilgrims of Hope" (1885, in *Commonweal*), a narrative poem based on the Paris Commune;

A Dream of John Ball (1886, in *Commonweal*), his evocation of the Peasant Uprising of 1381;

The House of the Wolfings (1888) and *The Roots of the Mountains* (1889), idealized reconstructions of early medieval tribal and communal life; and

News from Nowhere (1890, in *Commonweal*), the "romance" of utopian anticipation that is probably his most widely read work.

In seven years of intense political activity, Morris also prepared several thousand editorials and short "political notes" for *Commonweal;* kept a "Socialist Diary" in the early months of 1887; wrote the comedy *Nupkins Awakened, or the Tables Turned* for performance by the League the same year; co-authored, again for *Commonweal,* twenty-one articles with Ernest Belfort Bax, which later appeared in revised form as the book *Socialism: Its Growth and Outcome* (1893); and drafted scores of other essays on labor and art, collected in *Hopes and Fears for Art* (1882), *Signs of Change* (1888; later reprinted in volumes 22 and 23 of the *Collected Works*), May Morris's two-volume collection *William Morris: Artist, Writer, Socialist* (1936), and Eugene LeMire's anthology *The Unpublished Lectures of William Morris* (1969).

1. "The Lesser Arts," William Morris, in *The Collected Works of William Morris,* ed. May Morris, 24 vols. (London: Longmans, 1910–1915), 22:25; hereafter abbreviated as *CW.*

1

Despite the range and variety of Morris's socialist writings, two classes of critics have often dismissed them as irrelevant, naive, or worse. Apolitical commentators—some of them ardent admirers of his other accomplishments—have simply rejected much of his literature of the "Social Revolution" out of hand. Leftist critics, on the other hand, have often adopted a tone that might be called more-"scientific"-than-thou, and dismissed his socialist writings as a variety of bourgeois escapism at worst, and romantic anarchism at best. Morris intensely disliked the Victorian moralism and conventional realism of his time, and there is undeniably something lyrically counterfactual about all his work, including the socialist writings, for he strove throughout his life to blend psychologically liberating qualities of romanticism—subtle enjoyment of a kinetic beauty, and the restorative power of fluidity and fullness—with a growing respect for the quickening powers of human solidarity in sorrow and happiness, failure and success. More than his "scientific" critics, Morris also sensed—correctly—that the socialist commonwealth is a regulative ideal, a communitarian variant, in fact, of Kant's more openly counterfactual "realm of ends," and a visionary limit of the world as we know it.

Others have shared this vision, of course. In his 1976 postscript to *William Morris: Romantic to Revolutionary,* E. P. Thompson praised Morris's ability to create "Utopia's proper and new-found space: *the education of desire.*"[2] Marx himself was an ardent admirer of Greek and Shakespearean tragedy and German poetry who envisioned a "richness of *human* sensibility (a musical ear, an eye for beauty of form—in short, *senses* capable of human gratifications . . . ," and remarked that "the world has long dreamed of something of which it only has to become conscious in order to possess it in actuality."[3] Such appeals did not originate with Marx or end with Morris, for they are the essence of socialist humanism, and will survive its many distortions and betrayals. In "Marxism and Historicism," Frederick Jameson also appealed to such millenarian ideals when he summoned the past and a "Utopian future" to "judge" the present:

> The past will itself become an active agent . . . and . . . come before us as a radically different life form which rises up to call our own form of life into question and to pass judgment on us, and through us, on the social formation in which we exist. . . . This is the final reason why Marxism is not, in the current sense, a "place of truth," . . . only the Utopian future is a place of truth in this sense, and the privilege of . . . the present lies not in its possession [i.e., of the "truth"], but . . . in the rigorous judgment it may be felt to pass on us.[4]

2. E. P. Thompson, *William Morris: Romantic to Revolutionary,* 2d ed. (New York: Pantheon, 1978), 791.
3. Karl Marx to Arnold Ruge, May 1843, in *Writings of the Young Marx on Philosophy and Society,* ed. and trans. Loyd D. Easton and Kurt H. Guddat (New York: International, 1967), 214–15.
4. Frederick Jameson, "Marxism and Historicism," *New Literary History* 11 (1979): 70–71.

Such "judgment[s]" especially informed Morris's historical meditations, in which he blended ideals of past-in-future and future-in-past in complex ways. Recall again, for example, the famous exchange that concludes *News from Nowhere*. Ellen, in the "present" of the twenty-first century, tells "Guest" (Morris) to "Go back again, now you have seen us, and your outward eyes have learned that in spite of all the infallible maxims of your day there is yet a time of rest in store for the world, when mastery has changed into fellowship—but not before." Guest replies: "Yes, surely! and if others can see it as I have seen it, then it may be called a vision rather than a dream."[5]

Morris's utopian communism also reflected a mature and unillusioned appraisal of the nature of art in an exploitive society: once, for example, he closed a letter to a cautious social democrat with a wry but cheerfully blunt denunciation of "the Monopolists and their parasites—of which I am one."[6] He clearly saw in recorded and unrecorded history unending patterns of injustice and repression, and strongly believed that much serious art is inherently tragic. Among his longer works, *The Roots of the Mountains* and *News from Nowhere* are more "utopian" (meliorative; hopeful), while "The Pilgrims of Hope" and *The House of the Wolfings,* by contrast, are more "tragic." *A Dream of John Ball* is a complex and poignant mixture of the two: witness, for example, the priest's lovely final sermon, which modulates vindication of the doomed uprising into a kind of plagal cadence:

> Yea, forsooth, once again I saw as of old, the great treading down the little, and the strong beating down the weak, and cruel men fearing not, and kind men daring not, and wise men caring not; and the saints in heaven forbearing and yet bidding me not to forbear; forsooth I know once more that he who doeth well in fellowship, and because of fellowship, shall not fail though he seem to fail to-day, but in days hereafter shall he and his work yet be alive, and men be helpen by them to strive again and yet again; and yet indeed even that was little, since, forsooth, to strive was my pleasure and my life. . . .
>
> Therefore, I tell you that the proud, despiteous rich man, though he knoweth it not, is in hell already, because he hath no fellow; and he that hath so hardy a heart that in sorrow he thinketh of fellowship, his sorrow is soon but a story of sorrow.[7]

Not "escapism" but clear-sighted realism prompted Morris to look beyond the nineteenth century for the historical ironies and contrasts he sought to portray.

The aesthetic qualities and stoic historicism of Morris's socialist writings also refined forms of sensibility and awareness that had been present in his poetry

5. *CW,* 16:211.

6. Letter to James Mavor, *The Collected Letters of William Morris,* ed. Norman Kelvin, 2 vols. (Princeton: Princeton University Press, 1987), vol. 2, pt. 2 (1885–1888), 644.

7. *CW,* 16:233, 231.

from the first. His first major work, *The Defence of Guenevere* (1858), strained against the conventions of a romantic "medievalism" largely accepted by his predecessors and contemporaries (de la Motte-Fouqué, Scott, Tennyson, Rossetti); a similar ambivalence toward conventional heroism is also manifest in *The Life and Death of Jason,* in which the chief argonaut never reconciles his inconsistent desires for simple life and heroic reputation. Closer prototypes of Morris's later communist literature also appear in *The Earthly Paradise* (1870–1871), whose complex narrative texture blends the tales of several cultures and centuries in a communal vindication of human desire, effort, and loss. The tales are not narrated by a single "objective" author, but by a chorus of medieval speakers; their complex patterns of mutual empathy and recognition are reflected in the work's complexly echeloned frame-structure, simpler versions of which appear in *A Dream of John Ball, News from Nowhere,* and "The Pilgrims of Hope." *The Earthly Paradise*'s narrators are painfully aware of the heedless brutality of "great" historical events, and conscious also that they can only struggle to understand such events, admire those who have struggled well, and envision possibilities for future tranquility.

At some point, moreover, between his work on *The Earthly Paradise* and his visit to Iceland (1871–1873), Morris began to take personal comfort in a paradoxical, near-mystical belief in isolated instances of selfless action, as continuing sources of strength and solace, and to see such lost epiphanies, in effect, as a form of secular redemption. His curiously eloquent tribute to the doomed hero of his joint translation (with Eiríkur Magnússon) of the *Grettissaga,* for example ("Nay with the dead I deal not; this man lives"), anticipates not only his later, more serious eulogy of John Ball, but also the redemptive rhetoric of still later and more obvious resurrection myths:

> I dreamed I saw Joe Hill last night, / Alive as you and me. . . .
> Says I, "But Joe, you're ten years dead" / "I never died," says he.

Finally, Morris's socialist poems and other writings are distinguished most sharply from the hortatory prose of other well-known Victorian polemicists (not only Arnold and Ruskin, but also Marx and Engels), by their personal speaking voice. When he turned to a socialist audience of people who shared, or at least recognized, the goals he himself embraced, Morris's voice naturally assumed the infelt "we" and "you" of John Ball's "fellowship." The resulting straightforward speech is both resonant and intimate, and the mixture itself adds urgency and beauty to its rhythms:

> Art is long and life is short; let us at least do something before we die. . . . One
> man with an idea in his head is in danger of being considered a madman. . . . ten
> men sharing an idea begin to act, a hundred draw attention as fanatics, a thousand

and society begins to tremble, a hundred thousand and . . . the cause has victories tangible and real; and why only a hundred thousand? Why not a hundred million and peace upon the earth? You and I who agree together, it is we who have to answer that question.[8]

Similar instances of even-tempered encouragement and poignant doubt, historical distance and personal immediacy, suffuse all of Morris's socialist writings. They underlie their sensuous celebration of "The simple joys of the lovely earth";[9] their sense of compassion and conviction that shared effort and perception can be purposeful and renovative in themselves; their grief for failed revolutions, and ethical insistence on impassioned commitment; and finally, their persistent, equally impassioned hope that "we" may someday, after all, "answer that question." Far from "escapist," Morris's utopian communism was always tempered by many clear-eyed doubts, but sustained by the redemptive ideals he expressed in the climax of *A Dream of John Ball*:

> John Ball, be of good cheer. . . . thy name shall abide by the hope in those days to come. . . . by such grey light shall wise men and valiant souls see the remedy, and deal with it, a real thing that may be touched and handled, and no glory of the heavens to be worshipped from afar off.
> . . . it is for him that is lonely or in prison to dream of fellowship, but for him that is of a fellowship to do and not to dream.[10]

Gary Aho's *William Morris: A Reference Guide* lists 497 entries from the decade 1973–1982, and the last two decades have seen a sustained resurgence of interest in all aspects of Morris's work. The ten essays in this volume testify to the range of this interest.

The opening essay, Lawrence Lutchmansingh's "Archaeological Socialism: Utopia and Art in William Morris," provides a thorough analysis of Morris's deeply held views about the nature of work and its relation to artistic creation.

Five essays on *News from Nowhere* follow. Laura Donaldson's "Boffin in Paradise, or the Artistry of Reversal in *News from Nowhere*" argues that Morris's re-creation of a character from Dickens's *Our Mutual Friend* undercuts the social conventions of the nineteenth-century novel; Norman Talbot's "A Guest in the Future: *News from Nowhere*" considers Morris's subtle merging of frames and narrators. Lyman Sargent's "William Morris and the Anarchist

8. "Art under Plutocracy," *CW*, 16:191.
9. "The Society of the Future," in May Morris, *William Morris: Artist, Writer, Socialist*, 2 vols. (Oxford: Basil Blackwell, 1936), 2:454.
10. *CW*, 16:284–85, 234.

Tradition" compares the socialist commonwealths implicit in *Nupkins Awakened, A Dream of John Ball,* and *News from Nowhere,* and comments on the anarchist as well as socialist elements of Morris's utopian communism. Alex MacDonald's "Bellamy, Morris, and the Great Victorian Debate" surveys responses to Bellamy's work, and examines Morris's work as a countermodel to dystopian aspects of Bellamy's projections. Darko Suvin's "Counter-Projects: William Morris and the Science Fiction of the 1880s" identifies two examples of contemporary science fiction that included Morris as a *character,* and two other works, Edward Dering's *In the Light of the Twentieth Century* (1886) and Walter Besant's *The Inner House* (1888), whose structural features may have contributed to some aspects of Morris's plot.

Two essays consider other prose romances. Michael Holzman's "The Encouragement and Warning of History: William Morris's *A Dream of John Ball*" interprets Morris's work in the light of contemporary political conflicts, the histories available to him of the 1381 peasants' uprising, and his own parallel historical accounts, published in *Commonweal.* Carole Silver's "Socialism Internalized: The Last Romances of William Morris" defines several ways in which Morris's final, "escapist" prose romances continued to reflect essential elements of his socialist beliefs.

Finally, two essays discuss Morris's socialist poetry. Chris Waters's "Morris's 'Chants' and the Problems of Socialist Culture" offers the first sustained analysis of the substantial contemporary importance of Morris's socialist hymns, and examines the inherent limitations of literary and musical efforts by middle-class revolutionaries to speak for the working class. In "Narrative Design in *The Pilgrims of Hope*," I examine the complexities of the poem's narrative voice and feminist implications in the monologues spoken by the narrator's wife, and argue that the poem's political eloquence is strengthened, not weakened, by the elegiac subplot for which it is often criticized.

In order that this collection might serve as an introduction to its subject, I have also added a brief bibliography of complementary articles, book chapters, and dissertations. It is my hope that the collection as a whole reflects something of the freshness and innovation with which Morris managed to blend artistry and conviction in his socialist literary work.

LAWRENCE D. LUTCHMANSINGH⎯⎯⎯⎯⎯⎯⎯⎯⎯⎯⎯⎯⎯▬

Archaeological Socialism
Utopia and Art in William Morris

The awakening of the dead in those revolutions served the purpose of glorifying the
new struggles, not of parodying the old; of magnifying the given task in imagination,
not of fleeing from its solution in reality; of finding once more the spirit of
revolution, not of making its ghost walk again.

Marx, *The Eighteenth Brumaire of Louis Bonaparte* (1852)

In the recent emphasis upon the nature and the place of the utopian concept in
William Morris's work, three particular themes have been singled out: the
"moral realism" of his political position, the operation within it of "desire" and
imagination, and the degree to which his utopianism may be accommodated
within Marxism.[1] However, the significance of Morris's profound meditation on

1. See E. P. Thompson, "Postscript: 1976," in *William Morris: Romantic to Revolutionary*
(London: Merlin, 1977), 763-816, and Perry Anderson, ch. 6, "Utopias," in *Arguments within
English Marxism* (London: Verso, 1980), 157-75. The following are also relevant to this subject:
Eckart Bergmann, ch. 10, "Das irdische Paradies—Kunst als soziale Utopie," in *Die Präraffaeliten*
(Munchen: Heyne, 1980), 194-209; Paul Filmer, "The Literary Imagination and the Explanation of
Socio-Cultural Change in Modern Britain," *Archives Européens de Sociologie* 10, no. 2 (1969):
271-91; Michael Fisher, "The Literary Importance of E. P. Thompson's Marxism," *ELH* 50, no. 4
(Winter 1983): 104-25; Avery Gordon and Andrew Herman, "The Resurrection of Utopian
Socialism," *Review of Radical Political Economics* 15, no. 4 (Winter 1983), 104-25; Trevor Lloyd,
"How to Write a Utopia: William Morris's Medieval Interests and News from Nowhere," *Historical
Reflections* 2, no. 1 (Summer 1975): 89-108; Paul Meier, "The Necessity of Utopia," in *William
Morris: The Marxist Dreamer,* trans. F. Gubb (Hassocks, Sussex: Harvester Press, and Atlantic
Highlands, N.J.: Humanities Press, 1978), 1:260-75; Stanley Pierson, "William Morris: The
Marxist as Utopian," in *Marxism and the Origins of British Socialism* (Ithaca: Cornell University
Press, 1973), 75-89; Jeffrey L. Spear, ch. 4, "Morris: Revolution as Realised Romance," in
Dreams of an English Eden: Ruskin and His Tradition in Social Criticism (New York: Columbia
University Press, 1984), 201-39; Raymond Williams, *Politics and Letters: Interviews with New Left
Review* (London: Verso, 1981), 156-58; Williams, "Utopia and Science Fiction," in *Problems in
Materialism and Culture: Selected Essays* (London: Verso, 1981), 196-212; Williams, "William

the function of art in the history of human life and labor, and of its utopian prospects, has been relatively neglected, marginalized, or deposited among his *disjecta membra*. E. P. Thompson concluded in his monumental study of Morris that, "as a theorist of the arts—despite all his profound insight—he failed to construct a consistent system, and muddled his way around some central problems," so that his greatness lay elsewhere.[2] Perry Anderson was perhaps unduly suspicious of the apparent panaestheticism that would fill the "immense parenthesis" left by the withering away of history, politics, science, and education in Morris's quiescent utopia. The preferred line of development would have been toward a more positive engagement of history, capitalism, and the putative benefits of bourgeois civilization, in sum, toward an incremental social complexity. Hence, "there is no reason to think . . . that the practice of art could ever be reduced to a single existential standard, across or even within its different forms—Morris's theory of its springs, deriving from Ruskin, is plainly too narrow."[3] But the reduction is not Morris's. The specter of stasis that exercises Anderson stems partly from his somewhat foreshortened and limited construction of the aesthetic principle in Morris's utopian vision. Its desideratum of "a much greater variety of aesthetic production" as "a more credible horizon for an emancipated society," with its disconcerting echo of a consumer's cornucopia, would make of art as a humanizing praxis the mirror image of capitalism itself, a process that had already matured in Morris's day and earned his skepticism.[4]

In his own day too, Morris had despaired of his position being properly understood—so far had the process of capitalist deformation of human labor and the bourgeois misappropriation of the creative faculties penetrated the popular consciousness. The consequent ignorance of and callous insensitivity to art and history were to be demonstrated, for example, by the tragic record of the destruction and the so-called "restoration" of ancient monuments (to combat which, Morris, of course, founded the Society for the Protection of Ancient Buildings in 1877). When he learned of the alterations being made to St. Mark's in Venice in 1887, Morris wrote that he became "incoherent with rage," and lamented that "a few archaeologists, and archaeological Socialists, cannot resist civilization."[5] The startling conflation of archaeology and socialism here is emblematic of a complex series of synchronic forces in Morris's historical and artistic consciousness, at the heart of which lies a distinctive utopian moment; it is the purpose here to unravel at least part of that moment.

Morris, Questions of Work and Democracy," in Institute of Contemporary Arts, *William Morris Today* (London, 1984), 122–25; and Vincent Geoghegan, *Utopianism and Marxism* (London and New York: Methuen, 1987), 63–65.

2. Thompson, "Postscript: 1976," 717.

3. Anderson, "Utopias," 168.

4. Ibid.

5. "William Morris's Socialist Diary," ed. F. Boos, *History Workshop Journal* 13 (Spring 1982): 23.

A reciprocal inflection of the terms "archaeology" and "socialism" makes of the one something more than a mechanical curatorship of the artifacts and monuments of the past, and of the other something else than that reductive combination of scientism and economism that has made of Marxism "simply another industrial scheme" and a confirmation of "capitalist rationality."[6] So when Morris apostrophizes, "The History of Art! what is that history indeed but the history of the World, since it alone tells us of the deeds of the people, and what they thought of and hoped for? through this and this alone can we look upon times past as they really were and see them alive,"[7] he does not invoke a mere archival practice. He points, rather, to a concrete, pre-ideological history, in which we relive the very deeds by means of which those who have labored have at once met the demands of necessity and sustained their humanity in giving form to beauty and to the hope of what they might yet achieve. No sooner does Morris contemplate the art of the late Middle Ages and early Renaissance (when, he maintained, genuine popular art had reached its summit), than he leaps imaginatively into the future, from which vantage he redirects his historical vision to his own age. But what he finds is not encouraging. For when the people of the future look to the nineteenth century, "to see these days and seek for evidence in their handiwork of the lives of those who lived by their labour, they will be baulked and have to stop short." They will find scattered evidence in novels of middle-class notions of the workers and some record of their social and political activity, "but of the real story of their lives and the daily labour which was so great a part of them they will know nothing; a blank page will be the history of the popular art of the 19th century" (*AWS*, 2:386).

Here then, for Morris, lay the great scandal of history under capitalism—that for those who worked for its immense achievement time will have come to a stop; they will have, as it were, been erased from the record, and future generations will see in the historical annals an emptiness precisely where there should have been a body of work matching that of the past. It was from this vantage point that Morris in his socialist majority undertook his inquiry into the conjoined history of art and labor, to fix upon the moment of its greatest expression, but most of all, to ponder the fate of its victims. He thereby found one epoch of that history indicted by another, and his historical sense winced at the sheer incongruity of Homer then and Huxley now (*CW*, 23:280). His position anticipated a contemporary formulation of the dynamics of historical study, according to which "it is

6. Russell Jacoby, *Dialectic of Defeat: Contours of Western Marxism* (London and New York: Cambridge University Press, 1981), 33.

7. Morris, "Art and the People," in *William Morris: Artist, Writer, Socialist,* ed. May Morris (Oxford, 1936), 2:385, hereafter referred to as *AWS;* subsequent parenthetical in-text references are to this edition. See also Morris, "Making the Best of It," in *Collected Works,* ed. May Morris, 24 vols. (London: Longmans, 1910–1915), 22:81, hereafter referred to as *CW;* subsequent parenthetical in-text references are to this edition.

not we who sit in judgment on the past, but rather the past, the radical difference of other modes of production . . . which judges us, imposing the painful knowledge of what we are not, what we are no longer, what we are not yet."[8]

Among the thinkers whom Morris claimed as having provided the premise for this mode of historical thinking was Thomas More. In Morris's 1893 foreword to *Utopia* he claimed of More that "his imaginations [*sic*] of the past he needs must read into his political vision, together with his own experiences of his time and people," an intellectual maneuver which made it possible to reassess the book's value for socialists, whom Morris called upon "to look upon it as a link between the surviving Communism of the Middle Ages . . . and the hopeful and practical and progressive movement of today."[9] Indeed, the connection between More and modern times followed from the notion that "the past is not dead, but is living in us, and will be alive in the future which we are now helping to make" (*AWS*, 1:288). But to attempt to live that past in the present, and to contemplate its great works, meant doing so under a sort of interdiction, that is, in the ironic knowledge that such works are impossible under present conditions. Hence the necessity of an active but contrary memory which might shore up the past against the bleak present and pass it on to do its work of transforming the future. In that imperative lay the generating force of Morris's utopia.

When reviewing another utopia, Edward Bellamy's *Looking Backward*, in 1889, Morris suggested that every utopia is but "the expression of the temperament of its author" (*AWS*, 2:502), while elsewhere he defined the ideological aspect of those histories whose authors "were compelled to look on life through the spectacles thrust on them by the conventional morality of their times," or were simply "servile flatterers in the pay of the powers that were" (*CW*, 22:297). As against such falsifying accounts, Morris believed that the student of history could discern a "genuine life which exists in those written records of the past," and he even reclaimed a heuristic value for the "negative evidence" of the very lies told by some writers (*CW*, 22:297). The signal deficiency of Bellamy's temperament, "the unmixed modern one, unhistoric and unartistic," would not surprisingly lead to the purblind meliorism, the "economical semifatalism," and the anaesthetic system-mongering to be found in that author's book (*AWS*, 2:502, 504). The indispensable historical and artistic principles which Morris, for his part, demanded of utopian thinking, would look into the lives of those who made civilization, and upon the works—the arts, artifacts, and monuments—in which they did so.

This privileging of monuments and artifacts put to a more dramatic historical use and endowed with a greater explanatory power a practice which Carlyle and

---

8. Frederic Jameson, "Marxism and Historicism," *New Literary History* II, no. 1 (Autumn 1979): 70.
9. Morris, "Foreword to More's *Utopia*," *AWS*, 2:289–90.

Ruskin, among other writers, had previously employed. When examining the effects of industrialization on life and work in his 1829 essay, "Signs of the Times," Carlyle had written:

> On every hand, the living artisan is driven from his workshop, to make room for a speedier, inanimate one. The shuttle drops from the fingers of the weaver, and falls into iron fingers that ply it faster. The sailor furls his sail, and lays down his oar; and bids a strong, unwearied servant, on vaporous wings, bear him through the waters. [10]

It is therefore instructive to observe Carlyle, in another essay only a year later, "On History," turning his eye from the nineteenth century back to the long-forgotten predecessors of the artists and artisans being displaced by machinery:

> Which was the greatest innovator, which was the more important personage in man's history, he who first led armies over the alps, and gained the victories of Cannae and Thrasymene; or the nameless boor who first hammered out for himself an iron spade? . . . Laws themselves, political Constitutions, are not our Life, but only the house wherein our Life is led: nay they are but the bare walls of the house; all whose essential furniture, the inventions and traditions, the daily habits that regulate and support our existence, are the work not of Dracos and Hampdens, but of Phoenician mariners, of Italian masons and Saxon metallurgists, of philosophers, alchymists, prophets, and all the long-forgotten train of artists and artisans; who from the first have been joyfully teaching us how to think and how to act, how to rule over spiritual and over physical Nature. [11]

Morris echoes this spirit:

> When men say popes, kings, and emperors built such and such buildings, it is a mere way of speaking. You look in your history-books to see who built Westminster Abbey, who built St. Sophia at Constantinople, and they tell you Henry III, Justinian the Emperor. Did they? or rather, men like you and me, handicraftsmen, who have left no names behind them, nothing but their work? (*CW*, 22:7)

To the retrospection whereby Carlyle would rehabilitate the degraded worker Morris now gives a concrete and vital object: "For though history (so-called) has forgotten [the people], yet their work has not been forgotten, but has made another history—the history of Art" (*CW*, 22:32). They will have been actors on the stage of history not simply because the historian chooses to favor them with

10. Thomas Carlyle, "Signs of the Times," in *Thomas Carlyle: Selected Writings*, ed. A. Shelston (Harmondsworth, Middlesex: Penguin, 1971), 64.
11. Carlyle, "On History," in *Critical and Miscellaneous Essays* (London: Chapman and Hall, 1872), 2:256.

his backward gaze, but because they can truly be said to have made civilization. "History (so-called)," says Morris, "has remembered the kings and warriors, because they destroyed; Art has remembered the people, because they created" (*CW*, 22:32).

In view of the complex and perhaps ambivalent connection between Morris and Ruskin on this issue, it should be helpful to recall the latter's idealizing tribute to the worker:

> Ascending from the lowest to the highest, through every scale of human industry, that industry worthily followed, gives peace. Ask the labourer in the field, at the forge, or in the mine; ask the patient, delicate-fingered artisan, or the strong-armed, fiery-hearted worker in bronze, and in marble, and with colours of light; and not one of these, who are true workmen, will ever tell you that they have found the law of heaven an unkind one—that in the sweat of their face they should eat bread, till they return to the ground; nor that they ever found it an unrewarded obedience, if, indeed, it was rendered faithfully to the command—'Whatsoever thy hand findeth to do—do it with thy might.'[12]

Carlyle's positive acknowledgment of the worker's contribution to human progress and Ruskin's celebration of work's redemptive moral power were valuable to Morris only up to a point. For their Tory utopianism, complete with worker obedience until the grave and submission to "the law of heaven," still harbored an element of condescension, which would, in the end, render a genuine and revolutionary politics impossible.

A more fruitful lesson was to be derived from Ruskin's specific analysis of the condition of divided labor under industrialism, and a comparison with Morris proves useful here. In *The Stones of Venice* (1851–1853), Ruskin wrote:

> It is not truly speaking the labour that is divided; but the men:—Divided into mere segments of men—broken into small fragments and crumbs of life; so that all the little piece of intelligence that is left in a man is not enough to make a pin, or a nail, but exhausts itself in making the point of a pin or the head of a nail. (*Works*, 10:196)

But note Morris's quotation from Marx's *Capital* of 1883: "It is not only the labour that is divided, sub-divided and portioned out between divers men, it is the man himself who is cut up, and metamorphosed into the automatic spring of an exhaustive operation."[13] This understanding was what Morris had in mind when he claimed in his 1892 preface to a reprinting of "The Nature of Gothic" (the

12. John Ruskin, "Sesame and Lilies," in *The Works of John Ruskin,* ed. Edward Tyas Cook and Alexander Wedderburn (London: George Allen, 1903–1912), 17:175.
13. Morris's free translation from the French edition of *Capital,* vol. 1, ch. 13, section 5, cited in Thompson, *William Morris,* 38.

title of the chapter of Ruskin's work from which the preceding passage was taken) that Ruskin had found the key to the problem of industrial labor, which had eluded Robert Owen and Charles Fourier. That key was of an "ethical *and* political" nature, precisely that aspect of Ruskin's work "which has had the most enduring and beneficent effect on his contemporaries, and will have through them on succeeding generations" (*AWS,* 1:294–95).

Yet even at this point Morris expressed the reservation that Ruskin had been his guide only up to the time of his "consciousness of revolution" and his commitment to "practical Socialism" (*CW,* 23:279–80). For Ruskin had never satisfactorily resolved a contradiction that ran through his work and would have been noticed by Morris in a passage just a few sentences before the one already quoted concerning the division of labor. "The foundations of society," wrote Ruskin, "were never yet shaken as they are at this day. It is not that men are ill fed, but that they have no pleasure in the work by which they make their bread" (*Works,* 10:194). Confirmed as he was in the principle of the power of work to redeem base human nature, Ruskin showed a cold indifference to the condition of the rest of the worker's life. While acknowledging and elevating the principle of pleasure in work, Morris's problem would be one of substantiating his early intuition that the great works of the past sprang directly from a general "popular impulse," and that "their roots are founded in human nature" (*CW,* 22:81).

In his pre-socialist days, Morris apparently held the view that the privations of the artisan's life were a separate issue from the quality of his work, and that fine workmanship, equated variously with art, beauty, the instinct of humanity, the solace of life, and the reverence of nature, was the crown of existence.[14] These last metaphors contain a principle of cleavage, so that Morris could maintain that when art was at its finest it had no share in the slavery of the time and in the same breath attribute the decline of art to the fact that "the men of the Renaissance lent all their energies, consciously or unconsciously, to the severance of art from the daily lives of men."[15] Morris's search for a basis of totality merely yielded the proposition that art (and its synonyms) can be separated from everyday life only to their detriment (*CW,* 22:162).

Of course, a genuine totalization could only be conceived in a revolutionized society. Morris had to learn in his education as socialist and revolutionary how to translate the concept of totality from its approximate yet paradigmatic medieval embodiment—at once splendid and irretrievable—into a conscious utopian moment in the present. The value of More to Morris lay primarily in suggesting how the tragically interrupted history of art and labor might give rise to something more than mere nostalgia, might make the mute artifacts speak again

14. See "The Prospects of Architecture," *CW,* 22:125; "The Lesser Arts," *CW,* 22:17; "The Beauty of Life," *CW,* 22:53–57; and "Art and Beauty," *CW,* 22:158–59.
15. Morris, *CW,* 22:159 and 162.

and inspire a revolutionary hope. Morris accordingly reasoned that although Victorian artists were severed from cooperative (medieval) tradition and craft-practice, they were not irreparably severed, for through their newly won sense of living history they could be united with the past.

> So that if in the future that shall immediately follow on this present we may have to recur to ideas that today seem to belong to the past only, that will not be really a retracing of our steps, but rather a carrying on of progress from a point where we abandoned it a while ago. On that side of things, the side of art, we have not progressed; we have disappointed the hopes of the period just before the time of abandonment: have those hopes really perished, or have they merely lain dormant, abiding the time when we, or our sons, or our son's sons, should quicken them once more? (*CW*, 22:371)

The reconnection with an interrupted history, the poignant hope of a future restoration, and the accompanying revolutionary commitment—these were, for Morris, the necessary dialectical counterstatement to the hatred he felt toward the world about him.[16] If late medieval artistic production spoke of the free expression of the worker and the spirit of the people at large, the work of the nineteenth century showed precisely their absence (*CW*, 22:44). We have seen Morris pointing to the nullity at the heart of industrial production. The complex imagery of his numerous references to the era of capitalism evokes a lost and helpless people, in the iron grip of forces they can barely understand or discipline. Modern man uses his resources "blindly, foolishly, as one driven by mere fate," the victim of some "phantom," toiling "in a dream"; what passes for the popular art of the nineteenth century is "a blank space"; the people are oppressed by a "nightmare of riches and poverty"; the time since the Renaissance is one of "death or cataleptic sleep"; the present condition of life is a "murky smoked glass"; civilization is in a "blindness and hurry"; commercial competition is "bestial only"; society faces a "bankruptcy."[17]
This dizzying catalog takes us close to the inner movement of an imagination convulsed by what it perceives to be the great scandal at the heart of capitalist triumph: the systematic occlusion of the worker from the archaeological and historical record of modern times. But the orientation of this historical consciousness is an antinomian one, measuring the emptiness of the present moment against the achievement of the past, and looking back upon the latter only to be reminded of its subsequent undoing. "The sad truth," Morris observes, "is that

16. See "How I Became a Socialist," *CW*, 23:280.
17. Morris, "How We Live and How We Might Live," *CW*, 23:231; "Art and the People," *AWS*, 2:386 and 401; "The History of Pattern Designing," *CW*, 22:231; cited in Meier, *William Morris*, 272; "The Art of the People," *CW*, 44; "Art under Plutocracy," *CW*, 173; and "Individualism at the Royal Academy," *AWS*, 2:140.

there is no popular art today, no art which represents the feelings and aspirations of the people at large, as for example the buildings of the Middle Ages represented the feelings and aspirations of the people . . . of the period" (*AWS*, 2:391). But this sad and mild truth is for Morris only the surface register of a deeper, more sinister process:

> Just this is the end of competitive commerce, the getting people to live and breed in order that they may toil and go on living and breeding and by their toil produce a profit for certain people who call themselves masters: other things may be good, says this gospel, but this thing is necessary, that workmen should live and breed to produce a profit for their masters: this makes the true greatness of a country, this is prosperity, this is civilization.[18]

Morris's utopian reflection is thus located squarely upon the desperate contestation of power in the bourgeois era. If, then, "the fundamental failure of the utopian socialists for Marx and Engels is the lack of a concept of class struggle," Morris must be acknowledged as having developed the concept with a force and originality unique in the utopian socialist tradition.[19] And the effectiveness of his achievement is in part predisposed by his simultaneous use of both a restitutive and debunking analytic, or of what Jameson terms the "twin, irreconcilable characteristics, that of demystification and that of an essential restoration of access."[20]

The superordinate place which Morris accords to medieval art and the centrality of the aesthetic in his analysis have ironically contributed to the underestimation of his utopian vision. This probably began with Engels's sneering reference to Morris in 1886 as "a settled sentimental Socialist," and his dismissal of him and some other leaders of the Socialist League as "faddists and emotional socialists."[21] Medievalism itself has had an interesting place in the Marxist tradition. As an instance, Morris's general position was closely and perhaps surprisingly echoed by George Lukács in 1911:

18. *AWS*, 2:396. Note also the following: "The basis of all change must be, as it has always been, the antagonism of classes. . . . Commercialism, competition, has sown the wind recklessly, and must reap the whirlwind: it has created the proletariat for its own interest, and its creation will and must destroy it: there is no other force which can do so." From a letter of October 1883, in *The Letters of William Morris to His Family and Friends*, ed. Philip Henderson (London: Longmans, 1978), 190 (hereafter referred to as *Letters*). See also "True and False Society," *CW*, 33:215–37.

19. Douglas Kellner and Harry O'Hara, "Utopia and Marxism in Ernst Bloch," *New German Critique* 9 (Fall 1976): 29.

20. Frederic Jameson, *Marxism and Form: Twentieth-Century Dialectical Theories of Literature* (Princeton: Princeton University Press, 1971), 120.

21. Frederich Engels, Paul and Laura Lafargue, *Correspondence, 1868–1886* (Moscow: Foreign Languages Publishing House, 1959), 1:370, and William Otto Henderson, *The Life of Friedrich Engels* (London: Cass, 1976), 2:681.

The system of socialism and its view of the world, Marxism, form a systematic unity—perhaps the most unrelenting and rigorous synthesis since medieval Catholicism. When the time comes to give it an artistic expression, this will necessarily take a form as severe and rigorous as the genuine art of the Middle Ages (Giotto, Dante), and not that of the purely individual art, pushing individualism to the extreme, which is produced in our own times.[22]

According to Max Weber, "one thing became evident to Lukács when he looked at the paintings of Cimabue . . . and this was that culture can only exist in conjunction with collectivist values."[23] Marx himself gave to the proposition that "different kinds of spiritual production correspond to the capitalist mode of production and to the mode of production of the Middle Ages" the corollary that "capitalist production is hostile to certain branches of spiritual production, for example, art and poetry."[24] In the British Romantic tradition, too, from Cobbett to Ruskin, medievalism played a central role.[25] But it was Morris above all who redirected this originally conservative and nostalgic impulse toward a revolutionary heuristic purpose and incorporated its historical force into a dynamic utopian vision.

Morris singled out as a most telling historical fact of the Middle Ages the new lease of freedom it gave to the workers after the slavery of Greece and Rome. "In the earlier days the workman had nought to do but grind through his day's work, stick tightly to his gauge lest he be beaten or starved . . . but now he is rising under the load of contempt that crushed him, and could do something that people would stop to look at no less than the more intellectual work of his better-born fellow."[26] Under the new conditions of life and labor, "whatever a man thought of that he might bring to light by the labour of his hands. . . . Whatever a man had thought in him of any kind, and skill in him of any kind to express it, he was deemed good enough to be used for his own pleasure and the pleasure of his fellows" (*CW*, 22:188). And the necessary adjunct to this was that the work thus produced expressed the spirit of the people at large.

Morris saw in the late Middle Ages the summit of popular art. Even before his socialist "conversion" he had drawn out of Carlyle's and Ruskin's general

22. G. Lukács, cited in Michael Löwy, *George Lukács—From Romanticism to Bolshevism*, trans. Patrick Camiller (London: New Left Books, 1979), 96.

23. Cited in Löwy, *George Lukács*, 96.

24. Karl Marx, "Theories of Surplus Value," in *Marx and Engels on Literature and Art*, ed. Lee Baxandall and Stefan Morawski (Moscow: Progress Publishers, 1976), 140–41.

25. See Charles H. Kegel, "Medieval-Modern Contrasts Used for a Social Purpose in the Work of William Cobbett, Robert Southey, A. Welby Pugin, Thomas Carlyle, John Ruskin, and William Morris" (Ph.D. diss., Michigan State University, 1955), and A. Chandler, *A Dream of Order: The Medieval Ideal in Nineteenth-Century English Literature* (London: Routledge and Kegan Paul, 1971).

26. *CW*, 22:229. See also William Morris and E. Belfort Bax, *Socialism: Its Growth and Outcome* (London: Swan Sonnenschein, 1893), 55–56.

recuperation of common labor the more specific consequence that that labor, under certain historical conditions, would manifest the popular consciousness. This was the reverse of the modern practice whereby "fine" art is produced by an exclusive and specially skilled group. To the question, Who produced the great medieval works? Morris responds:

> The great architect, carefully kept for the purpose, and guarded from the common troubles of common men? By no means. Sometimes, perhaps it was the monk, the ploughman's brother; oftenest his other brother, the village carpenter, smith, mason, what not—"a common fellow," whose common everyday labour fashioned works that are today the wonder and despair of many a hard-working "cultivated" architect. . . . And I will assert, without fear of contradiction, that no human ingenuity can produce work such as this without pleasure being a third party to the brain that conceived and the hand that fashioned it. (*CW*, 22:41)

The principle of pleasure invoked here is not merely a libidinal mechanism. The dynamic of pleasure in medieval collective work is inconsistent with the kind of individuality and hierarchism that mark bourgeois art. "For least of all things could it abide to make for itself kings and tyrants: every man's hand and soul it used, the lowest as the highest, and in its bosom at least were all men free."[27] As if in anticipation of the later call for international working-class unity, medieval production even "cast down the partitions of race and religion. . . . Christian and Mussalman were made joyful by it; Kelt, Teuton, and Latin raised it up together; Persian, Tartar, and Arab gave and took its gifts from one another" (*CW*, 22:158).

Part of the explanation for the subsequent renunciation of the principle of pleasure in work lay, therefore, in the ascetic code promulgated by capitalism (*CW*, 22:42). Indeed, capitalist modes of production were not simply counteractive to art and poetry, as Marx alleged. In a deeper and more sinister sense, Morris added, they gave rise to an ascendant and privileged class who "have a sort of Manichean hatred of the world (I use the word in its proper sense, the home of man)," people who "must be both enemies of beauty and the slaves of

27. Morris, "The Prospects of Architecture," *CW*, 22:133. Cf. also the following from "The Lesser Arts," *CW*, 22:18: "For as was the land, such was the art of it while folk yet troubled themselves about such things; it strove little to impress people either by pomp or ingenuity; not unseldom it fell into commonplace, rarely it rose into majesty; yet was it never oppressive, never a slave's nightmare nor an insolent boast: and at its best it had an inventiveness, and individuality that grander styles have never overpassed: its best too, and that was in its very heart, was given as freely to the yeoman's house, and to the humble village church, as to the lord's palace or the mighty cathedral: never coarse, though often rude enough, sweet, natural and unaffected, an art of peasants rather than of merchant-princes or courtiers." It should be noted that no contradiction is entailed in Morris's use in this passage of the concept of "individuality." For he generally maintained that in the traditional situation, unlike the modern one, production was grounded in human needs, so that manifestations of "individuality" were accidental rather than final. See "Art and Its Producers," *CW*, 22:351–52.

necessity" (*Letters,* 150). And in wantonly destroying the monuments of the people's handiwork, they would not only manifest their blindness to beauty but also, at another level, erase from the archaeological record the effective presence of those by means of whose exertions they ascended in the first place.

A symptomatic but critical result of what Morris construes as an active "repression of the instinct for beauty" was that "the interest in the mere animal life of man has become impossible to be indulged in in its fulness by most civilized people."[28] He makes this development a central concern of his politics, for no matter how the systems of production and exchange are rearranged in the future, "we shall not be happy unless we live like good animals."[29] Civilization as it is takes away from us what barbarism gave in full measure. So, ironically, we must nourish our hope on the latter, but in so doing we sustain the utopia of Morris's dialectical imagination:

> For if we live in the present on such crumbs as we can pick up amidst the general waste and ruin, we live generously in the future; and one part of our pleasure in the ordinary life of today, the animal life I mean, and the goings on in field and flood and sky and the rest of it, comes from the fact that we see in them the elements of which the life of the future will be built up far more than of the thought of today, its literature, its so-called art, its so-called science.[30]

There has been little discussion of the issue of pleasure in mainstream Marxism. Russell Jacoby has even suggested that "Asceticism is the conceptual center of gravity of orthodox Marxism. . . . The object is to become an object; hence the hatred for the subjective" (p. 35). But Morris proposes that there is a specific politics of pleasure, and puts the issue at the center of his analysis of the history of art and labor. If there is in his demand for the restoration of unfettered and pleasurable work an explicit political dimension, there is, conversely, a repressed politics in the curtailment of such work. The restrictive assimilation of Morris's position to a "libidinal utopianism," therefore, runs the danger of slighting its political aspect, a move abetted by his apparent failure to define the mechanism of change and to provide the blueprint of the socialist future. But he sees the very concept of a libidinal domain as a historical product of the dissolution by capitalism of unified medieval work procedures. It is also an effect which Morris was concerned to expose and combat, especially in its reinvestment in the modern concept of leisure. He supposed labor as the satisfaction of strict necessity to be itself the site of pleasure, where people tested their skills,

28. Morris, "Art under Plutocracy," *CW,* 23:169–70. See also "How We Live and How We Might Live," *CW,* 22:17, and "The Society of the Future," *AWS,* 1:457.
29. Morris, "How Shall We Live Then," ed. Paul Meier, in "An Unpublished Lecture of William Morris, *International Review of Social History* 16 (1971): 228.
30. Ibid., 227.

expressed their thoughts and their hopes of yet greater mastery and pleasure, and prefigured to themselves a fuller life. Indeed, in Morris's view the healthy experience of pleasure and the discipline of imagination are indissolubly linked to their operation within the constraints of natural necessity and craft technique:

> Men whose hands were skilled in fashioning things could not help thinking the while, and soon found out their deft fingers could express some part of the tangle of their thoughts, and that this new pleasure hindered not their daily work, for in the very labour that they lived by lay the material in which their thought could be embodied; and thus, though they laboured, they laboured somewhat for their pleasure and uncompelled, and had conquered the curse of toil; and were men.[31]

The disarrangement of this pattern of work under industrialization results in manufactures bereft of human signs on the one hand, and on the other in works of "fine art" incomprehensible to the majority.

Industrial manufacture and "fine art" are the two main categories of production consequent to the disintegration of medieval crafts. The qualifications which Morris usually attaches to his use of the term "art" indicate an attempt to define simultaneously a practice which had almost ceased to exist in the present and its authentic, undivided medieval prototype. Today the division also expresses itself in the distinction between mental and manual labor, and within the plastic arts, between the "fine" and the "decorative" categories. In the integral culture of the Middle Ages, Morris claims,

> There was an intimate connexion between [the] two kinds of art; nay moreover . . . in those times when art flourished most, the higher and the lower kinds of art were divided by no hard and fast lines; the highest of the intellectual art had ornamental character in it and appealed to all men, and to all the faculties of a man; while the humblest of the ornamental art shared in the meaning and deep feeling of the intellectual; one melted into the other by scarce perceptible gradations; or to put it in other words, the best artist was a workman, the humblest workman was an artist.
> (*AWS*, 2:387)

To the question, What must our alternatives be when we lack such a consummation? Morris answers,

---

31. *CW*, 22:236. See also "Making the Best of It," *CW*, 22:81. In a critique of Adam Smith, Marx noted, "Smith has no inkling whatever that [the] overcoming of obstacles is in itself a liberating activity—and that, further, the external aims become stripped of the semblance of merely external natural urgencies, and become posited as aims which the individual himself posits—hence as self-realization, objectification of the subject, hence real freedom, whose action is, precisely, labour." *Grundrisse, Foundations of the Critique of Political Economy*, trans. M. Nicolaus (New York: Random, 1973), 611.

> One of two miseries must happen to us: either the necessary work of our lives must
> be carried out by a miserable set of helots for the benefit of a few lofty intellects; or
> if, as we ought to do, we determine to spread fairly the burden of the curse of labour
> over the whole community, yet there the burden will be, spoiling for each one of us a
> large part of [the] sacred gift of life. (*CW*, 22:358)

The socialist alternative, on the other hand, is to overthrow the present social
order, with its uncertain balance of asceticism and rampant consumerism, and
restore to labor the condition of freedom and creative possibility lost under
capitalism. This argument is less an illustration of Jameson's dictum that "the
persistent valorization of handicraft production [is one of the] desperate attempts
to think away the unthinkable reality of alienated labor" than the reverse.[32]
Morris's enshrinement of handicraft production (as well as his close study and
exceptional practice of it) entail a comprehensive analysis of its attendant
economic, social, and psychological conditions, and it has the effect precisely of
exposing the nullity and the alienating effect of industrial manufacture, and of
offering a glimpse of what disalienated labor might be under socialism.

The blindness of mainstream socialism to the necessity of a new basis of
artistic production stems not only from a preoccupation with economic and
political "realities," but equally from the marginalization of the aesthetic as a
secondary or "superstructural" effect. This latter move is based precisely upon
an uncritical acceptance of the bourgeois redefinition of art, however, and it
prevents socialists from seriously considering, as Morris puts it, "the due
relation of art to society" (*CW*, 22:256). Morris claims that socialism, "as an all-
embracing theory of life," must have an ethic and a religion, but also an
aesthetic, all of its own (*CW*, 22:255). Comparing such a proposition with the
prevailing "commercialist" one, he points out that,

> To the Socialist a house, a knife, a cup, a steam engine, or what not, anything . . .
> that is made by man and has form, must either be a work of art or destructive to art.
> The Commercialist, on the other hand, divides "manufactured articles" into those
> which are prepensely works of art, and are offered for sale in the market as such,
> and those which have no pretence and could have no pretence to artistic
> qualities. . . . The Commercialist sees that in the great mass of civilized human
> labour there is no pretence to art, and thinks that this is natural, inevitable, and on
> the whole desirable. The Socialist, on the contrary, sees in this obvious lack of art a
> *disease* peculiar to modern civilization and hurtful to humanity; and furthermore
> believes it to be a disease which can be remedied. (*CW*, 22:256)

But to this day socialists continue to remain in large measure indifferent to the
issue which was so central to Morris's political vision, apparently not realizing

---

32. Jameson, "Marxism and Historicism," 57.

that their indifference harbors another instance of condescension, that is, toward the products of the labor of those whom they would liberate.

In his later years, Morris hinted at an aspect of the problem of modern production and its "remedy," but did not develop it at any length. This was the question of the nature of human needs under the respective regimes of commercialism and socialism. In common with Ruskin and the other leaders of the Arts and Crafts Movement, Morris favored the principle of a few, beautifully designed furnishings for the home, for example, as against the notorious Victorian clutter, and applied it to production and consumption in general. "In looking forward toward my utopia of the arts," he says, "I do not conceive to myself of there being a very great quantity of art of any kind . . . apart from the purely intellectual arts" (*CW,* 22:295). The ideal stems partly from a concept of the purity of design and of beauty without ostentation. But it has a deeper basis, for when, as in the Middle Ages, "the mental qualities necessary to an artist, intelligence, fancy, imagination [have] not to go through the mill of the competitive market," and when craft (in keeping with the etymology of the word) manifests the power of the worker, both mental and manual, the thoughts and aspirations of the people, and the accumulated technical knowledge inherited across generations, then another, symbolic kind of beauty makes its appearance (*CW,* 23:175). This quality has largely disappeared from commercial production, geared as it is to profit rather than use, and regulated as it is by asceticism on one side and luxury on the other.

The distinction has recently been refined in Jean Baudrillard's proposition that the pre-capitalist artisan, whose work is not yet determined by the finality of value, "lives his work as a relation of symbolic exchange, abolishing the definition of himself as 'laborer' and the objects as 'product of his labor.'" In that world before the reign of productive finality, furthermore, "the work of art and to a certain extent the artisanal work bear in them the inscription of the loss of the finality of the subject and the object, the radical incompatibility of life and death, the play of ambivalence that the product of labor as such does not bear since it has inscribed in it only the finality of value."[33] On this basis, we may come closer to an understanding of how Morris conceives of capitalism as appropriating labor to its central purpose in a manner that simultaneously ensures the effacement of the worker's human presence from the historical and archaeological record.

It is, therefore, to this symbolic character of artisanal work, made into a mere thing of the past by the capitalist process, that Morris appeals as the historical guarantee of what production as well as consumption might again be. In the absence of such a symbolic dimension of experience, capitalist production

33. J. Baudrillard, *The Mirror of Production,* trans. M. Poster (St. Louis: Telos Press, 1975), 98–99.

generates the mechanical and insatiable psyche of modern consumerism, which Morris sees as being in irreconcilable conflict with his own ideals of aesthetic pleasure and meaningful simplicity. Observing how the visitors to an art gallery were momentarily impressed by a dull but costly Raphael or by an analyzed beefsteak in a glass case, but went blank before Holbein, Van Eyck, and Botticelli—who spoke to the mind through the power of the eye of "tales of the past, the present, and the future"—Morris reflected upon the spasmodic nature of the consumer mentality and the dynamic of its perpetual excitation (*AWS*, 2:464). As an alternative, he grounds aesthetic experience in certain basic biological and psychological needs, such as those which figure in his utopian romance, *News from Nowhere,* which would appear at first glance to be of a relatively "static" sort. Morris's position leads us to ask, by analogy, what measure of further complication we might expect in a socialist future when it comes to the pleasure of sexual experience, for example, or of eating.

This vision is at odds with Marx's ideal of human development through ever increasing consumption.[34] But a more specific and crucial point of difference would lie in Marx's supposition that "the potential for individual development [is] itself a historic potential that has only come into being under the civilizing influence of capitalism, and therefore could not feature among the needs of those living in earlier epochs."[35] To this, Morris has, in a sense, already responded to the effect that the history of art teaches otherwise; and that where they can be called such, the benefits of capitalist progress have accrued only to a minority, and at the horrific cost of the domination and brutalization of labor.

The thinker in the Marxist tradition whose utopian vision comes closest to Morris's may be Ernst Bloch (1885–1967). For Bloch, Marxism would be truest to its intention if it became the prototype of the utopian tendency of bringing to light and undertaking to actualize the possibilities of mankind which have been repressed or foreclosed by history. Such potentialities, lodged in the major human achievements of the past as hopes and anticipations, send signals, as it were, beyond the horizon of the actual, so that to look at the past is to imagine and to have intimations of the future consummation of human possibilities. The two lines of thinking supplement each other in some suggestive ways, but there are also some crucial points of divergence. The first concerns Bloch's universal proposition that "the permanence and greatness of major works of art consist precisely in their operation through a fulness of pre-semblance and of realms of utopian significance."[36] The restriction to "major" works of art would appear to be based upon the modern bourgeois definition, which Morris contested. But

---

34. Marx, *Grundrisse,* 408–9.

35. Kate Soper, *On Human Needs: Open and Closed Theories in a Marxist Perspective* (Brighton, Sussex: Harvester Press, and Atlantic Highlands, N.J.: Humanities Press, 1981), 99.

36. Ernst Bloch, "Utopia in Archetypes and Works of Art," in *A Philosophy of the Future,* trans. J. Cumming (New York: Herder and Herder, 1970), 94.

more significant is Bloch's underestimation of the issue of class and power in the history of production. For Morris, the historical trajectory that leads to the genuinely utopian auguries of the cathedrals and their ornamentation, for example, is quite another from the one that leads to the programmatically ugly and meretricious goods of industrial manufacture, or from the one in the classical world which produced wonders on the basis of slavery and according to an aesthetic of perfection so narrow as to suppress a great part of the worker's own fancy, imagination, and wit.[37]

But the most compelling point of argument, based as it is on Morris's study of the history and practice of the crafts, is that the evidence of the artifacts and monuments tells a different story; indeed, one epoch of production stands above others as a point of reference for the revolutionary utopian imagination. Further, the history of the people shows too many instances of domination of and brutal violence against them, as well as a pattern of inequitable distribution of privileges and sheer abortions of their creative power; such a history makes it impossible for all works to be redeemed by the same utopian resonance.

The differences raise the question of the conceptualization of the historical basis upon which, and of the concrete intellectual processes whereby, consciousness in the dystopian present is enabled to envisage a revolutionized society. After pointing to the untenability of Platonic recollection (anamnesis), Bloch states that "the *genuine* reference-and-return is towards what is still in the future, and therefore *what has not come to be in the past;* ultimately it is a return to the *still underived derivation* of all that happens."[38] Bloch grounds this "justification" exclusively in a forward-looking perspective, for its aim is a radical *novum* which has "nothing in common with a receptive renewal of anything that already has been, and *happened,* and is merely *lost.*"[39] On this basis, the history of art and labor becomes merely a vast museum of presentiments, valuable only or primarily for its surviving clues to the future. To a craftsman studying the cumulative skills inscribed in artifacts, to a historian convinced of the continuous rather than the supersessive growth of history, and to the utopian who would restore the condition of freedom which once prevailed and was catastrophically terminated, the principle of one-way progress valorized by Bloch is only of limited value.[40] For if "that which is authentic in the world is still in expectancy" and "waiting . . . to be realised through the labor of

37. *CW*, 22:209–11 and 217–19; "Of the Origins of Ornamental Art," in *The Unpublished Lectures of William Morris,* ed. Eugene D. Le Mire (Detroit: Wayne State University Press, 1969), 144–45; "Art and Labour," in Le Mire, *Lectures,* 96–97; and "Gothic Architecture," in *William Morris,* ed. G. D. H. Cole (London, 1948), 477–79.

38. Ernst Bloch, "Incipit Vita Nova," in *Man on his Own: Essays in the Philosophy of Religion,* trans. E. B. Ashton (New York: Herder and Herder, 1970), 83.

39. Ibid., 83.

40. See Morris, in Le Mire, *Lectures,* 87.

socialized men," we may once again risk a condescension to the past, this time in a mysticism of the future, and perhaps in a way that would render Morris's reliving and recuperation of the best of the past impossible.[41]

Morris's position is in partial agreement with the Blochian postulate that "existing man is not final man but only partial man—man as he has arrived so far," so that "his full human nature and his real humanity still lie ahead."[42] What Morris would add to this is the historical deduction that a token of that fulfillment has already been given to us. He thus claims that his vision of an authentic popular art, for example, "is not a mere dream of something which might have been," for "it has in many times and places solaced the lives of toiling men," indeed, "it has always been in advance of the apparent progress of the times that produced it" (*AWS*, 2:385). Where Bloch locates the principle of disjunction between mankind's incomplete present and its future fulfillment, Morris finds it already evident in those times and places in which the workers seize the opportunity of freedom and register in their production a condition of humanity in advance of the general historical condition. In order to answer the question of what socialist humanity would be, we have neither to grope in the dark nor to speculate upon the uncertain future. For when Morris bids us to "judge there-fore, how I must love the Art of the People," he speaks not only of a love whose historical coordinate is the compounded fatality by which capitalism vitiates mankind's movement toward its own fullness of being, as Bloch would have it, but also of its curtailment of a vivid revelation of that progress.

This study has attempted to suggest that "utopia" in Morris refers more to a phenomenology than to a topography. For it is a kind of dialectical posture to the world in this tragic interregnum of art and labor, by means of which we sustain the broken hopes of the past and the revolutionary expectation of their future recovery, and of which the society prefigured in *News from Nowhere* is an imaginative instance. If Bloch discerned the utopian in the "not-yet" and in the foretellings of human experience, Morris emphasizes that it is implicated in history, is the outcome of determinate conditions, and so is subject, as Baudrillard reminds us, to the inscription of both hope and frustration; Morris further suggests that this utopian truth, though awaiting a future realization, was nevertheless already circumstantiated in the past history of labor. For behold, the much-traduced worker was there first! And if it be claimed that those who labor and those who exploit that labor both have their utopian moments, it is only the former who hold in store the authentic and universal promise of mankind's future.

41. Jürgen Habermas, "Ernst Bloch—a Marxist Romantic," *Salmagundi* 10-11 (Fall 1969–Winter 1970): 319.
42. David Gross, "Ernst Bloch: The Dialectics of Hope," in *The Unknown Dimension: European Marxism since Lenin,* ed. Dick Howard and Karl Klare (New York and London: Basic Books, 1972), 117.

What it in fact meant to Morris to live this utopian moment is indicated in a letter of 1884 which he wrote to Emma Lazarus:

> You see I have got to understand thoroughly the manner of work under which the art of the Middle Ages was done, and that that is the *only* manner of work which can turn out popular art, only to discover that it is impossible to work in that manner in this profit-grinding society. So on all sides I am driven towards revolution as the only hope, and am growing clearer and clearer on the speedy advent of it in a very obvious form, though of course I can't give a date for it.[43]

Yet Morris did partly work in the medieval handicraft manner and achieved a success which helped to revolutionize modern design. The proof of the achievement in turn demanded the active utopian hope and revolutionary commitment. So it was that in a similar interchange of times at the end of *News from Nowhere*, Ellen admonished her guest from an earlier, prerevolutionary era: "Go back and be the happier for having seen us, for having added a little hope to your struggle. Go on living while you may, striving with whatsoever pain and labour needs must be, to build up little by little the new day of fellowship, and rest, and happiness."[44] Having prospectively witnessed the new society, the guest can resume with new assurance the struggle toward its actualization. So Morris, having contemplated the glorious presence of the long-forgotten craftsman in his work and personally attested to its possible recovery, commits himself to bringing about the change that would symbolically redress the irreparable violation of work and actually put the worker at the center of civilization once again.

43. Appendix to Emma Lazarus, "A Day in Surrey with William Morris," *The Century Magazine* 32, no. 3 (July 1886): 397.
44. *CW*, 16:211.

LAURA DONALDSON

Boffin in Paradise, or the Artistry of Reversal in *News from Nowhere*

There were not always novels in the past and there will not always have to be. . . . All this is to accustom you to the thought that we are in the midst of a mighty recasting of literary forms, a melting down in which many of the opposites in which we have been used to think may lose their force.

Walter Benjamin, *Reflections*[1]

In the throes of the nineteenth-century fin de siècle, many writers experimented with the novel in response to the growing ambiguity of its status and purpose, and the loss of historical time as a novelistic medium. Even though such "modernist" authors frequently commented upon the processes of society through this experimentation, specific political goals seemed beyond the appropriate boundaries of what the novel ought to encompass. William Morris, like many modernist writers, attempted a new formulation of the genre. Unlike these artistic counterparts, however, he imbued his experimentation with a definite sociopolitical aim: a revolution, true to its etymological roots of a complete cycle of change altering the basis of both society and the art it produced. This experimentation becomes especially important in *News from Nowhere* (1891), Morris's utopian fantasy of England in its idyllically socialist future. To discover what this welding of aesthetics and politics into a single link might augur for the future of the novel and for Morris's own political vision, one must pause before an image in *News from Nowhere* whose innocence belies its heuristic importance for this question.

> I looked over my shoulder, and saw something flash and gleam in the sunlight that lay across the hall; so I turned round, and at my ease saw a splendid figure slowly

1. Walter Benjamin, *Reflections,* ed. Peter Demetz (New York, London: Harcourt, Brace, Jovanovich, 1978), 224.

sauntering over the pavement; a man whose surcoat was embroidered most copiously as well as elegantly, so that the sun flashed back from him as if he had been clad in golden armour. The man himself was tall, dark-haired, and exceedingly handsome, and though his face was no less kindly in expression than that of the others, he moved with that somewhat haughty mien which great beauty is apt to give to both men and women. He came and sat down at our table with a smiling face, stretching out his long legs and hanging his arm over the chair in the slowly graceful way which tall and well-built people may use without affectation. He was a man in the prime of life, but looked as happy as a child who had just got a new toy.[2]

This paragraph describes the first impression the appearance of one "Boffin" makes upon the narrator of *News from Nowhere*. While Guest, the narrator, is rather startled to encounter "such a dignified-looking personage" named for the celebrated Dickensian character, he readily accepts the explanation that the title merely expresses a nuance of Nowherian humor "partly because he is a dustman, and partly because he will dress so showily" (*CW*, 16:22). This futuristic Golden Dustman possesses one weakness, however: he whiles away the utopian hours in Nowhere by writing "reactionary" novels and is very proud of getting "the local colour right, as he calls it." Confronted with this allusion to Boffin, we can dismiss it neither as a puzzling distraction, nor as a picturesque use of the nineteenth-century literary tradition. Although Boffin's entrance is certainly picturesque, his "dazzling" quality reveals the transformation that his character projects, a transformation that becomes much clearer when we compare the passage in *News from Nowhere* with Dickens's own description of Boffin in *Our Mutual Friend*:

a broad, round-shouldered, one-sided old fellow in mourning, coming comically ambling towards the corner, dressed in a pea overcoat, and carrying a large stick. He wore thick shoes, and thick leather gaiters, and thick gloves like a hedger's. Both as to his dress and to himself, he was of an overlapping rhinoceros build, with folds in his cheeks, and his forehead; and his eyelids, and his lips, and his ears; but with bright, eager, childishly-inquiring grey eyes, under his ragged eyebrows, and broad-brimmed hat.[3]

In the narrative of both Dickens and Morris, the reader initially perceives Boffin from a distance. In *Our Mutual Friend*, Boffin is a dark "fellow in mourning" who comically ambles along; in *News from Nowhere*, a gleaming "splendid figure slowly sauntering" whose brightness dazzles one's vision.

2. William Morris, *News from Nowhere Or An Epoch of Rest*, in *The Collected Works of William Morris*, ed. May Morris, 24 vols. (London: Longmans, 1910–1915), 16:20–21; subsequent parenthetical in-text references are to this edition and are cited as *CW*.
3. Charles Dickens, *Our Mutual Friend*, intro. E. Salter Davies (London: Oxford University Press, 1952), 46; subsequent parenthetical in-text references are to this edition.

Thus, Morris's first sentence duplicates the flow of Dickens's narrative, yet reverses its content by replacing darkness with light, and the leisure of a comic "amble" with a dignified saunter. The next clause, describing Boffin's dress, has the same effect. Instead of his predecessor's thickly padded pea overcoat, complemented by thick shoes, thick gaiters, and thick gloves, the utopian Boffin swathes himself in a "surcoat" that is "embroidered most copiously as well as elegantly." The Dickensian Boffin sports the build of an "overlapping rhinoceros," with folds in his cheeks and forehead; the Morrisian Boffin is "tall, dark-haired, and exceedingly handsome," and moves with an unaffected and confident grace. Both authors end their respective descriptions with conditional "but" clauses that establish analogies between Boffin and the qualities of a child. For Dickens, Boffin's "bright, eager, childishly-inquiring grey eyes" enliven his animal-like qualities, while for Morris, he was a man in the prime of life who "looked as happy as a child who had just got a new toy."

In fact, one could characterize this appearance of Boffin as the manifestation of a "dialectic reversal," or the paradoxical turning around of a phenomenon into its opposite.[4] In *Marxism and Form,* Frederic Jameson identifies this reversal as the basic movement of dialectical thought and observes that its transformative qualities involve an

> essentially critical, negative, rectifying moment . . . which forces upon us an abrupt self-consciousness with respect to our own critical instruments and literary categories. . . . Such a shock is constitutive of and inseparable from dialectical thinking, as the mark of an abrupt shift to a higher level of consciousness, to a larger context of being.[5]

This reversal also demands that we grasp the reality of what a thing is through the simultaneous awareness of what it is not.[6]

An instructive example of this phenomenon surfaces in the development of the Theater of the Absurd, whose practitioners depended so heavily upon the audience's socialized expectations of both theatrical content and form. Without this predisposition toward certain kinds of artistic values, no reversal could have occurred; more specifically, without the audience's awareness of the social and religious constructs they adopt to render human existence intelligible, no reversal of attitudes concerning mankind's purpose in the world would be possible. Ionesco's dictum that the "absurd is that which is devoid of purpose. . . . Cut off from his religious, metaphysical and transcendental roots, man is lost," depends upon an anguished recollection of this vanished center for its subversive power. Further, "the means by which the dramatists of the Absurd express their

4. Frederic Jameson, *Marxism and Form* (Princeton: Princeton University Press, 1971), 309.
5. Ibid., 375.
6. Ibid., 311.

critique—largely instinctive and unintended—of our disintegrating society are based on suddenly confronting their audiences with a grotesquely heightened and distorted picture of a world that has gone mad. This is a shock therapy that achieves what Brecht's doctrine of the 'alienation effect' postulated in theory but failed to achieve in practice."[7] While Martin Esslin calls this confrontation "shock therapy" rather than "epistemological shock," the dynamics of both phenomena are similar. For example, Beckett's "wearish old man" Krapp, listening to the tape recorder revealing his own disembodied voices of past years, forms just such a "grotesquely heightened and distorted" image. Its shocking presentation attempts to reverse the audience's belief in a complacent and stable notion of the self to one which is alienated and protean.

Like Morris, the Theater of the Absurd uses an epistemological shock to achieve its dialectic reversal. Both seek to catapult humanity from an inauthentic existence that is unconscious and mechanical into an abrupt consciousness of its own self-deception. The Theater of the Absurd differs from Morris, however, in its lack of concern whether this "shock therapy" communicates some moral or social lesson; rather, it expresses a pattern of poetic imagery that rejects the literary, the empathetic, and the anthropomorphic.[8] In terms of Boffin, the remarkable grammatical similarity between the passages of Morris and Dickens, and the precise physical opposition of the two figures suggests Morris's deeply held Marxist conviction that change involves a transformed content seeking its adequate expression in form. While Morris would emphatically agree with the Theater of the Absurd's refusal to accept art forms based on the continuation of invalid standards and concepts, he departs from them in grounding the reversal on certainty—of socialism's ultimate value and society's utopian meta-morphosis.

If the figure of Boffin in *News from Nowhere* embodies Morris's goals for the transformation of nineteenth-century cultural and literary values, the question remains: transformed from what to what? Since our first introduction to Boffin in *Our Mutual Friend* occurs in the midst of a business deal enabling him to experience some "fine bold reading, some splendid book in a gorging Lord-Mayor's-Show of wollumes," we assume that the social and political ramifications of this situation form the core of Morris's transvalued sensibilities. His collaborator in this enterprise is one Silas Wegg, a wooden-legged street vendor whom he regards with "haw" and "hadmiration." When Boffin asks, " 'How can I get that reading, Wegg?" the response from Wegg is immediate: " 'By,' tapping him on the breast with the head of his thick stick, 'paying a man truly qualified to do it, so much an hour (say two-pence) to come and do it' " (p. 50).

7. Martin Esslin, *The Theatre of the Absurd* (Garden City, N.Y.: Doubleday, Anchor Books, 1969), 360.
8. Ibid., 354.

His greed thoroughly aroused, Wegg responds favorably to the request. He wonders, however, "was you thinking at all of poetry?"

> "Would it come dearer?" Mr. Boffin asked.
> "It would come dearer," Mr. Wegg returned. "For when a person comes to grind off poetry night after night, it is but right he should expect to be paid for its weakening effect on his mind." (p. 51)

Thus, the Dickensian Boffin seeks a transformation of his sensibilities through the commercial purchase of literary pleasure: " 'This night, a literary man— *with* a wooden leg'—he bestowed an admiring look upon that decoration, as if it greatly enhanced the relish of Mr. Wegg's attainments—'will begin to lead me a new life!' " (p. 97).

Morris readily accepted Marx's designation of the consciousness of profit and loss as the distinguishing feature of modern capitalism, and such an ethic certainly characterizes the activities of Boffin in the world of nineteenth-century London. Despite the highly altruistic motives behind his pretended corruption by the one-hundred-thousand-pound Harmon legacy, Boffin nevertheless perceives his world in terms of contractual obligations rather than the collectively determined relationships of earlier societies. Despite his undeniable love for his daughter, Bella, in defense of whose honor the charade is conducted, the Dickensian Boffin becomes "prey to prosperity" by succumbing to that attitude which turns all connections of value to account and restricts humanity's artistic capabilities to the level of a commodity.

Rather than this reduction of art to money, the Boffin of *News from Nowhere* literally turns money into art. The "Golden Dustman" of his name refers to the gold embroidery on his coat, a fact which emphasizes the value of money only in terms of its aesthetic properties. When Guest attempts to pay for his ferry ride across the Thames, his companion replies: "As to your coins, they are curious, but not very old; they seem to be all of the reign of Victoria; you might give them to some scantily-furnished museum" (*CW,* 16:11). The quantification of society through the perspective of profit and loss has completely disappeared from the psyche of the Nowherian people, and money acquires value only by the merit of its artistic design. Thus, Morris's use of Boffin—one of the most famous images depicting the degrading effects of class-based wealth in nineteenth-century literature—not only raises the question of the novel's dependence on the attitudes and technology of commercialism, but also suggests why Morris so inseparably intertwines the transformation of society and the transformation of the novel as genre. Although Silas Wegg's greed for money seems relatively insignificant compared with the voraciousness of contemporary mass-marketing, writers in both milieus are aptly described by Jasper Milvain in *New Grub Street:* "Your successful man of letters is your skilful tradesman. He thinks first and foremost of the markets; when one kind of goods begins to go off slackly, he is ready with something new and appetising."[9] Guest, the narrator of *News from Nowhere* and often the voice of Morris himself, corroborates this observation by admitting that "in the land whence I come, where the competition, which produced those literary works . . . is still the rule, most people are thoroughly unhappy" (*CW* 16:152). This deprecatory perspective on the novel is the main reason Boffin's utopian comrades gently chide him for his "weakness" of writing "reactionary," that is, realistic, novels.

Morris's ambivalence toward the novelistic tradition of the nineteenth century is illuminated by the fact that in Greek, the same word can mean "guest" and "alien." Since Morris's translations of Homer provide eloquent testimony to his fluency in Greek, one must conclude that his choice of the name "Guest" for the narrator of *News from Nowhere,* and its connotations of both exclusion from and inclusion within, can hardly exist as a random feature of the character who articulates society's socialist metamorphosis to the reading public. This ambiguous state of a coeval existence both within and without utopian society becomes clearer in light of several comments that Guest makes during the course of the narrative. Upon his first sight of the lovely Ellen, Guest responds: "Though she was very lightly clad, that was clearly from choice, not from poverty, though these were the first cottage-dwellers I had come across; for her gown was of silk, and on her wrists were bracelets that seemed to me of great value" (*CW,* 16:148). Guest, still trapped in his bourgeois perspective, instinctively perceives Ellen's worth in terms of monetary value. The pathos of this situation is emphasized during his reawakening in the "dingy" Hammersmith of industrial England: "I lay in my bed in my house . . . thinking about it all; and trying to consider if I was overwhelmed with despair at finding I had been dreaming a dream. . . . Or indeed was it a dream? If so, why was I so conscious all along that I was really seeing all that new life from the outside, still wrapped up in the prejudices, the anxieties, the distrust of this time of doubt and struggle" (*CW,* 16:210).

Morris, like Guest, is irrevocably a man of his time and thus unable to actualize fully the dream whose possibilities he so fervently imagined. In terms of the novel, however, he does reach a higher point on his revolutionary spiral through an experimental engagement of realism and romance. Creating the social and political imagination he believed that his predecessors lacked, Morris hoped that such an interaction would eventually create the "due" art and literature of "healthy bodily conditions, a sound and all round development of the senses, joined to the due social ethics which the destruction of all slavery will give us."[10]

9. George Gissing, *New Grub Street,* 3 vols. (London: Smith, Elder, 1891), 1:8–9.
10. William Morris, "The Society of the Future," in *William Morris: Artist, Writer, Socialist,* ed. May Morris, 2 vols. (Oxford: Basil Blackwell, 1936), 2:465.

The realism that constitutes the first term of the dialectic assumes a subversive role and refuses to perpetuate the illusions Morris perceived as the basis of nineteenth-century bourgeois realism. Old Hammond, Dick's great-grandfather and custodian of books in the British Museum, comments on the fallacious premises of bourgeois realism when he observes that

> in the nineteenth-century, when there was so little art and so much talk about it, there was a theory that art and imaginative literature ought to deal with contemporary life; but they never did so; for, if there was any pretense of it, the authors always took care . . . to disguise, or exaggerate, or idealise, and some way or another make it strange; so that, for all the verisimilitude there was, he might just as well have dealt with the times of the Pharaohs. (*CW,* 16:102)

More specifically, the blinded vision of bourgeois realism, while it made some attempt to depict the plight of the poor and oppressed, ultimately submerged its portrayal in the social melioration of the happy ending. Through its artifice, "we must be contented to see the hero and heroine living happily in an island of bliss on other people's troubles" which occurs only "after a long series of sham troubles (or mostly sham) of their own making, illustrated by dreary introspective nonsense about their feelings and aspirations" (*CW,* 16:151).

For Morris, realism does not involve either illusion or blindness. Instead, as Frederich Engels characterizes it, realism conjures a searing truthfulness which, "by conscientiously describing the real mutual relations . . . breaks down the conventionalized illusions dominating them, shatters the optimism of the bourgeois world, causes doubt about the eternal validity of the existing order."[11] This characterization certainly depicts the thrust of Old Hammond's harrowing account of the socialist struggle for England: his plain and direct discourse, thick with details of the phenomenal world, give it a substantiality and objectivity that makes it seem "real" to the listener or reader. Guest, in fact, defines Hammond's language as a "scientific disquisition" that convinces him of the truth that socialism actually overcame the culture of capitalism and produced the utopian society of Nowhere. Turning this shattering power to his own use, Morris attempts to undermine the sensibilities of his readers and to create a disillusioned perspective allowing the vision of socialism to take root.

As a socialist who intended to supplant "discontent with hope of change that involves reconstruction," however, Morris realized the limits of this subversive realism.[12] Without another, more creative perspective to fill the void, one can only lament with Guest the coldness of a life "where I was, so to say, stripped bare of every habitual thought and way of acting" (*CW,* 16:103). Morris uses

11. Frederich Engels, letter to Minna Kautsky, 26 November 1885, in *Marx and Engels on Literature and Art,* ed. Leo Baxandall Stefan Morawski (New York: International General, 1973), 114.
12. Morris, "Art under Plutocracy," *CW,* 23:189.

romance, the second term of the dialectic, to transcend this critical emptiness, and through it, furnishes socialism with a reconstructive direction. John Stevens defines the essential quality of romance as that of "experience liberated"; the essential romance experiences, he writes, "are idealistic. The quality which is 'liberated' or 'disengaged' from all our vulgar communities is expressive of a supreme claim (in a medieval world where realities are spiritual and transcendental), or of a supreme aspiration (in a modern world where man's own feelings are the final realities)."[13] It is just this ability of romance to liberate experience from the bourgeois ethic that makes romance so necessary in order to achieve the goals of reconstructive socialism.

The fact that Morris encircles Hammond's realistic account and prosaic, analytical style with Guest's lyrical pastoralism and lush first-person narration illustrates the importance he assigns to romance. For example, after Hammond lectures Guest on "the lack of incentive to labor in a communist society," the next chapter immediately plunges the reader into a scene whose ambience is molded by the wall-pictures of "queer old-world myths and imaginations," or fairy tales representing "the child-like part of us that produces works of imagination" (*CW*, 16:102). For Morris, this creative power exists as the essential space of imaginative freedom, which nurtures the utopian vision and allows it to grow within humanity. Even the chapter titles reinforce this juxtaposition. In the chapters which Guest narrates, the titles are descriptive of places, actions, or persons—"A Morning Bath," "Children on the Road," "Going Up the River"; in the chapters that Old Hammond narrates, the titles are didactic and reminiscent of a scholastic treatise—"Concerning Love," "Questions and Answers," "Concerning the Arrangement of Life." The former connote vision and experience, the latter, erudite detachment and precisely ordered thought.

Morris's use of romance highlights its status as "the place of narrative heterogeneity and of freedom from the reality principle to which a now oppressive realistic representation is the hostage. Romance now again seems to offer the possibility of sensing other historical rhythms, and of . . . utopian transformations of a real now unshakably set in place."[14] The subtitle of Morris's novel, "an epoch of rest: being some chapters from a utopian romance," suggests that he intended to use the visionary dilation that romance provides as a central part of his transformation of values. For John Ruskin, one of Morris's most important mentors, art makes visible to us realities that could neither be described by science nor retained by memory; for Morris, romance creates alternatives to existing society that could neither be envisaged by realism

13. John Stevens, *Medieval Romance: Themes and Approaches* (New York: W. W. Norton, The Norton Library, 1973), 28.
14. Frederic Jameson, *The Political Unconscious: Narrative as a Socially Symbolic Act* (Ithaca: Cornell University Press, 1981), 104.

nor experienced in capitalist society. Through its gift of those "waste places" where the imagination can cavort without constraint, romance allows Morris "the pleasure of the eyes without any of that sense of incongruity, that dread of approaching ruin, which had always beset me hitherto when I had been amongst the beautiful works of art of the past, mingled with the lovely nature of the present" (*CW* 16:140–41).

The narrative and social fruits of Morris's experimentation engender what Mikhail Bakhtin calls an "intentional novelistic hybrid," that is, an artistically organized system that has as its goal the "carving-out of a living image of another language."[15] The word "hybrid" lends an especially relevant context to Morris's transvaluation of literature and culture, for it connotes a cross-breeding and an evolution of structure in order to meet a changing environment, a process essential to the implementation of socialism's goals. In the narrative of *News from Nowhere,* the languages of realism and romance fertilize each other and germinate a new breed of novel whose formal elements draw upon, yet transcend, their predecessors. An examination of this process in *News from Nowhere* in terms of two of the nineteenth-century novel's most important features—an individualist perspective and a highly plotted structure—yields rich insights into Morris's literary experimentation with specific social and political goals.

Morris moves beyond the nineteenth-century novel's privatistic communication of individual author with individual reader through the collectivism of utopian story-telling, and its emphasis on the narrative imagination as a common human experience. The practice of story-telling enables mankind to experience a genuinely shared community, for its theme, as George Lukács observes, "is not a personal destiny but the destiny of a community. And rightly so, for the completeness, the roundness of the value system creates a whole which is too organic for any part of it to become so enclosed within itself, so dependent upon itself, as to find itself as an interiority—i.e., to become a personality."[16] A lovely example of this dynamic occurs in Morris's description of the summer softness of a Nowherian evening:

> We had quite a little feast that evening, partly in my honour, and partly, I suspect, though nothing was said about it, in honour of Dick and Clara coming together again. The wine was of the best; the hall was redolent of rich summer flowers; and after supper we not only had music (Annie, to my mind surpassing the others for sweetness and clearness of voice, as well as for feeling and meaning) but, at last we even got to telling stories, and sat there listening, with no other light but that of the summer moon streaming through the beautiful traceries of the windows, as if we

15. Mikhail Bakhtin, *The Dialogic Imagination: Four Essays,* ed. Michael Holquist (Austin, London: University of Texas Press, 1981), 361.

16. George Lukács, *The Theory of the Novel,* trans. Anna Bostock (Cambridge: The MIT Press, 1971), 66.

had belonged to a time long passed when books were scarce and the art of reading
somewhat rare. (*CW,* 16:140)

That story-telling is free and depends on neither the attitudes nor the technology of capitalism so vividly portrayed by the Dickensian Boffin certainly
demonstrates its affinity with Morris's socialist ethic. But, even more impor-
tantly, story-telling promotes that "sound and all round development of the
senses" which is so central to Morris's revaluation of values. In fact, the passage
just cited utilizes the totality of the senses in its portrayal of story-telling: the
feast, which serves as the context for the stories, involves tasting; the voices of
the story-tellers, hearing; the redolence of the flowers, smelling; the light of the
moon, seeing; the physical closeness of the participants, touching. This radically concrete quality of story-telling overcomes what some critics have called
the distancing frame of the novel as genre. Thackeray's model of the author as
stage manager and manipulator of the character-puppets (and by implication, the
reader), in many ways exemplifies the alienation that Morris perceived as
permeating all levels of the nineteenth-century novel. Contrasted to this distancing narrative frame, one could describe story-telling as "part of the de-alienat-
ing, re-personalizing process to which Morris is committed."[17] In the fair of
vanity which is bourgeois society, the potential for endowing life with a more
holistic quality remains profoundly limited. However, for the socialist utopia of
Nowhere, there are no fairs but only feasts—those communal celebrations of a
revolutionary people whose narrative expression is story-telling.

The syntactical ambiguity surrounding the person of the narrator also emphasizes Morris's reinvention of the collective. In the introductory chapter, a fellow
activist of the Socialist League relates his dream of a journey through Nowhere
to the apparent narrator. " 'But,' says he, 'I think it would be better if I told them
in the first person, as if it were myself who had gone through them.' " To whom
does the "I" of this phrase refer—our friend or his companion? In this passage,
one cannot syntactically separate the two, and thus the "I" of the narrator seems
to imply the pluralistic "we" of those struggling to achieve justice, and to reflect
the ethic of a literal socialism, that is, the joining together of the particular into a
larger collectivity.

Jameson notes that only this emergence of a post-individualist social world and
its reinvention of the collective can concretely achieve the "decentering" of the
individual subject called for by the Marxist diagnosis of society.[18] For Morris,
only the sensuality and freedom of utopian story-telling can effect such a
transformation. Its communal dynamic seeks to "restore the coordinates of a

---

17. Michael Wilding, *Political Fictions* (London, Boston, Henley: Routledge and Kegan Paul,
1980), 55.
18. Jameson, *The Political Unconscious,* 104.

face to face storytelling institution which has been effectively disintegrated by the printed book and even more definitively by the commodification of literature and culture."[19] The dissolution of the novel in utopian story-telling reflects a larger fulfillment of Morris's socialist praxis: its complete union of theory and practice causes the backward and forward movement of socialism's revolutionary spiral to cease, creating the "epoch of rest" which is the utopian society of Nowhere.

The second element of the nineteenth-century novel which Morris seeks to transform is a highly plotted structure intimately yoked to the "reactionary" novels for which the utopian Boffin possesses such a definite predilection. This pejorative label stems from a plot structure suggesting the inevitability of conflict, power and competition. In many ways, the most appropriate metaphor for its highly structured character is that of the machine, or, as Morris puts it, "a geared contrivance for the transfer of power from one character to another. In a plotted novel, it is by way of plot that characters mesh. (And we might also note that the passive gear may rotate in the same direction as the active one, or in the opposite direction: complicity or conflict.)"[20] The observation of Ellen's grandfather that "good sound unlimited competition was the condition under which they were written,—if we didn't know that from the record of history, we should know it from the books themselves," mirrors Morris's own view that the machinations of plot in the novel possess intimate links to the ethics of capitalism (*CW*, 16:149). He himself bridges the chasm between the geared Victorian plot and the complete absence of such contrivance in the utopian story through the dialectic of realism and romance. *News from Nowhere* has very little plot in the traditional sense of the word; it exhibits a dearth of activity, and even fewer situations motivated by the temptations of social ambition. What it does have, and that in abundance, is a creative tension produced by the engagement of romantic and realistic modes and the vision that such a relationship produces. The transformation of perspectives rather than the transfer of power provides the "controlled propulsion" of Morris's narrative.

Ironically, it is just this competitive power of the nineteenth-century plot that reveals the positive dimension of Boffin's hobby. The inclusion of the adjective "good" in the statement by Ellen's grandfather points to a more profound motivation underlying Boffin's devotion to such allegedly decadent forms of fiction. The danger of an "epoch of rest" is that its serenity will turn into political and spiritual inertia, and its tolerance into an inability to act. Although Nowherian citizens contend that the novels engendered by their past perpetuate oppressive economic and social structures, they nevertheless perceive the "spirit of adventure in them, and signs of a capacity to extract good out of evil which our

19. Ibid., 155.
20. David Goldknopf, *The Life of the Novel* (Chicago: University of Chicago Press, 1972), 107.

literature quite lacks now" (*CW,* 16:150). These novels exude an energy and a vital zest for all that life offers—qualities central to the ultimate success of Morris's proletarian revolution. Recognizing the possibility that Nowherian society might grow too complacent in its utopian perfection, thereby losing its social vision, Morris ingeniously creates Boffin's "curious" habit as a preventive measure against such a tragic loss.

Through the artistry of reversal in *News from Nowhere,* a vision emerges in the concreteness of a utopian Boffin—a vision that Morris ultimately enlarges to include all dimensions of society. We find this vision not only when comparing the figures of Boffin in Morris and Dickens, but also when comparing the voyages their respective novels depict. In *Our Mutual Friend,* the reader journeys up the Thames in "a boat of dirty and disreputable appearance," which ferries its passengers into the horrors of an industrialized society; in *News from Nowhere,* the reader travels in "a pretty boat, not too light to hold us and our belongings comfortably, and handsomely ornamented." Dickens's nineteenth-century river voyage literally forces its oppressed to become fishers of corpses rather than men, while Morris's journey up the utopian Thames imbues its participants with the "excited pleasures of anticipation of a holiday." A journey through the waters of *Our Mutual Friend* sucks readers down into the miasma of society, and we become "allied to the bottom of the river rather than the surface, by reason of the slime and ooze with which it was covered." In stark contrast, Guest's journey upriver infuses him with "a deep content, as different as possible from languid acquiescence," so that he is, "as it were, really new-born" (*CW,* 16:164). Thus, the context of these respective journeys parallels the dialectic reversal embodied by the figure of Boffin: through his wedding of aesthetics and politics, Morris replaces dark with light, despair with hope, capitalist decay with utopian regeneration. Leading us into the heart of Morris's transvaluation of literature and culture, Boffin in paradise represents narrative form as radical practice, offering us a paradigm of a just world. Morris seeks to endow the reader's imagination with this paradigm and to enable its implementation in the realm of the actual.

NORMAN TALBOT
A Guest in the Future
News from Nowhere

I

William Morris was the first great English man of letters to declare himself a Communist, and to devote his extraordinary talents to changing the hearts and minds of his countrymen in preparation for the revolution. This study of *News from Nowhere,* while acknowledging the book's honorable membership in the category of utopian fiction, is concerned with another and profounder aspect of its achievement, its use of the narrator-protagonist.

In 1887 Morris had written *Nupkins Awakened,* the first English example of agitprop.[1] Influenced by medieval pageant-drama, the play has obvious weaknesses and genuine strengths. The heroine's two big set-piece speeches have a plain eloquence akin to the slightly earlier time-travel novella *A Dream of John Ball,* and the exuberant farce of the trial scene of the first act is still enjoyable. In several aspects, including the necessary placing of the revolution proper between the two acts, the play has an illuminating kinship with *News.*[2] Not the least of these aspects are the consciously Dickensian title (or subtitle, since it was staged as *The Tables Turned, or Nupkins Awakened*) and the paradoxically sympathetic presentation of Nupkins in the second act. The revolution complete, Nupkins wanders England's green and pleasant land, still enmeshed in his assumptions about security, power, and property, a useless lackey in a world with no employment for lackeys. This elderly alien represents a link between the images of Scrooge amid Christmas cheer and William Guest and Ellen's grandfather amid the renewed innocence of Nowhere. A recent descendant is the Beggar-

1. "Agitprop," from the Russian *agitatsiya* and the Latin *propaganda,* is a dramatic style of social protest expressing Marxist values, especially characteristic of street theater.
2. *News from Nowhere,* hereafter called *News,* was first published in the Socialist League's—which meant Morris's—periodical *Commonweal,* January–October 1890. Quotations are from *The Collected Works of William Morris,* ed. May Morris, 24 vols. (London: Longmans, 1910–1915), vol. 16; subsequent parenthetical in-text page references are to this edition.

man, in Tirin's play of that name, in Ursula K. Le Guin's "ambiguous utopia" *The Dispossessed*.[3]

Nupkins Awakened shows most of the limitations of agitprop. Such plays have a palpable design upon us and our convictions, and depend on the collective and assenting responses of a crowd. Thus it has a rather repulsive clarity, because it fulfills precisely its explicit tendencies and possibilities. Such work becomes almost lifeless to the reader, who has no fellows to join in communal assent or resolution.

Morris was also well acquainted with the other extreme of literary affect, since his reputation was made by *The Life and Death of Jason* and *The Earthly Paradise*. These expansive works were accepted as balm for weary minds, to console and entertain those enervated by commercial and social strivings (and their unconscious accompaniment of self-disgust). *News from Nowhere* makes explicit both the opposed principles, agitprop and consolation, in its rich and vigorous treatment of the protagonist and the consequent responses of its audience.

It may seem, to very traditional literary critics, a dubious matter to generalize about how the audience of a book responds to it. However, the exercise is illuminating, not only in terms of propaganda effects but also the implied, encoded or specifically putative reader, invoked and evoked by the text.[4] The reader of *News* is a socialist, one of the tiny band of subscribers to *Commonweal*, and no author can have had a clearer idea of his specific audience, nor they of him. The encoded reader knows a substantial amount about Morris, relishes the open secret that the narrator and protagonist is Morris, and regards him, literally, as a comrade.

It is impossible to get to the energy-core of *News* without recognizing its author's special availability. Far from being "extra-literary," his presence has an obvious influence on the text. Nor, though it does cater to the pleasure of unsophisticated readers, is the effect of this influence necessarily a simple one. By definition, a utopia is an extreme form of fictional lying, of projected opinion and emotion, what is called a "wish-fulfillment," which means a synthesis of the principles of agitprop and consolation. Morris delights in this amphibious form of fiction, and in making a totally honest, vulnerable journey out of it. The sublime frustration of wish-fulfillment in *News*, addressed like the whole of the frame-tale to socialists weary of strife and division, consoles and enheartens them as a "happy ending" could not. Guest is back among us, more resolute than ever.

It is no part of this essay's purpose to evaluate sources, but there can be no

3. Ursula K. Le Guin, *The Dispossessed* (New York: Avon, 1974), 47.
4. *The Implied Reader* is the title of a study by Wolfgang Iser (Baltimore: Johns Hopkins University Press, 1974).

doubt that Bellamy's *Looking Backward* was an immediate stimulus to *News*.[5] Morris's important review of the book in 1889, in *Commonweal* of course, makes not only the adverse points about a mechanistic world that any reader of Morris would expect, but also some profound points about how to read utopias. The only safe way to do so, he says, "is to consider it as the expression of the temperament of the author"; Bellamy's temperament is "the unmixed modern one, unhistoric and unartistic." The review is intensely aware of the implied reader as well as the concealed author, and of how dangerous for naive readers the wrong utopia can be, whether or not they feel themselves to be identifiable as the implied reader. If the vision displeases them, such readers may accept the work as prophecy and turn away from many good and valuable tasks, disheartened. If the vision pleases them, on the other hand, they may accept the work as a conclusive statement of facts and rule for action, thus warping their own faith and actions by accepting "all its necessary errors and fallacies (which such a book *must* abound in)."

It is clear that Morris distinguished between prophetic vision, which is true in its own terms, and prediction, true in external terms. In *News* he therefore lays out his own vision as a personal story on a highly personal map. The map is reassuring and recognitive for the implied reader, but it also insists on the subjectivity of the journey. The enduring vitality of *News* is partly due to our knowledge that Guest is "really" Morris, and partly to the resultant confidence that we can identify—and choose whether or not to be identified with—his experiences and reactions.

The first chapter of *News* offers a small maze of misleadings, none of them capable of bewildering such old friends and perceptive socialists as us, the encoded readership. The storyteller quotes a "friend" who relates what happened to somebody else again, a fellow member of the Socialist League. Since there are as many opinions in the League as there are members, it is amusing, but by no means difficult, to work out which one would have "finished by roaring out very loud, and damning all the rest for fools" (p. 3). The friend says the roarer is "a man whom he knows very well indeed," and proves it by making genial, confident fun of him, exactly as one laughs at oneself.

The blurring of friend into roarer is accomplished by well-placed and half-ambiguous "he" pronouns, until they can overtly become one, in the last sentence of the chapter:

> But, says he, I think it would be better if I told them [the adventures] in the first person, as if it were I myself who had gone through them; which, indeed, will be the

5. Edward Bellamy's *Looking Backward,* published in 1888, was read eagerly by many socialists, including many of Morris's friends. Although James Redmond (introduction to *News from Nowhere* [London: Routledge and Kegan Paul, 1970]) says Morris reviewed it "very unfavourably" in January 1889, the review actually appeared in *Commonweal* on 22 June 1889, p. 195. However, it was certainly unfavorable.

easier and the more natural to me since I understand the feelings and desires of the comrade of whom I am telling better than anyone else in the world does. (p. 5)

Our own shrewdness in perceiving this as a mere autobiographical fantasy, an obviously suspect wish-fulfillment, cajoles us into building an intimate portrait of the "I" whose lifestyle, tastes, and expectations present Nowhere. We can tell ourselves to relax and enjoy the story because we "understand the feelings and desires" of our comrade very well. Our expanded self-esteem paradoxically encourages us to share the hopes and fears of the narrator: a professional novelist might deceive us, but not good old unsubtle William Morris!

Our world of division, disappointment and spiritual discontent (not unmixed with guilt) is left behind for an unpretentious dream whose motive power is a prayer: "If I could but see a day of it; if I could but see it!" (p. 2). Like many a dreamer, our narrator is partly objective about what he sees and seeks to understand, but his subjective responses are so convincing, so literally lifelike, that they actually increase the believability of the dream. The most convincing aspect of the encoded reader's induced *ad hominem* logic is the knowledge that this Nowhere is precisely what the dreamer needs. That is, it is the wish-fulfillment we immediately suspected when the frame-narrator who says "says a friend" disappears.

Nothing much is going on in Nowhere. As in our world, if Guest had begun by ordering Dick to "take me to your leader" there could have been no response. He has arrived at the easiest, most idyllic time of the year, in a luxuriously fine June at the hay harvest, so that he can contribute nothing obvious to the world that he enters. There are no great people and events. Nobody needs him—as far as they know.

He needs them, of course. The human dimension, the individual as measure, is the only way of testing a society; indeed, it defines society. After the withering away of the state, social authority and personal freedom are no longer antithetical but synthesized. Guest wants to know, intellectually, how this synthesis came about, since most people where he came from couldn't believe in its inevitability. Even Guest can't do so, which is why he needs the epoch of rest this new "reality" offers. And that is why that "reality" is so convincing to us.

Nowhere's first delight is physical and sensory, but the physique and senses are those of Morris. They tell him that this is a utopia thoroughly worth living in. His incomprehension of the waterman not only enables us to laugh a little but also tells us that this world will be difficult to contribute to. Guest needs this epoch, not as an earnest of personal rewards but because he claims to be angrier, more frustrated, even more discouraged than fellow Leaguers, and therefore temperamentally more vulnerable than his reader. When he returns to being William Morris, refreshed and wholehearted, he refreshes and enheartens his reader.

If the greatest poverty is not to live in the physical world, as Stevens says,

Morris is the wealthiest man in history. He offers the phenomena of being alive with clarity, simplicity, and directness; authenticity is guaranteed by humor and sensory alertness. The book is designed to enliven the reader's awareness of the world we already have, as well as the one it might become.

The emotions are not skilled workers, however, so intensity is a mixed blessing. In Nowhere one form of competition still degenerates into conflict: sexual desire can ravage even paradise. In other respects human fellowship is supreme: commodities are made when someone wants to make them or needs them, and external nature and social imagination can be identified one with the other. But sex is neither a commodity nor merely an objective natural fact. Apart from this, alienation is rare, and few things can obstruct the joy of being alive, the satisfaction of contributing oneself to the folk. Even the occasional naysayer, who mistrusts everything the rest like, is free to do so and can even be a stimulating element. Ellen's grandfather, for example, is one reason why she (unlike most of those around her) realizes that the world's and humanity's beauty may stand in need of defense.

The epoch of rest grew out of bad times, culminating in a very bloody revolution and a difficult period of physical and social remaking. Times and challenges just as grievous may be ahead—though no one seriously expects them. In any case, sufficient unto the day is the good thereof; the folk take no thought for the morrow except to plan the next festival and anticipate the next winter. Neither beauty nor work is taken for granted; the former is the object of a thousand endeavors, conspicuous or humble, while the latter is savored and saved up. The lifestyle of Nowhere, and those who live it, are a dream come true.

Well, of course they are a dream come true. Those are the only terms in which we could accept them. We are encouraged to accept not only specific Morrisian wish-fulfillments but also the Morrisian locations where they become evident. We read *News* knowingly, as Morris's book, and every detail is potentially ironic.

The term is meant literally; we are offered two recognitions at once: "how beautiful and sensible" is immediately joined by "how exactly right for poor old Morris!" The reader becomes a co-conspirator with Nowhere, anticipating how it will next ratify and clarify the narrator's wildest dreams. As soon as the winter of his discontent is invaded by a feeling of simple pleasure, we can predict that winter will be transformed into glorious summer. What the narrator believes in principle unfolds before him in fact, to his astonishment; we are a jump ahead, less astonished, and able to nod patronizingly. "Obvious wish-fulfillment," we mutter, just as we are meant to. Behind the stalking-horse of his lovably unthreatening personality, Morris controls our every response.

We know, then, who Guest really is, where he lives (we've probably attended a meeting in the old coachhouse) and what he believes in. Nothing he hopes for will surprise us. Every correlation delights and privileges us; perhaps especially, as among those commemorated, we are touched to see the plaque in the

Guest house (which part of our mind accepts as Morris's Kelmscott House, so that Guest-Hall equals Morris-Hall): "Guests and neighbours, on the site of this Guest-Hall once stood the lecture-room of the Hammersmith Socialists. Drink a glass to the memory! May 1962."[6]

The frisson of the autobiographical utopia is there, but it has become the reader's frisson. Where we expect to see Morris's name we see our own. All Guest's supposed "wandering," quite unlike that of any other utopian viewpoint character, is as locatively perfect and inevitable as this; his journey must follow his longing, and the reader recognizes every step. Guest determinedly collects "objective" history, but we instantly correlate it with his personal history. The enduring vitality of the book is not in its ideas alone but in the structuring self that lives them and is identified with them. Instead of a stock wandering enquirer we have a dreamer fulfilled, exploring with delight all that fulfills him. . . . And losing it.

The poignancy of the love affair with Ellen, so unlike the sentimental "love interest" in predecessors like *Looking Backward, A Crystal Age* and *Erewhon,* leads us to the final pages in which the frame-tale rather than the dream is fulfilled, and the dreamer is emptied of narrative hope. The law of the conservation of fictional energy, it seems, is that whatever wishes you have put into your fantasy must be taken out at the end. Indeed, to write a fantasy to escape self-knowledge is like taking an express train to escape from railway lines.

II

The meeting with the waterman is where Guest's consciousness enters Nowhere, as his body is rather briefly baptized in the new Thames. With vigorous directness that meeting drowns the assumptions of the class society to which Morris and his implied reader have become forcibly habituated. Guest seems to be a confused, illogical old eccentric to Dick and a trembling, half-adoring, half panic-stricken alien to himself. But what does he seem to us?

As guests in his longings, which have begotten a world superficially alien to him but which we already know to be his own, self-projected, we watch Morris turn into Guest with fascination and sympathy. Yet we also smile, because we see into the nature of things in Nowhere far more quickly than Guest. This is the inbuilt privilege of the spectator and the core of dramatic irony.

Dick is the first and representative Nowherian, casually nonintellectual but obviously on the best of terms with art, craft, and high culture as well as with his muscles and their proper uses. In this first meeting he makes a score of benevolent assumptions about Guest that must be accepted with mingled bewilderment and gratitude. He is also utopia's agent in identifying, in a naive

6. P. 16. The plaque is already there, although Hammersmith has not yet become Nowhere.

and unthreatening way, many of the assumptions about the nature of human community that Guest is soon glad to abandon. We, in turn, see Guest's assumptions from the outside while employing his bad guesses and specific mistakes to test our exploratory skills, without losing faith in him or ceasing to respect his unique relationship with the world of Nowhere, so we soon become eager for Dick to respect and accept him, too.

Dick later develops a fascinating relationship with the idea of spiritual childhood, of being born again, but in these early pages Nowhere calls forth distinct child-aspects of Guest, which are urgently needed since his own time has aged him (as he begins to realize) unnaturally fast. A shocking question about his age is engendered by a conceptual discussion about his birthplace near Epping Forest, but subconsciously by the smell of balm: "Its strong, sweet smell brought back to my mind my very early days in the kitchen-garden at Woodford, and the large blue plums which grew on the wall behind the sweet-herb patch—a connection of memories which all boys will see at once" (p. 17). The smell-taste stimulus (long before Proust) brings back intense and protective delight in the physical world, which leads to his incautious reminiscence. This naive time traveler needs our amused sympathy as well as that of the Nowherians.

Without self-conscious commentary, Morris continually lays himself open to our understanding, so that Guest can be seen binocularly, as unique and "real" as well as representative of us, those who live in the prerevolutionary world. It is impossible to suspect Morris of bad authorial faith when he is overtly so much less shrewd than we, so we travel gladly into London and history as his allies, while also imaginatively receiving him into his kingdom and longing to explain it all to him. We cling gratefully to the rules of politeness to elderly and confused strangers, as Guest does, while noting for his benefit that a public and communal society involves more respect for privacy than a bourgeois and divided one.

When Dick takes him to visit Old Hammond, we are amused by our ability to infer that the elderly sage of Bloomsbury may be Morris's own grandson; if so, Dick is also a descendant of his guest, being Hammond's great-grandson. Subliminally, we may wonder if the whole of this blessed society is not descended directly from Morris as well as from the socialist faith of the author and his small band of allies, that is, from the implied reader of *News*. Just as Dick guides Guest through the physical byways of redeemed London and the Thames Valley with truly filial devotion, so Hammond guides him through the intervening centuries to the when of Nowhere.

Both journeys are necessarily internal, too, quests for the self and its purposes. At Hammersmith Guest-Morris has found motifs from his own work on the frieze of the Guest-Hall, and quotations from his works in the sleeping-room. The mixture of gruffness and coyness with which these are presented amuses the implied reader (because such a response is intensely Morrisian) as much as the comic self-portrait of the first chapter:

The subjects I recognised at once, and indeed was very particularly familiar with them. (pp. 13–14)

. . . the pale but pure-coloured figures painted on the plaster of the wall, with verses written underneath them which I knew somewhat over-well. (p. 141)

So, the reader acquainted with Morris may murmur, Morris is the forefather of this whole society he is dreaming of, and has at last got the recognition he deserves.

When the journey up the Thames begins, we know that Morris knows every reach of the river and we feel certain the destination must be either Oxford or his beloved Kelmscott. However, as with our other geographical expectations, we are inexact: what Guest recognizes is not the Thames that Morris knew, but what the Thames should have been. A Platonist might say the Thames is transformed into its true self. If the inward power of the narrative is derived from the sense of the narrator coming home to himself, we wonder, is some similar transformation about to work upon him?

At the narrative level, Guest knows Dick longest among the Nowherians, and undoubtedly learns from him. Dick's alliance of art, craft, and uninhibited muscle-stretching has already been mentioned, but his combination of instinctive tact and good temper with emotional vulnerability and the capacity for righteous indignation does much to prevent Nowherians from seeming either tedious or effete. Dick's furious disgust in reaction to the question about prisons is striking, but so, in a general context of summer luxury, is the strong emphasis upon his passion and his past emotional failure. His relationship with Clara has been stormy, full of misunderstanding and pain, sexual incompatibility and jealousy, though with Guest as catalyst it promises better days.

In parallel, and implying Dick's representative stature, a manslaughter has occurred near Reading, and the whole community is still recovering. Guest witnesses the effect Ellen has upon the males who meet her and learns that nothing can prevent the turmoils of romantic love and sexual longing, even when all economic and class-based obstacles are removed.

This aspect of Nowhere contrasts radiantly with the bland, etiolated love experienced in *Looking Backward,* where every family is of the upper-middle classes, knowing and speaking to nobody; in that world Edith can only offer a sickly, obsessive love, miraculously answered by Julian's entry from the past. In Morris's work, what Guest learns from Dick, as the admirably normative Nowherian, is a subtler matter.

III

Guest has entered a society of humans no longer alienated from the totality of that society, from their work, or from external nature. In spite of the long expositions by Old Hammond, these people may be in danger of alienation from their own history, and it is not clear from Dick's relationship with Clara whether individuals in Nowhere are much better at avoiding alienation from themselves and from individual lovers than the rest of us are. This submerged theme, of potential alienation even within an earthly paradise, contrasts in the Bloomsbury chapters with the historical ballast, and offers itself as an antithesis, intelligible through folk mythology.

Guest has begun to think of Nowhere as a golden age, but such an age cannot exist either at the beginning or the end of history. It is, rather, always at an angle to history, and always within the imagination of humanity. The childhood of the race occurs many times, and for Morris as for Engels it echoes earlier states.[7] The innocence and openness, the happy physicality of Nowhere, and especially the ability of most individuals to submerge self-consciousness in work and social responses, signals this as a childhood of the race, and the Bloomsbury chapters link this matter to the questions raised by an art-life dichotomy.

Old Hammond has emphasized that Nowhere's attitude to work is that of an artist, but his description is also applicable to an engrossed child:

> "*All* work now is pleasurable: either because of the hope of gain in honour and wealth with which the work is done, which causes pleasurable excitement, even when the actual work is not pleasant; or else it has grown into a pleasurable *habit,* as is the case with what you may call mechanical work; and lastly (and most of our work is of this kind) because there is conscious sensuous pleasure in the work itself: it is done, that is, by artists." (p. 92)

It is not clear what is meant by "wealth" in this sentence (we can be sure it does not mean "riches"), but the boyish self-satisfaction with which Dick regards his metalwork and anticipates his mowing and road mending exemplifies the third and second clauses.

The child, born in travail but now deeply enchanted by learning, work, and play alike, is part of the deep structure of *News*. Leading Guest to dinner in the Bloomsbury Market Hall, Clara takes his hand "as an affectionate child would" (p. 99), leaving her reconciled ex-husband and her dear counselor Hammond to follow "as they pleased." As so often in Morris, the body-language introduces the art-language. Guest looks at the murals in the hall: "I saw at a glance that their subjects were taken from queer old-world myths and imaginations which in yesterday's world only about half a dozen people in the country knew anything about" (p. 100).

7. See the final section of this study. Engels expounds his view of human history in *The Origins of the Family, Private Property and the State,* trans. Alec West (1884; reprint, New York: International Publishers, 1972), which borrows heavily from Lewis Morgan, *Ancient Society* (Chicago: Charles H. Kerr, 1877).

His surprise surprises his companions. Hammond says,

> "I don't see why you should be surprised; everybody knows the tales; and they
> are graceful and pleasant subjects, not too tragic for a place where people mostly eat
> and drink and amuse themselves, and yet full of incident."
>
> I smiled and said: "Well, I scarcely expected to find record of the Seven Swans
> and the King of the Golden Mountain and Faithful Henry and such curious pleasant
> imaginings as Jacob Grimm got together from the childhood of the world, barely
> lingering even in his time: I should have thought you would have forgotten such
> childishness by this time." (p. 100)

The reader is invited to disapprove of this backhanded version of a pleasurable
recognition. Dick is surprised too, and a little insulted:

> "What do you mean, Guest? I think them very beautiful, I mean not only the
> pictures but the stories; and when we were children we used to imagine them going
> on in every wood-end, by the bight of every stream: every house in the fields was the
> Fairyland King's House to us. Don't you remember, Clara?"
>
> "Yes," she said: and it seemed to me as if a slight cloud came over her fair face.
> (pp. 100–101)

It is not surprising that Clara should feel some regret for the innocent past,
having been long estranged from her husband and childhood sweetheart. Perhaps she also thinks of the shadow this estrangement may have cast upon their
daughters' upbringing. She may even feel some guilt because the childhood bond
has not endured. An alternative reading suggests, however, that the separation
may have been partially caused by Dick's persisting naiveté, his lack of adult
forethought (even when a parent), along with related and half-perceived inadequacies, unresolved aspects of the childhood bond, as well as by her own
response to another man.

Morris does not insist upon any interpretation of the renewed bond between
Clara and Dick, and we could not believe in any attempt by Guest to analyze it.
Through the typical Nowherian blend of openness and reticence, we may
perhaps detect that Clara is still wary, suspecting the lack of some edge, of some
unchildlike complexity or tension that has not yet developed in their relationship.
After dinner she returns to the subject of the pictures:

> "How is it that though we are so interested with our life for the most part, yet
> when people take to writing poems or painting pictures they seldom deal with our
> modern life, or if they do, take good care to make their poems or pictures unlike that
> life? Are we not good enough to paint ourselves? How is it that we find the dreadful
> times of the past so interesting to us—in pictures and poetry?" (pp. 101–2)

Hammond's reply argues that artists have always done this, even in the nineteenth century (Guest's presence forces him to refer to that terminal period of tory-capitalist anarchy) when the critics disapproved. However, Dick's naive reply is more apt:

> "Well," said Dick, "surely it is but natural to like these things strange: just as when we were children, as I said just now, we used to pretend to be so-and-so in such-and-such a place. That's what these pictures and poems do: and why shouldn't they?"
>
> "Thou hast hit it, Dick," quoth old Hammond; "it is the child-like part of us that produces works of imagination. When we are children time passes so slow with us that we seem to have time for everything."
>
> He sighed, and then smiled and said: "At least let us rejoice that we have got back our childhood again. I drink to the days that are!" (p. 102)

Guest feels alienated from their childlikeness, and confuses it with childishness. Hammond's cordial toast stretches him out over the gulf of his own self-knowledge:

> "Second childhood," said I in a low voice and then blushed at my double rudeness, and hoped that he hadn't heard. But he had, and turned to me smiling and said: "Yes, why not? And for my part, I hope it will last long: and that the world's next period of wise and unhappy manhood, if that should happen, will speedily lead us to a third childhood: if indeed this be not our third. Meantime, my friend, you must know that we are too happy, both individually and collectively, to trouble ourselves about what is to come hereafter."
>
> "Well, for my part," said Clara, "I wish we were interesting enough to be written or painted about." (pp. 102–3)

Clara is in the presence of a writer who does indeed find them interesting—more interesting than his own disastrous times—and this is more satisfactory as a reply than Dick's loverlike flattery.

After the awkward silence in which they contemplate the problem of being both happy and interesting, Dick courteously invites Guest to choose one of several ways to spend the evening, to be entertained. In context, Guest's reaction seems very adult, very alien:

> I did not by any means want to be 'amused' just then; and also I rather felt as if the old man, with his knowledge of past times and even a kind of inverted sympathy for them caused by his active hatred of them, was as it were a blanket for me against the cold of this very new world, where I was, so to say, stripped bare of every habitual thought and way of acting, and I did not want to leave him too soon. (p. 103)

So the older folk are left together, Guest seeking a comforter because old people do feel the cold to which happy children are oblivious. History does not, however, prevent his feeling a further chill when the lovers return and Dick responds to him as "a being from another planet," which is Hammond's convention to cover the fact that he has guessed when Guest has come from. Dick's imagination is vigorous and appropriate: "I was half suspecting as I was listening to the Welshmen yonder that you would presently be vanishing away from us, and began to picture my kinsman sitting in the hall staring at nothing and finding that he had been talking a while past to nobody" (p. 135).

Without consciously intending to, Dick has frightened Guest. But he has also begun to intuit Guest's nature; he adds later that meeting Guest has helped him to understand Dickens better. The most apt connection here is with Arthur Clennam, who dismisses himself as a spiritless "nobody," too old and used up to belong in the lover-world of the childlike (and childish) Pet Meagles. The protagonist's painful awareness of the age-gap and the ebbing of his vital forces is as important here as in *Little Dorrit,* and later this alienated protagonist also meets youth, love, and beauty by the Thames.

Hammond's sly reply to Dick is really an attempt at prophecy for Guest, so, as with other children listening to the subtleties of grown-ups, Dick does not understand it:

> "Don't be afraid, Dick. In any case, I have not been talking to thin air; nor indeed to this new friend of ours only. Who knows that I may not have been talking to many people? For perhaps our guest may some day go back to the people he has come from, and may take a message from us which may bear fruit for them, and consequently for us." (p. 135)

Although his responses are beautifully understated, Hammond in this chapter has become certain of Guest's origin in the prerevolutionary past. He seems also to have recognized that he and Guest are parts of a time-loop by means of which his own record of the revolution is helping to create it; therefore he is in a sense begetting himself and his world, as in many of the paradoxes of time travel. Guest must return, bearing witness, or there will not have been a Nowhere to return from.

This chapter is rich with the illogical awarenesses that contrast most effectively with Hammond's lengthy and rationalistic historical exegesis. Clara, too, receives implications from the darkened hall and the darker history that has been evoked there. She senses that Guest is also Ghost, mainly because she has toyed with the idea that he might renew his youth by immersion in the childlike commonweal:

> "Kinsman, I don't like this: something or another troubles me, and I feel as if

> something untoward were going to happen. You have been talking of past miseries to
> the guest, and have been living in past unhappy times, and it is in the air all round us,
> and makes us feel as if we were longing for something we cannot have." (p. 136)

She has picked up from Guest his own fears about having to return to his own
dark century, since he literally lives (as she says the conversation has meta-
phorically made *both* older men live) "in past unhappy times." What he is
longing for is what she has, a life worth living and a community worth living in.

Hammond gently warns Clara to go on living in the present, but he cannot
deny the aura that surrounds Guest. He asks, with some subtlety, "Do you
remember anything like that, Guest, in the country from which you come?"
Guest understands him perfectly, as few commentators have, and replies, "Yes,
when I was a happy child on a sunny holiday, and had everything I could think
of." It is Clara's specific feeling he is being asked about, not some general
impression that utopia is nice; he recognizes her percipience, like Dick's more
conceptual response, as partaking of the happy child's vague awareness of the
vulnerability of its happiness. This echoes neatly the simpler child-response
Guest had caught on smelling balm at Hammersmith, and foreshadows Ellen's
acceptance of her vocation.

The Bloomsbury section of the story ends with another and even more specific
prophecy in Hammond's reply:

> "So it is," said he. "You remember just now you twitted me with living in the
> second childhood of the world. You will find it a happy world to live in: you will be
> happy there—for a while."
> Again I did not like his scarcely veiled threat, and was beginning to trouble myself
> with trying to remember how I had got amongst this curious people. (p. 136)

This "threat," really a valuable foreshadowing, is reiterated on their parting,
before being swamped by Dick's determined effort to reestablish present and
active life as the true topic of concern. His "boisterous" comments on the
physical challenge of the hay harvest (which he regards much as a second-row
forward regards the annual match against the Old Boys' fifteen) are not stupid,
but represent a strenuous attempt to change the subject. This soon turns into a
clumsily erotic celebration of how beautiful Clara will be when her arms are
tanned to contrast with the whiteness of her less public parts. Hard outdoor
work, he adds optimistically, will also get "some of those strange discontented
whims" out of her head. Fortunately, the reverse happens: Dick gets some
strange discontented whims of his own into his head (or admits their presence
there), and is all the better for them.

Guest delights in this world of strong, warm-hearted children, but the greater
his commitment to them the subtler his self-consciousness becomes. At Ham-

mersmith he loves the story-telling at night, "as if we had belonged to a time long passed, when books were scarce and the art of reading somewhat rare" (p. 140). His going to bed is a climax of contentment, set off against the inveterate shadow that must fall behind the joys of Morris:

> Here I could enjoy everything without an after-thought of the injustice and miserable toil which made my leisure; the ignorance and dulness of life which went to make my keen appreciation of history; the tyranny and the struggle full of fear and mishap which went to make up my romance. The only weight I had upon my heart was a vague fear as it grew toward bedtime concerning the place where I should wake tomorrow: but I choked that down. (p. 141)

Bedtime and waking are the times when the edge of the dream is nearest to consciousness, but the "over-night apprehension" helps to fix Hammond's predictions in the reader's awareness even as it and they are banished from Guest's.

Delightfully, as the journey up the Thames begins, Guest feels some measure of childhood response come back to him. This occurs first because of the clothes made for him: "I dressed speedily, in a suit of blue laid ready for me, so handsome that I quite blushed when I got into it, feeling as I did so that excited pleasure of anticipation of a holiday, which, well remembered as it was, I had not felt since I was a boy, newly come home for the summer holidays" (p. 141). His renewed delight is sharpened for us by his memory of how haymaking had looked in the nineteenth century, but as far as his conscious mind is concerned he merely longs to forget all that.

The rush of sexual responsiveness appropriate to summer hayfields is one reason for Guest's renewal. He has to remind himself that a woman as lovely as Annie is bound to have a lover of her own age, and he is fascinated by Clara's open pleasure in Dick's beautiful body. Thus it is partly sex that kindles his love of (and self-acceptance amid) the summer greenery: "I almost felt my youth come back to me, as if I were on one of those water excursions I used to enjoy so much in those days when I was too happy to think that there could be much amiss anywhere" (p. 144).

Along the Thames, Arthur Clennam's response was one of humiliatingly muted desire, where Guest's is one of developing desire. The visit to Hampton Court reminds us of *Little Dorrit,* just as Boffin had reminded us of *Our Mutual Friend,* and both are very much Thames-side books—though not more so than *News.* But nothing in Dickens is so redolent of sexual consciousness and response as Guest's journey up the Thames. Even in his "three's-a-crowd" alertness Guest thoroughly enjoys this aspect, and is taught by Dick's unselfconsciousness and Clara's erotic awareness not to turn his emotions away from their sexual course, as the Victorian nineteenth century had tried to do:

> She looked at him fondly, and I could tell that she was seeing him in her mind's eye showing his splendid form at its best amidst the rhymed strokes of the scythes: and she looked down at her own pretty feet with a half sigh, as though she were contrasting her slight woman's beauty with his man's beauty; as women will when they are really in love. (p. 145)

It is no wonder, since he is learning a lesson in healthy sensuality from Clara and Dick, and since he has met the even more definitively beautiful Ellen, that Guest does not say much about the power-barges and other technological aspects of the England through which he is passing. That would have been bad art, divorcing us from Guest's feelings, the reawakening desires of youth, at this crucial moment when he can love both the Thames and Ellen most poignantly.

Insensitive critics who expect prediction instead of prophecy, high-tech guess-work about solar batteries or fusion cells instead of the felt life of Guest's dream, never give any reason why Guest should dream about such things. Indeed, he has a deep-seated anxiety not to be told, which matches his underlying prejudice for low-level technology (mills and looms rather than power units), his emotional state, and his natural wariness, as a time traveler, about giving himself away.

> I took good care not to ask any questions about them, as I knew well enough both that I should never be able to understand how they were worked, and that in attempting to do so I should betray myself, or get into some complication impossible to explain: so I merely said,
> "Yes, of course I understand." (p. 162)

Dick and Clara do not teach Guest anything specific to the future except its abiding kinship with childhood and sexual desire. The wisdom of history comes from Old Hammond. The crucial enlightenment comes in the Thames journey, through Ellen, and links with both the present-wisdom of the lovers and the past-wisdom of Hammond to develop authentic future-wisdom.

IV

Ellen is the most effective image of liberated womanhood in *News,* although she has not Clara's relish for the male as sex-object, nor any conscious drive for dominance. Mistress Philippa, of the Obstinate Refusers, has the necessities of art to force her to influence others, and we are free to imagine Ellen, inspired by her strange male muse, also becoming a woman of conscious power. If she feels that humanity is in danger of falling back out of Nowhere into bad old ways, this will give her a mission such as she has been seeking. It will also account for the intensity of her attraction to Guest, and for the physical world of midsummer

England which others might perhaps be tempted to think invulnerable, as Hammond prefers to.

Where almost every woman is attractive, Ellen stands out; she even tests the newly reforged bond between Dick and Clara. This is not a merely decorative glamour, but enables the issues of the Bloomsbury chapters to be summarized and ratified. In dispute with her grandfather, loving and exuberant as she is, she sets stern limits on the authority of fiction. She points to the lovers as Nowhere's books, which provides an exuberant answer to Clara's wish that "we were interesting enough to be written . . . about." After all, like the rest of us, Clara cannot know that she is in fact a character in a book!

The next stage of her attack on fiction indicts specifically such novels as *Little Dorrit,* as well as novels in general:

> "As for your books, they were well enough for times when intelligent people had but little else in which they could take pleasure, and when they must needs supplement the sordid miseries of their own lives with imaginations of the lives of other people. But I say flatly that in spite of all their cleverness and vigour, and capacity for story-telling, there is something loathsome about them. Some of them, indeed, do here and there show some feeling for those whom the history-books call 'poor' and of the misery of whose lives we have some inkling; but presently they give it up, and towards the end of the story we must be contented to see the hero and heroine living happily in an island of bliss on other people's troubles." (p. 159)

Certainly the remainder of Ellen's description embraces far inferior fictions, but the presence of Dickens in the imagination of Nowhere is well established. Significantly, Guest goes to sleep that night with the pleasure of the evening Ellen adorns quite extinguishing the fear he had felt the night before, that he would wake up back in the century of Dickens and Morris.

Dick and Clara, next morning, together reaccept the child-wonder of folk tale, this time without any forebodings from Clara, and they do it by watching Ellen:

> "Doesn't it all look like one of those very stories out of Grimm that we were talking about up in Bloomsbury? Here are we two lovers wandering about the world, and we have come to a fairy garden, and there is the fairy herself amidst of it: I wonder what she will do for us."
>
> Said Clara demurely, but not stiffly: "Is she a good fairy, Dick?" (p. 155)

Of course Dick says she is, but Guest notices that the story has omitted all reference to himself. With offhand precision Dick remedies the omission, saying that Guest has the "cap of invisibility," the Tarnhelm, and is "seeing everything, yourself invisible."

Clara is naturally very conscious of Ellen's beauty, and has dressed like her as far as possible—a very naive way of coping with a potential rival. In the same way, though less consciously, Ellen puts on the intellectual dress of Guest in offering her grumbling grandfather her home-truths about life in the glamorous past. Guest is "much moved," and haunted by Ellen's wild beauty as the three travelers re-embark. Clara, too, remains aware of her influence, and is consequently very affectionate toward Dick. This relieves Guest (he assumes because of his fatherly attitude to the lovers). He reasons that Dick could not have welcomed such caresses if "at all entangled by the fairy." As the reader realizes, Guest is himself "entangled."

What Guest has experienced, and what gives him a "keen pang" on leaving Ellen, is not just beauty but a response to visionary power. Since his vision has brought him to her, it is a thrill to encounter in her an equivalent vision. She is drawn to the elderly, haggard stranger too, and makes him her muse. However, the reader is aware, consciously or unconsciously, that Guest is also the author, so the evocation of Ellen is of his muse, in a perfectly reciprocal irony that does not depreciate either term, or deny the erotic nature of their attraction.

Thus Ellen rows after Guest, determined to stay with him, anticipates and absorbs his ideas and perspectives, and at the same time attracts and inspires him. As in Shelley's allegory of the poet's imagination, "Alastor," Ellen's "voice was as the voice of his own soul,/ Heard in the calm of thought." But since the dream has created the dreamer's soul-mate, it cannot allow their total union, any more than *Epipsychidion* can allow the total mutual annihilation of the poet and Emily. Such a union would sentimentalize the dream-frame and trivialize the doubleness of the reader's response to Morris and Guest. In fact, it would also depreciate the air of hard-earned wisdom that balances the book's sweet-tempered delight.

As Guest comes closer to the fateful return to his own time (a necessary element in all utopias, or how could they be written?) and the inevitable loss of personal wholeness such as he feels in the love of Ellen, two processes reach their climax. The first is the joy itself, the delight that for once involves no guilty privilege; it entails both love and a reborn sense of being usable, the narrative expression of which is his being allowed to row and his teaching Ellen about the past and the Thames. The second is the personal division and alienation that adds poignancy and courage to that joy, and becomes yet another test of the man who had lain down to dream.

In fairness to the dream-aspect of *News*, it must be admitted that not only Ellen but all the significant characters have a resemblance to Guest and Morris, especially in their negative characteristics. For example, if Old Hammond is like Guest as an aged, eccentric and anomalous man, fascinated enough by the past he hates to be almost a living museum, he is distinct in his quietly benevolent support of Clara in her marital tangles, and in his total identification with the young society around him. To Hammond, but never to Guest, Nowhere is "we."

Dick resembles his great-great-great-grandfather in his gruff bewilderment about sex and women, his seeking for consolation for such troubles in good hard work, his glib no-nonsense attitude toward high art, and his devotion to community. He is dissimilar in his ability to forget himself, even as he takes a naive pride in his body and its purposes.

Ellen's grandfather, the old grumbler, is so deeply wrong in underestimating his own day as to revere the surviving art of a much inferior time. Yet what he loves Guest also appreciates, and might even accept as one of the best things to be said about a bad Empire. What the grumbler does not admit is that Nowherians who "like" their world can also appreciate Thackeray. Still, the grumbler is secretly happy, using his grumbling to tease and test the beautiful people around him.

Ellen has a special relationship to Guest. As muse, she is full of knowledge, passion, and wisdom, accepting a vocation to chasten and toughen a future that might otherwise forget the past. Her passion might be that of an isolated Cassandra, except that she is determined to inherit Hammond's function at a more affirmative level, striving always to express her love of the physical world. Among the benefits of a soul-bond with Guest is her eschewing of Hammond's temptation to praise Nowherians for being "too happy . . . to trouble ourselves about what's to come hereafter" (pp. 102–3). She is tender with the anomalous and cross-grained aspects of humanity rather than sponsoring conformity, because she knows there are seeds of wisdom even in the wrong-headed, and all are worth loving. She will link Guest's past to Nowhere's future, as the healer links illness with health in preventive medicine, striving to understand both. As pupil and lover, she is both protector and purpose for Guest.

Old Hammond and his great-grandson are clearly contrasting figures; while the latter finds the past puzzling, repulsive, and (after the Renaissance) eventually boring, the former is ratified by the fullness of his recognition of Guest's temporal aura, as it were. Still, despite the human interest of the Bloomsbury chapters, Hammond's historical account is the least dramatic part of *News,* and to confuse "news" with history, as readers concentrating on those chapters have done, is a serious error.

That is not to say that history does not matter, but instead that the book is written in the right order. It is from history that Ellen will learn to prevent a repetition of history: "Who knows? Happy as we are, times may alter; we may be bitten with some impulse towards change, and many things may seem too wonderful for us to resist, too exciting not to catch at, if we do not know they are but phases of what has been before; and withal ruinous, deceitful, and sordid" (p. 198).

Indeed, if Guest is her muse, he is the equivalent of Clio, not of Erato, and he is very conscious that, however arousing her beauty and however intimately they know themselves to be linked, she cannot regard him primarily as a sexual lover. As his imagination becomes keener and healthier, he introduces her to aspects of the Upper Thames without even needing to name them (so closely can he identify them with their ideal forms in his other role, as wish-fulfilling author). What more inspiring gift can a muse offer than one's own country?

They are both lovers of the place, as well as of each other. Ellen utilizes the ominous or deathlike elements in Guest and takes the brunt of those shadow-powers as they gather for his life's climacteric around his beloved Kelmscott manor and village. Her undirected prayer that she might but say or show how she loves "the earth and the growth of it and the life of it," is the author's too, and through him it is granted.

Again this is achieved by a double or ironic effect. Ellen is confirmed by meeting Guest to be a healer of spiritual blindness; she will teach her children, and those of all Nowhere, to become vigilant against all signs of law, organization and mechanism, the beginnings of anti-ecological brutalism or power- and profit-seeking exploitation, the first symptoms of cant, ambition, or progress. In this sense she becomes the inheritor and purpose of Guest's time in Nowhere.

Guest's loss has an opposite effect: he has left the hideous travesty of London and the Thames, and discovered the true London and Thames. He has been carried along the currents of history to hear of the best and worst of times, forward in time and back through mounting social, erotic, and natural delight, toward the source of himself. Yet at the climacteric, when he reaches the *locus amoenus,* the sacred central place from which he should be reborn, his own renewal cannot take place.

At the personal level, the wish-fulfillment's climax might have been in the bed at Kelmscott with Ellen. But even if it had to be purely social, it ought to have taken place at the tables of the folk, especially since they are in Kelmscott church. Both are forbidden. Guest was never more than a guest of the community of Nowhere, and suddenly the Tarnhelm that Dick had evoked descends upon him. He sees faces that have forgotten him, or for whom he never was. He becomes unstuck in time, in a "disaster long expected," encounters the travesty of a countryman who represents his own time, and a black cloud sweeps to meet him, "like a nightmare of my childish days," which is precisely where the energy of the whole vision had come from. This reestablished dream-frame possesses both a fierce precision and a genuine plangency, as Guest is dismantled from the consciousness of his own creation, the children of his own longing. He even reads Ellen's last conscious glance toward him as explaining that "you cannot be of us . . . our happiness even would weary you" (p. 210).

All utopias, not just ironically insulated ones like Lemuel Gulliver visited, must remain at a distance, always lost as soon as emotionally accepted, or how could they still be Nowhere? And Guest has, after all, contributed to the community that seemed to have everything. He has not only inspired his soul-maiden, Ellen, but also offered a temporal gift to much less sensitive spirits.

In that beautiful and poignant last chapter, he bathes for the second time in the

Thames in the company of Dick, the quintessential Nowherian. Dick has guided the time-spirit without much apparent danger to his own serene world view, though we know his serenity is not unshakable. Now he introduces the final time-transaction with an amazing but convincing reflection. First, he comments that it is in autumn that one "almost believes in death"—and the reader may reflect that one definition of childhood is that time of life before one imaginatively accepts one's own mortality. Guest feels that Nowherians are "like children" about the phenomena of the seasons, sympathizing with their gains and losses (as if Ruskin had never isolated "the pathetic fallacy"!). Now he suggests that Dick should respond as keenly to winter and its trouble and pain as to the summer luxury now all about them. Dick replies that he does so, but as a worker within the seasons rather than a spectator merely appreciating them. Like other aspects of *News,* this chimes with a discussion in *The Dispossessed,* when Shevek admires the beauty of the long view of Urras but Takver says she would rather be fully involved in the phenomena of life, however messy and unglamorous.[8]

For the first time, Dick becomes introspective rather than merely thoughtful: "One thing seems strange to me . . . that I must needs trouble myself about the winter and its scantness, in the midst of summer abundance. If it hadn't happened to me before, I should have thought it was your doing, guest; that you had thrown a kind of evil charm over me" (p. 207). The charm has indeed been cast, though by Guest's presence rather than his will, and it is a most valuable rather than an evil one. Dick cannot dismiss now what he had previously pushed out of his mind, because he has had to put it into words. The inertia of a Golden Age such as that described by the Greeks is vulnerable to many corruptions, and time-consciousness gives resilience even to an epoch of rest.

When Guest returns to the world of William Morris, passing on to his contemporary and later readers something of his own longings and warmhearted striving, he also leaves behind a better, tougher Nowhere. Human endeavor can improve even utopia.

V

Although *News* is influenced by several writers, like Jeffrey and Bellamy, who overtly discuss the future of humanity, Charles Dickens seems to be the major literary presence. Indeed, a socialist Dickens would have been Morris's ideal reading. Scrooge, the isolated old man upon whom *A Christmas Carol* focuses, probably inspired some of Morris's physical contrasts between alien and child-like community joys, for instance, as well as making a spectacular journey into the darkest of Victorian futures.

8. Le Guin, *The Dispossessed,* 153–54.

Certain aspects of Dickens's nobody-figures, especially Clennam in *Little Dorrit* and Rokesmith and Headstone in *Our Mutual Friend,* walk the Thames beside Guest. More subtly, the complexities of the first-person narrator as protagonist, of which Dickens was abidingly conscious and to which he committed substantial amounts of autobiographical material, seem to have taught Morris a good deal. Like David Copperfield, Guest uses himself up in a Kuenstlerroman about how he came to write the tale, and like David he is by no means prepared to guarantee that he is the hero of it.

Pip and Esther Summerson are examples of Dickensian narrators whose stories use them up in a more dangerous sense. The shadows that gather around Guest's identity as he looks in on the feast in Kelmscott Church are less like Scrooge's temporary isolation from other people's Christmases than like those shadows that begin to shroud Pip's early identity when he realizes that Biddy and Joe have attained a family status he must not look to have. Beginning as Bildungsroman of a muted kind, Esther's and Pip's stories evolve into retrospectives of wearied contentment and accepted social duty, tales that bear testimony to a past chaos of feeling. Pip and Esther are not divided from their true loves by the gulfs of time and the ironies of art, as Guest is, but they have striven devotedly "to build up little by little the new day of fellowship, and rest, and happiness," a goal Ellen's final look presents to Guest. From the distance of Nowhere, Guest has gone into as complete a death—and as brave and selfless a death so that others may live—as Sydney Carton.

Beside this sober Dickensian self-acceptance can be placed Morris's specific human faith as a socialist—for Esther could otherwise never have used a phrase like "the new day." Guest's journey into the future is also into the past, seeking the true childhood of the race, from which renewal comes. Old Hammond suspects that Nowhere is the third childhood rather than the second, probably in honor of the finest aspects of the thirteenth and fourteenth centuries. Dickens would have responded more to Jesus' use of "born again," as a necessary re-start before we can enter the Kingdom, but for a revolutionary socialist the new day is an equivalent kind of death for individual life-habits as well as for power-greed and social division.

Morris may not have accepted the mythical Golden Age preexisting society, but he did revere the High Barbaric or heroic age as admirable, courageous, and communal.[9] Like Old Hammond in *News,* Morris and Bax, in their "Socialism from the Root Up," also give full honor to the medieval period's vestiges of communism and the vigorous popular arts and crafts associated with them.[10]

9. See note 5. For Morris, "heroic age" denoted the worlds of tales like the *Iliad* and *Odyssey,* the *Volsungasaga, Beowulf,* and the *Kalevala.* Historically, the Goths who resisted Rome, and Bronze Age cultures all over Europe, merited the epithet.

10. "Socialism from the Root Up" was first published in *Commonweal* in 1887 and later presented in book form as *Socialism: Its Growth and Outcome* (London: Swan Sonnenschein, 1893).

This is not to agree with James Redmond, who asserts with his usual casual disregard of evidence that Morris "looked back to the fourteenth century as an epoch of rest, when there had been beauty in the daily lives of Englishmen whose nineteenth-century descendants were blighted by the squalor of capitalist industrialism" (p. xiv).

Undoubtedly, there are superficial and conceptual similarities between the fourteenth century and Nowherian concepts of art and community, for example, but Morris was a distinguished and perceptive cultural historian. He knew far too much about the period ever to believe it "an epoch of rest," any more than he could have believed that High Barbarism was communally equitable or its devotees likely to be as thrilled with horror by a single manslaughter as the inhabitants of Nowhere's Thames Valley were.[11]

These two periods do, however, offer societal childhoods analogous to that of post-revolutionary Nowhere. Human societies can at times spring into intense and admirable life, and these childhoods are similar to each other, though never in the sense that one spring is identical with all other springs. Dick sees life and nature like a Heroic Age warrior, to a limited extent, and he dresses and designs metalwork rather as a fourteenth-century craftsman would, but he himself is not like either.

Morris was far ahead of his socialist contemporaries in at least this aspect of sociocultural theory. He did not accept that history had proceeded or would proceed by straight-line "developments," either the "historical inevitability" of naive social optimism or, for that matter, the "progress" of the naive capitalist meliorist, or any "natural decadence," either from a naively imagined Golden Age or by analogy with the seasonal cycle. Morris and Bax were the first socialists to posit a cyclic theory of historical change, recognizing the repetition of principles in a context of wide and vital variation. The analogies they employ offer powerful links between diverse periods, but they also illuminate contrasts and discontinuities. It is this cyclic sensitivity that Ellen's wisdom will develop into an invaluable instrument, as distinct from Dick's response to the seasons and Hammond's historical "long view," as from the assumptions about social decadence posited half-seriously by her grandfather.

What Guest has lost to stimulate this gift is considerable. He has understood the fulfillment of human history according to Hammond, the energies of free humanity exemplified by the wild beauty of Ellen and the confident, active

---

The meticulous discussion by Paul Meier in *William Morris: The Marxist Dreamer,* trans. Frederick Gubb, 2 vols. (Sussex: Harvester Press, 1978), emphasizes the originality and quality of Morris's perspective.

11. Morris's first three major prose fictions are a preparation in this as in other ways for *News,* his fourth. In *A Dream of John Ball* he explores his limited kinship with fourteenth-century radicals, then in *The House of the Wolfings* (1889) and *The Roots of the Mountains* (1890) he tests the social worlds of earlier and later heroic age peoples. All three are, however, war-focused stories.

openness of all her folk, and the simplicity of a community reconciled in work, in play, and even sometimes in sexual love. And having understood the community that results, he must depart from it, never to return.

He has also lost something more personal, his own created place and his soulmate in one (which entails losing his childhood and his achieved self in one). In Nowhere his work and faith and life are valued—except by name—and make perfect heroic sense. In Nowhere his young and passionate muse is grateful and supportive; she understands him, often, even before he speaks. In Nowhere his love of Ellen, mankind, and the Thames Valley makes him a kind of *genius loci*. As the pair row the Upper Thames, names fall away and the places are offered to Ellen as if new-created—as if Guest is creating them! It is not surprising that as the value of the experience increases, so his forebodings increase, until he is expelled from the *locus amoenus*, the heart of his paradise.

As we, along with the original reader of *News,* still encoded in the text, share Guest's loving and humble discovery and become guests in Nowhere, we also share Nowhere's sympathetic and protective attitude to Guest—and to the author so amusingly visible behind him. Morris has invited us to laugh at him, especially in the opening pages, but his presence is also highly purposeful. The integrity of *News* becomes so much a matter of the reader's own concern, as a co-enthusiast with Morris, that the failure and return of Guest guarantees the triumph of both the book and Nowhere itself, for which our imaginations are all working.

LYMAN TOWER SARGENT
William Morris and the Anarchist Tradition

Any discussion of the relationship of William Morris and anarchism must begin by recognizing that Morris vehemently rejected the connection, opposed the contemporary anarchists in England, and called himself a Marxist or communist. Much of the recent literature on Morris's political ideas—and it is substantial—insists that we stop there. Such authors argue that Morris was a self-proclaimed communist who opposed anarchism; therefore, there can be no relationship between the two. [1]

Admitting that these descriptions of Morris's position are generally correct, I argue that Morris was more of an anarchist theorist than perhaps even he recognized. However, I am not going back to an earlier school of Morris interpretation that tried to depict him as essentially apolitical or alternatively argued that the political activity that took up so much of the last years of his life was an aberration. I accept the importance of political activity in Morris's life; I accept that he saw himself as a Marxist or a communist; and I accept that he fought with the anarchists over the control of the journal *Commonweal* and the Socialist League. [2] Anarchism has two forms, collectivist and individualist. The parallels between Morris and anarchism are all to a form of collectivist anarchism usually labeled communist anarchism and most commonly identified with Kropotkin. Morris displayed no affinities with a second form of collectivist anarchism, called anarcho-syndicalism, which stresses trade union activity, and Morris ridiculed individualism; therefore, I shall only discuss communist anarchism here.

---

1. For variations of this position, see Paul Meier, *William Morris the Marxist Dreamer,* trans. Frank Gubb, 2 vols. (Hassocks, England: Harvester, 1978); A. L. Morton, "Introduction," in *Political Writings of William Morris,* ed. A. L. Morton (New York: International Publishers, 1973), 11–30; and E. P. Thompson, *William Morris: Romantic to Revolutionary* (New York: Pantheon, 1977).
2. Evidence on the relationship between Morris and the London anarchists can be found in "William Morris's Socialist Diary," ed. Florence Boos, *History Workshop* no. 13 (Spring 1982): 1–75; John W. Hulse, "William Morris: Pilgrim of Hope," in *Revolutionists in London: A Study of Five Unorthodox Socialists* (Oxford: Clarendon Press, 1970), 77–110; Hermia Oliver, *The International Anarchist Movement in Late Victorian London* (London: Croom Helm, 1983); and John Quail, *The Slow Burning Fuse: [The Lost History of the British Anarchists]* (London: Paladin, 1978).

Morris rejected the tactics of the anarchists of his time—specifically their advocacy of violence—but a comparison of the anarchist tradition with Morris's political writings shows him to be part of that tradition despite his denials. The works of Morris that I shall use to make my argument include *News from Nowhere* (1889-1890), *A Dream of John Ball* (1886-1887), a number of essays, including "The Society of the Future" (1889), "The Beauty of Life" (1880), and "Looking Backward" (1888)—his criticism of Bellamy, and a little known play, "The Tables Turned" (1887). Of these writings only *News from Nowhere* has been carefully analyzed by a variety of scholars concerned with Morris's political attitudes, and they disagree about as fundamentally as possible.

John Quail has argued that discussing whether or not Morris was an anarchist or a communist diminishes Morris because it fails to see him as "a powerful and original thinker."[3] I do not want to reduce Morris's stature as a thinker, and I believe Quail is correct that, in one sense, it does not matter much if Morris is called a libertarian Marxist or a communist anarchist with strong leanings toward Marxism. In another sense, however, it does matter, because, as I hope to show, Morris's creativity as a political thinker was within the anarchist tradition.

The Anarchist Tradition

The popular image of anarchism that relates it to violence and even the scholarly image that frequently stresses the individualism of anarchism and excludes its communal side are simply wrong. Anarchism is a political theory advocating social order without coercion.[4] It is a consensual theory, not, except in a minority position, an individual-centered theory.

Peter Kropotkin (1842-1921) once defined anarchism as:

> the name given to a principle or theory of life and conduct under which society is conceived without government—harmony in such a society being obtained, not by submission to law or by obedience to any authority, but by free agreements concluded between the various groups, territorial and professional, freely constituted for the sake of production and consumption, as also for the satisfaction of the infinite variety of needs and aspirations of a civilized being.[5]

3. Quail, *Slow Burning Fuse,* 28.
4. For general studies of anarchism in English, see April Carter, *The Political Theory of Anarchism* (London: Routledge and Kegan Paul, 1971); James Joll, *The Anarchists,* 2d ed. (London: Methuen, 1979); Alan Ritter, *Anarchism: A Theoretical Analysis* (Cambridge: Cambridge University Press, 1980); and George Woodcock, *Anarchism: A History of Libertarian Ideas and Movements* (Cleveland: World, 1982). This section is based on the chapter "Anarchism" in Lyman Tower Sargent, *Contemporary Political Ideologies: A Comparative Analysis,* 7th ed. (Homewood, Ill.: Dorsey Press, 1987), 178-95.
5. Peter Kropotkin, "Anarchism," in *Encyclopedia Britannica,* 11th ed., 1:914.

To the extent that a definition of anarchism is agreed upon, this is it.

As a political philosophy, anarchism advocates a society in which no person is in a position to coerce another. This result is achieved through freedom within a community. As Alexander Berkman (1870–1936) put it, "Anarchism teaches that we can live in a society where there is no compulsion of any kind. A life without compulsion naturally means liberty; it means freedom from being forced or coerced, a chance to lead the life that suits you best."[6] Anarchists believe coercion (the exercise of power) corrupts both the person using power and the person on which it is used. Therefore, a social organization must be developed where the possibility of coercion is dramatically lessened or, ideally, eliminated.

The reduction or elimination of coercion does not eliminate the need for social organization and order, but anarchists believe noncoercive order is better on almost any measure than coercive order. "Given a common need, a collection of people, by trial and error, by improvisation and experiment, evolve order out of chaos—this order being more durable than any kind of externally imposed order."[7] A communally evolved order will be "(1) voluntary, (2) functional, (3) temporary, and (4) small."[8]

In communist anarchism, the commune or collective is a fundamental social unit. These collectives would be small and membership voluntary, as would participation in the commune's daily affairs. One of the underlying assumptions of communist anarchism, however, is that there are some subjects on which only the community can make decisions. This assumption is combined with the belief that such subjects are very limited and that no coercion will be needed.[9]

The central problem of anarchism is how to balance individual liberty, particularly the right to withhold cooperation, with the daily needs of the society. This balancing act requires that there be an understanding of what areas of life are to be solely under personal control and which areas require collective decision making. A basic premise of anarchists is that many areas of life now under community control can be shifted easily to personal decision making. Such areas of personal control would include, for example, marriage, the family, and education.

Decisions are reached by consensual agreement with an emphasis on reasoned argument; this distinction is a key to the similarities and differences between Morris and anarchism. The same approach is used within both an institution like the workplace and the community as a whole. If there is a disagreement on any

6. Alexander Berkman, *ABC of Anarchism,* 3d ed. (London: Freedom Press, 1964), 10.

7. Colin Ward, "Anarchism as a Theory of Organization," *Anarchy 62* 6 (April 1966): 103.

8. Ibid., 101. See also Terry Phillips, "Organization—The Way Forward," *Freedom* 31 (22 August 1972): 3.

9. This section is based on Lyman Tower Sargent, "Social Decision Making in Anarchism and Minimalism," *The Personalist* 59, no. 4 (October 1978): 358–69.

issue, consensus would be achieved through informal discussion followed by a meeting in which a solution would be proposed and debated. Discussion would continue in and out of meetings, with participation dependent on interest in the specific issue, until a consensus is reached or it is clear that no consensus can be reached.

If consensus cannot be reached, the established practice continues. At the same time, minorities would be expected to give way to the majority unless the minority felt very strongly about the issue. And the majority would be expected to accommodate the concerns of the minority. Consensus means agreement reached through the acceptance of and adjustment to the positions of others in the community.

Such a decision-making process would mean many meetings and much debate. This is one of the implicit reasons for limiting areas of social decision making. If all possible questions had to be discussed in such a way, everyone would be in meetings all the time.

Collectivist anarchists are federalists. While stressing the small community, they propose a federal structure for issues that extend outside these small communities.[10] As George Woodcock wrote, "The village would appoint delegates to the regional federations, which in their turn would appoint delegates to the national federations. No delegate would have the power to speak for anything but the decisions of the workers who elected him, and would be subject to recall at any time."[11] Woodcock goes on to say that the delegates would be chosen for a short period of time, and although their expenses might be paid, they would receive exactly the same wage as in their regular jobs.[12]

An alternative model is to have delegates or administrators with more authority to make decisions. Still, such decisions would have to be confirmed by the community. The administrators would not have coercive authority. They would not govern; they would arrange the general scheme of production, distribution, and consumption. They would not regulate daily life in any detail because the people themselves do that. Administration is a political activity, however, and anarchists recognize that strict accountability to the collectivity is an essential component of anarchist administration.

Anarchism, then, can be characterized as a social theory opposing coercion and advocating a community-centered life with great amounts of personal liberty. Social decision making is reduced and personal decision making expanded. Life in an anarchist society would be a free life within a community. Measured against this model, William Morris was an exponent of anarchism.

10. See, for example, C. Berneri, *Peter Kropotkin: His Federalist Ideas* (London: Freedom Press, 1942).

11. George Woodcock, *New Life to the Land* (London: Freedom Press, 1942), 26.

12. On this point, see also P. S., "Anarcho-Syndicalism—The Workers' Next Step," *Freedom* 26 (30 January 1965): 5.

William Morris

Morris is probably remembered today primarily for his printing, his wall-papers, and some of his romances reprinted in response to the popularity of fantasy fiction.[13] During his lifetime he was probably best known for his poetry, though he also earned a reputation for a general advocacy of craftsmanship expressed through his printing, wallpapers, dyeing, and furniture. His role in the movement to preserve ancient buildings added to his reputation. And this many-faceted man was widely recognized for his political involvement.

For some time after his death Morris's politics were deliberately forgotten. For example, the twenty-four volumes of his collected works excluded most of

13. The literature on Morris is simply enormous. For a few examples, see R. Page Arnot, *William Morris: The Man and the Myth* (New York: Monthly Review Press, 1964); Florence Boos and William Boos, "The Utopian Communism of William Morris," *History of Political Thought* 7, no. 3 (Winter 1986): 489–510; Ian Bradley, *William Morris and His World* (London: Thames and Hudson, 1978); Patrick Brantlinger, "*News from Nowhere:* Morris's Socialist Anti-novel," *Victorian Studies* 19, no. 1 (September 1975): 35–49; Robert Currie, "Had Morris Gone Soft in the Head?" *Essays in Criticism* 129, no. 4 (October 1979): 341–56; Peter Faulkner, *Against the Age: An Introduction to William Morris* (London: George Allen and Unwin, 1980); Gustav Fritzsche, *William Morris' Sozialismus und anarchistischer Kommunismus: Darstellung des Systems und Untersuchung der Quellen,* vol. 3 of *Kölner Anglistische Arbeiten* (Leipzig: Bernard Tauchnitz, 1927); John Goode, "William Morris and the Dream of Revolution," in *Literature and Politics in the Nineteenth Century,* ed. John Lucas (London: Methuen, 1971), 221–80; Philip Henderson, *William Morris: His Life Work and Friends* (London: Thames and Hudson, 1967); Jack Lindsay, *William Morris: His Life and Work* (London: Constable, 1975); Robert E. Lougy, "The Politics of William Morris's *News from Nowhere:* The Novel as Psychology of Art," *English Literature in Transition* 13, no. 1 (1970): 1–8; J. W. Mackail, *The Life of William Morris,* 1-vol. ed. (1899; New York: Benjamin Blom, 1968); Nancy D. Mann, "Eros and Community in the Fiction of William Morris," *Nineteenth-Century Fiction* 34, no. 3 (December 1979): 302–25; R. D. Mathews, *An Introductory Guide to the Utopian and Fantasy Writing of William Morris* ([London:] William Morris Centre, 1976); Paul Meier, *La Pensée utopique de William Morris* (Paris: Editions sociales, 1972); Meier, "L'Utopie de William Morris—aboutissement ou étape," *Journal of the William Morris Society* 1, no. 3 (Spring 1963): 10–13; Meier, *William Morris: The Marxist Dreamer* (Atlantic Highlands, N.J.: Humanities Press, 1978); Lionel M. Munby, "William Morris' Romances and the Society of the Future," *Zeitschrift für Anglistik und Amerikanstik* 10, no. 1 (1962): 56–70; John Middleton Murray, "The Return to Fundamentals: Marx and Morris," *Adelphi* 3 (October–November 1932): 19–29, 97–109; Michael Naslas, "The Concept of the Town in the Writings of William Morris," *Architectural Association Quarterly* 11, no. 3 (1979): 21–31; T. M. Parssinen, "Bellamy, Morris and the Image of the Industrial City in Victorian Social Criticism," *Midwest Quarterly* 14 (Spring 1973): 257–66; Graham Stanhope Rawson, "William Morris's political romance 'News from Nowhere'. Its sources and its relationship to 'John Ball' and Edward Bellamy's political romance 'Looking Backward' " (Ph.D diss., Jena, 1914); Silvia Rota Chibaudi, "Utopia e propaganda: il caso William Morris," *Il Pensiero Politico* 9, nos. 2–3 (1976): 519–20; Angele Botros Samaan, " 'A Poet's Vision of the Socialist Millennium.' *News from Nowhere* and Its Critics," *Bulletin of the Faculty of Arts,* (Cairo University) 24, no. 2 (December 1962); E. P. Thompson, *William Morris: Romantic to Revolutionary* (New York: Pantheon, 1977); Paul Thompson, *The Work of William Morris* (New York: Viking, 1967); Geoffrey Tillotson, "Morris and Machines," *Fortnightly Review* 141 (April 1934), 464–71; Anna A. Von Helmholtz-Phelan, *The Social Philosophy of William Morris* (Durham: Duke University Press, 1927); and *William Morris: The Critical Heritage,* ed. Peter Faulkner (London: Routledge and Kegan Paul, 1973).

the political essays, apparently at the publisher's behest. (The essays were published later and provide the basis for part of the argument in this essay.) People chose to ignore the fact that Morris called himself a Marxist and a communist; he saw himself working for a revolution that would almost certainly be violent. Morris's greatest contribution to political thought, as seen from 1989, is in the literary pictures he drew of the society developing after—probably long after—that revolution. It is these pictures that I shall now examine.

A Dream of John Ball. John Ball probably led peasant uprisings in 1381 against landlords, and most of Morris's work is taken up with a presentation of contemporary conditions and the successful uprising; there are some passages, however, in which Morris describes through Ball a future society without masters. For example, at one point Ball observes,

> Ye shall not lack for the fields ye have tilled, nor the houses ye have built, nor the cloth ye have woven; all these shall be yours, and what so ye will have that all the earth beareth; then shall no man mow the deep grass for another, while his own kine lack cow-meat; and he that soweth shall reap, and the reaper shall eat in fellowship the harvest that in fellowship he hath won; and he that buildeth a house shall dwell in it with those that he bideth of his free will; and the tithe barn shall garner the wheat for all men to eat of when the seasons are untoward, and the raindrift hideth the sheaths in August; and all shall be without money and without price.[14]

Here Morris presents an idealized peasant society with a touch of the golden age or the arcadia. *A Dream of John Ball* is an agrarian utopia of peace and plenty where work is easy and all humankind is part of a single fellowship. But such felicity will only come about through violence. The likelihood of a violent transition to the better society is always part of Morris's vision even though it is sometimes easy to miss in his pictures of a peaceful future. For example, violence is present in the background of the utopia in *News from Nowhere*, where a long, bloody revolution was necessary to bring about the good society.

Morris once said that what was needed to improve society was action, not prophecy,[15] thereby indicating that he followed Marx in the notion that the point of the revolution was to change the world. Still, we remember Morris mostly for his visions of the future.

14. William Morris, *A Dream of John Ball,* in *The Collected Works of William Morris,* ed. May Morris, 24 vols. (London: Longmans, 1910–1915), 16:47, hereafter cited as *CW;* parenthetical in-text page references are to this edition. It was first published serially in *Commonweal* 2–3, nos. 44–54 (November 1886–January 1887) and in book form in London (Reeves and Turner, 1888).

15. Morris, "The Society of the Future," in May Morris, *William Morris: Artist, Writer, Socialist,* 2 vols. (Oxford: Basil Blackwell, 1936), 2:453, hereafter cited as *AWS.* Subsequent parenthetical in-text references are to this edition.

The Tables Turned. *The Tables Turned,* one of Morris's earliest such pictures, is a didactic play with the first act set before the revolution and the second after. Before the revolution, Mr. Justice Nupkins is a standard tool of the dominant class meting out injustice with a free hand. The rich get off even if guilty; the poor are jailed even if innocent. The revolution comes because, as one of the characters—described as a Socialist Ensign—says, "The Revolution we were all looking forward to had been going on all along, and now the last act has begun. The reactionists are fighting, and pretty badly too, for the soldiers are beginning to remember that they too belong to the 'lower classes.'"[16]

This revolution removes Justice Nupkins from the bench and, after the revolution, Citizen Nupkins is shown fleeing for his life—as he sees it—and from the new regime. As he worries to himself, "and then they will find out who I am, and then I shall be hanged—I shall be hanged—I, Justice Nupkins! Ah, the happy days when *I* used to sentence people to be hanged! How easy life was then, and now how hard" (*AWS,* 2:556). Nupkins's penchant for self-dramatization is evident.

Enter Mary Pinch, a typical laborer's wife (played by May Morris in the original; William Morris had a walk-on part as the Archbishop of Canterbury). The world she inhabits and represents is the world of *News from Nowhere,* and she is still marveling over the transformation that has been made in her life. Her new life reminds her of the joys of childhood. "Yes," she says, "I am my old self come to life again; it's all like a pretty picture of the past days" (*AWS,* 2:556–57).

Having discovered Citizen Nupkins (who had sentenced her to prison in the old days) cowering in the beeches, she invites him home, saying, "I'm like a child with a new toy, these days, and want to show new-comers all that's going on" (*AWS,* 2:558). Nupkins assumes that she plans to murder him. In fact, Nupkins is so obtuse that the audience was probably ready to murder him.

The community, meeting in traditional fashion under a tree, discusses important community business before getting around to dealing with Nupkins. The important business includes the repair of the town hall, trade with other communes, improvements in the silk mill, the wheat harvest, and a dog that is killing sheep. We are presented with a simple, agrarian and craft community making decisions by consensus and rotating any unpleasant job among themselves.

The problem of Nupkins, who remains unaware to the end, is dealt with by telling him that since he has no skills that might be useful to the community, he will be taught to dig potatoes. The play ends with the people dancing and singing and Nupkins in tears bewailing the fact that he must live in a world without lawyers, having "to dig potatoes, and see everybody happy" (*AWS,* 2:567). He will probably end his days being miserable because everyone else is happy.

The Tables Turned is a minor work in the Morris canon, but it illustrates

---

16. Morris, "The Tables Turned; or Nupkins Awakened," *AWS,* 2:555.

aspects of Morris's thought, including a slighting reference to Auberon Herbert, a contemporary individualist. In addition to the emphasis placed on the revolution, the collective nature of Morris's imagined better society is important, and the way it appears to function fits the analysis of anarchist society presented here. *The Tables Turned* serves best as an introduction to *News from Nowhere*, because that is where Morris most thoroughly describes his future utopia.

News from Nowhere.[17] *News from Nowhere* was written in part because Morris heartily disliked the best-selling American utopia, *Looking Backward* (1888) by Edward Bellamy. Bellamy's picture of a centralized socialist (Bellamy called his system nationalism) regime focusing on an industrial army and the reduction of labor appalled Morris. In a review of the book originally published in *Commonweal*, Morris wrote that the aim should not be to reduce labor as such but to reduce the "*pain of labor* to a minimum, so small that it will cease to be a pain."[18] He went on to argue that "the true incentive to useful and happy labour is and must be pleasure in the work itself" (*CW,* 16:506).

For Bellamy work was a burden to be reduced and life was to be lived during the enlarged hours of leisure, although there is little made of that leisure in *Looking Backward.* Bellamy did better at presenting a more rounded life in the sequel, *Equality* (1897). For Morris art was to weld leisure and work into an undivided whole: "Art, using that word in its widest and due signification, is not a mere adjunct of life which free and happy men can do without, but the necessary expression and indispensable instrument of human happiness" (*CW,* 16:507). Thus, Morris attacks Bellamy for presenting a truncated life shorn of meaning and the possibility of wholeness.

Morris makes this same point in his central political criticism of *Looking Backward*.

> It will be necessary for the unit of administration to be small enough for every citizen to feel himself responsible for its details, and be interested in them; that individual men cannot shuffle off the business of life on to the shoulders of an abstraction called the State, but must deal with it in conscious association with each other: that variety of life is as much an aim of a true Communism as equality of condition, and that nothing but an union of these two will bring about real freedom. (*CW,* 16:506–7)

17. William Morris, *News from Nowhere: or, An Epoch of Rest. Being Some Chapters from a Utopian Romance* (Boston: Roberts Bros., 1890). The novel was first published serially in *Commonweal* 6, nos. 209–47 (January–October 1890). Parenthetical in-text page references are to *CW,* vol. 16. On the textual problems, see Michael Raymond Liberman, "William Morris's *News from Nowhere:* A Critical and Annotated Edition" (Ph.D. diss., University of Nebraska, 1971).

18. Morris, "Looking Backward," *AWS,* 2:506. Originally published in *Commonweal* 5, no. 180 (22 June 1889): 194–95.

In this passage Morris makes two crucial points. First, he argues for the radical decentralization of social decision making stressing the need for individuals to control their own lives collectively. Second, he emphasizes variety or diversity as an absolutely essential concomitant of equality; this combination is the only guarantee of freedom. Both these points are developed in *News from Nowhere*.

In that book probably the best-known symbol of change in the governmental system is the use of the Houses of Parliament as a storehouse for manure, since Nowherians, it is noted, "have no longer anything which you . . . would call a government" (*CW,* 16:75).

> It is true that we have to make some arrangements about our affairs; and it is also true that everybody does not always agree with the details of these arrangements; but it is true that a man no more needs an elaborate system of government, with its army, navy and police, to force him to give way to the will of the majority of his *equals,* than he wants a similar machinery to make him understand that his head and a stone wall cannot occupy the same space at the same moment. (*CW,* 16:64; emphasis in original)

The point is reasserted later on: "We are very well off as to politics—because we have none" (*CW,* 16:85). Still, some social decisions which are made by a form of majority rule:

> In matters which are merely personal which do not affect the welfare of the community—how a man shall dress, what he shall eat and drink, what he shall write and read, and so forth—there can be no difference of opinion and everybody does as he pleases. But when the matter is of common interest of the whole community, and the doing or not doing something affects everybody, the majority must have their way; unless the minority were to take up arms and show by force that they were the effective or real majority; which, however, in a society of men who are free and equal is little likely to happen; because in such a community the apparent majority *is* the real majority, and the others know that too well to obstruct from mere pigheadedness; especially as they have had plenty of opportunity of putting forward their side of the question. (*CW,* 16:87; emphasis in original)

The first part of this description could have been used earlier in this essay to illustrate what is meant in anarchist theory by reducing the areas of social decision making and expanding the areas of personal decision making. The second part of this description poses a fundamental question regarding my argument: Can an anarchist theorist advocate majority rule? This is one basis on which Morris separated himself from the anarchists of his time. But when we look at his description of the exact procedure used in making decisions, Morris advocates majority rule only as a last resort:

"Some neighbours think that something ought to be done or undone: a new town-hall built; a clearance of inconvenient houses; or say a stone bridge substituted for some ugly old iron one—there you have undoing and doing in one. Well, at the next ordinary meeting of the neighbours, or Mote, ... a neighbour proposes the change, and of course, if everybody agrees, there is an end of discussion, except about details. Equally, if no one backs the proposer—"seconds him," it used to be called—the matter drops for the time being; a thing not likely to happen amongst reasonable men, however, as the proposer is sure to have talked it over with others before the Mote. But supposing the affair proposed and seconded, if a few of the neighbours disagree to it, if they think that the beastly iron bridge will serve a little longer and they don't want to be bothered with building a new one just then, they don't count heads that time, but put off the formal discussion to the next Mote; and meantime arguments *pro* and *con* are flying about; and some get printed, so that everybody knows what is going on; and when the Mote comes together again there is a regular discussion and at last a vote by show of hands. If the division is a close one, the question is again put off for further discussion; if the division is a wide one, the minority are asked if they will yield to the more general opinion, which they often, nay, most commonly do. If they refuse, the question is debated a third time, when, if the minority has not perceptibly grown, they always give way; though I believe there is some half-forgotten rule by which they might still carry it on further; but I say, what always happens is that they are convinced, not perhaps that their view is the wrong one, but they cannot persuade or force the community to adopt it."

"Very good," said I; "but what happens if the divisions are still narrow?"

Said he: "As a matter of principle and according to the rule of such cases, the question must then lapse, and the majority, if so narrow, has to submit to sitting down under the *status quo*. But I must tell you that in point of fact the minority very seldom enforces this rule, but generally yields in a friendly manner." (*CW*, 16:88–89)

It would be hard to produce a better description of consensual decision making in an anarchist society; such evidence is strong basis upon which to build the point that Morris was, in at least some senses, an anarchist theorist. A comparison with the description of anarchism provided at the beginning of this chapter shows Morris presenting almost precisely the same means of decision making.

Thus, the fundamental means of making social decisions is anarchist, but, as with any utopia, Morris's society possesses other aspects as well; these are anarchist also, in that they reject coercion. For example, education is mostly an apprenticeship system with little book learning. In addition, people choose freely where and with whom to live and are free to work at what they wish.[19]

News from Nowhere also reflects Morris's concern with individuality or

19. All these same arguments are made in Morris's "How Shall We Live Then?" ed. Paul Meier, *International Review of Social History* 16 (1971): 222–40.

diversity. It presents a society of diverse people—perhaps not greatly different but differing nonetheless—leading their lives in a community in which they are accepted and in which they can express themselves. In a way they are artists, at least in the sense of what Morris calls the "Democracy of Art, the ennobling of daily and common work."[20]

The Society of the Future. In "The Society of the Future" Morris reiterates the same points, writing that his "ideal is first unconstrained life, and next simple and natural life. First you must be free; and next you must learn to take pleasure in all the details of life."[21] Freedom, individuality, creativity, and simplicity are the keys to Morris's future world. Private property will be abolished, many machines will disappear, cities will be broken up, manufacturing will be decentralized, and some occupations will be abolished to improve the life of the workers. As Morris summarized his position in "The Society of the Future,"

> It is a society which does not know the meaning of the words rich and poor, or the rights of property, or law or legality, or nationality: a society which has no consciousness of being governed; in which equality of condition is a matter of course, and in which no man is rewarded for having served the community by having the power given him to injure it.
>
> It is a society conscious of a wish to keep life simple, to forgo some of the power over nature won by past ages in order to be more human and less mechanical, and willing to sacrifice something to this end. It would be divided into small communities varying much within the limits allowed by due social ethics, but without rivalry between each other, looking with abhorrence at the idea of a holy race. (*AWS*, 2:466)

In an essay entitled "Useful Work *versus* Useless Toil" (published in 1885 as *The Socialist Platform*),[22] Morris presents his analysis of work and its place both in modern life and in the future. He argues that the first task is to eliminate waste, and, having achieved that goal, it will be easy to provide the necessities of life for all. Then people will be able, within limits, to choose the work they want to do and make that work more enjoyable. As he wrote,

> We must begin to build up the ornamental part of life—its pleasures, bodily and mental, scientific and artistic, social and individual—on the basis of work undertaken willingly and cheerfully, with the consciousness of benefitting ourselves and our neighbours by it. Such absolutely necessary work as we should have to do would in the first place take up but a small part of each day, and so far would not be

20. Morris, "The Beauty of Life," *CW*, 22:79; originally entitled "Labour and Pleasure *versus* Labour and Sorrow" (1880).
21. Morris, "The Society of the Future," *AWS*, 2:459.
22. Morris, "Useful Work *versus* Useless Toil," *CW*, 23:98–120.

burdensome; but it would be a task of daily recurrence, and therefore would spoil our day's pleasure unless it were made at least endurable while it lasted. In other words, all labour, even the commonest, must be made attractive. (*CW*, 23:111)

Work, then, must be changed to become useful, interesting, varied, less time-consuming and undertaken in pleasant surroundings.[23] In order to achieve these ends, people must control their own lives rather than have them controlled by others.

As Morris wrote elsewhere, "The new order of things says . . . why have masters at all? Let us be *fellows* working in the harmony of associations for the common good, that is, for the greatest happiness and completest development of every human being in the community."[24] This "greatest happiness and completest development of every human being" has been the plea of every radical thinker of the past century-and-a-half. Communists and anarchists agree on this.

Conclusion

Since some areas of agreement do exist between communists and anarchists, there can be no certain conclusion to the quest to place Morris in one tradition rather than another, that is, Morris cannot be easily packaged. On the one hand, comparing Morris's views with communist anarchism would seem to be conclusive; Morris was a creative theorist of anarchism. Still, he vehemently denied it and called himself a communist. There is, as I indicated at the beginning, evidence to support this, though I am not accusing Morris of willful misrepresentation. He opposed some of the anarchists of his day and sided with the communists. But he also invited Kropotkin to contribute to *Commonweal*. In the day-to-day struggles of working for the revolution, Morris was a communist, but when he painted his picture of the future, he produced one with which no anarchist would disagree.

Marxists and anarchists tend to present very similar descriptions of revolution. They differ in their analyses of contemporary society and in the way they depict the society to come after the revolution. Morris used a class analysis of contemporary capitalism that might seem to place him with the communists, but so did anarchists like Kropotkin.

Further evidence is needed to support certain points. First, while we know Morris met Kropotkin, we do not know how close they were. We do know that they corresponded with some regularity, met fairly often, and apparently found each other's company congenial. Second, more evidence is needed regarding the

23. He makes the same point in "Art and Socialism: A Lecture Delivered Before the Secular Society of Leicester, 23rd January, 1884," *CW*, 23:192–214.
24. Morris, "The Dawn of a New Epoch," *CW*, 23:123; emphasis is in the original.

communist reception of *News from Nowhere* and Morris's utopia in general. It is possible that his futuristic society was acceptable as a picture of the final stage of communism—irrelevant to the current struggle but a valid long-term goal. Until such evidence is produced, Morris fits very nicely into the anarchist tradition, despite what he may have called himself.

ALEXANDER MACDONALD

Bellamy, Morris, and the Great Victorian Debate

There are few critical or biographical works about Edward Bellamy or William Morris, or indeed few general commentaries on utopian writing, that do not at least mention the contrast between the utopian visions of these two writers. Some references are strongly and emotionally worded, revealing that the choice between the two visions is perceived as an important one—not merely a squabble about the shape of never-never-land but something more fundamental.[1] That something is the fact that *Looking Backward* (1888) and *News from Nowhere* (1890), the most important utopian novels in a period rich in such books, embody between them much of the great Victorian debate about the future of humanity in modern industrial society. Although Bellamy and Morris did not know each other personally, they certainly knew of each other and recognized that essential issues were involved. After a brief look at the history of this "conflict in utopia," this essay will focus on these issues as embodied in the two famous novels, relate them to some other works by Bellamy and Morris, and consider, finally, how literary aspects of the novels can aid in understanding the contrast of their authors' ideas.

We know that Bellamy toyed with certain utopian notions in his notebooks of the 1870s. For example, he contemplated a state in which the government would "take hold of" procreation and manage an "enlightened sort of stock raising" for human beings. He imagined a utopia in which legislation would prohibit

---

1. For example, Bellamy was described as an "American petit-bourgeois Philistine" whose utopia was "vapid" and "counter-revolutionary" in R. Page Arnot, *William Morris: A Vindication* (London: Martin Lawrence, 1934), 26. Morris was charged with not giving up his "accustomed luxury or the privilege of self-expression made possible by the toil of others" in Arthur E. Morgan, *Edward Bellamy* (New York: Columbia University Press, 1944), 403. An edition of *News from Nowhere* dismissed *Looking Backward* as a "bureaucrat's paradise": James Redmond, "Introduction," *News from Nowhere* (London: Routledge and Kegan Paul, 1970), xxxvi. A Bellamy scholar suggested the problem was Morris's complete failure to understand Bellamy's objectives; see Peter Marshall, "A British Sensation," *Edward Bellamy Abroad,* ed. Sylvia Bowman (New York: Twayne, 1962), 93.

"coffee and tea, drinking, cards, late hours, foolish conversation, all love except matrimonial."[2] But a more consistent theme was the pouring of scorn upon socialist or utopian scheming,[3] and it was not until the mid-eighties, consequent upon what he termed his "discovery" of the industrial army idea, that he began to write *Looking Backward,* which was published in January of 1888. It soon became a best-seller and provoked Mark Twain to comment that Bellamy had invented a better heaven on earth.[4]

A surprising number of the readers of *Looking Backward* were inspired to write sequels of one kind or other. Some were admiring and emulative, like that by the New Zealander who wrote *Looking Upwards* and merely wanted "to show *how* we are to reach the state pictured by Bellamy."[5] There were satirical sequels in which Dr. Leete becomes a Big Brother figure,[6] or the head of the industrial army is General Dick Tator,[7] or in which Julian discovers to his horror that Edith, the consummate flower of the new age, is a laundress.[8] The author of one sequel confused Bellamy with the anarchist dynamiters and reminded us that: "GOD HIMSELF RECOGNIZED THE RIGHT TO HOLD PRIVATE PROPERTY."[9] There were also many letters, including one from A. L. McWhorter who, by his own account, lived in "a little sod shanty on the arid and poverty stricken plains of South Dakota"; McWhorter wrote: "at one reading I have finished *Looking Backward . . .* to you I bow in humble adoration."[10] A European correspondent wrote: "I was so struck with the truth and beauty of the ideas in [*Looking Backward*] that I instantly took the resolution of translating it into Hungarian."[11] Reverend E. Lewis of Ohio edited a "newspaper for the people" called *Plain Talk,* which proclaimed in its masthead, "Do right, Fear

2. Notebook, "Plots for Stories," no. 1, bMs Am 1181.6(2), 35, 36, Bellamy Papers, the Houghton Library, Harvard University, Cambridge, Mass.

3. In an article in the *Springfield Union* in 1877 he described a concept like the industrial army as "lunacy and something worse." Quoted in Sylvia E. Bowman, *The Year 2000* (New York: Twayne, 1958), 105.

4. Quoted in W. H. G. Armytage, *Yesterday's Tomorrows* (London: Routledge and Kegan Paul, 1968), 81.

5. Robinson Crusoe (pseud.), *Looking Upwards; or, Nothing New. The Upgrade: From Henry George Past Edward Bellamy on to Higher Intelligences* (Auckland, N.Z.: H. Brett, 1892), 7.

6. Richard Michaelis, *Looking Further Forward* (Chicago: Rand McNally, 1890), 27. Dr. Leete points out here that "ideas are little sparks. They may easily cause a conflagration if not watched."

7. W. W. Satterlee, *Looking Backward and What I Saw 1890–2101* (1890; reprint, New York: Arno, 1971).

8. Julian West (pseud.), *My Afterdream: A Sequel to the late Mr. Edward Bellamy's "Looking Backward"* (London: T. Fisher Unwin, 1900), 230. In fact, this could have been a response to *Equality,* in which Bellamy modified *Looking Backward*'s patronizing attitude toward women by giving Edith a role as a farm worker.

9. George A. Sanders, *Reality: or Law and Order vs Anarchy and Socialism. A Reply to Edward Bellamy's "Looking Backward" and "Equality"* (Cleveland: Burrows, 1898), 24.

10. A. L. McWhorter to Edward Bellamy, 6 December 1889, bMs Am 1181(280), Bellamy Papers.

11. Julius Csernyci to Edward Bellamy, 31 October 1891, bMs Am 1181(168), Bellamy Papers.

God and Make Money"; Lewis hailed *Looking Backward* as a "new gospel."[12]
And so the novel was indeed taken by those across the United States who
involved themselves in the Nationalist Movement by joining one of the many
(over one hundred and fifty) Nationalist and Bellamy clubs, which ranged in
complexion from ethical discussion groups to Fabian-type social action societies
to organizations sponsoring utopian colonies. Some of the clubs were criticized
for their snobbishness, for their tendency to attract retired military men with
command experience (lured, presumably, by the prospect of high rank in an
industrial army), for their exclusion of "the crank and the uneducated for-
eigner,"[13] and for the number of ladies involved rather than practical men of
affairs.[14] Bellamy's own participation in the movement was more indirect than
direct, as he put his energies into editorial work and, briefly, into Fabian politics
and Populism.[15]

William Morris might not have paid *Looking Backward* much attention had it
been only an American phenomenon but, of course, the novel became a British
phenomenon as well. It appeared first as a serial, in *Brotherhood,* between
January and July of 1889, after which Ebenezer Howard was instrumental in
bringing it out in book form.[16] According to the reminiscences of the artist
Henry Holiday, "piles" of *Looking Backward* were cleared off the bookstalls
every day.[17] No fewer than seventeen printings had appeared by December of
1889, although some reviewers were less than enthusiastic. *The Review of
Reviews* saw the novel as a "sign of the times" but found the story "dull as
ditchwater."[18] The *Saturday Review* printed two analyses, the first calling it "a
stupid book" which was "inexpressibly silly." The second review compared it to
a fantasy about an underground race and concluded that *Looking Backward* was
"much the more serious, more carefully wrought out, and less worth reading of
the two."[19] Despite such carping by the critics it was an enormous popular
success, leading to some interest in Bellamy's earlier works and to the inaugura-

12. E. Lewis to Edward Bellamy, 16 June 1889, bMs Am 1181(272), Bellamy Papers.
13. Speech by Cyrus Willard on the first anniversary of the Boston club, quoted in Howard H.
Quint, *The Forging of American Socialism: Origins of the Modern Movement* (1953; reprint, Indi-
anapolis: Bobbs-Merrill, 1964), 85.
14. Nicholas Gilman, "Nationalism in the United States," *Quarterly Journal of Economics* 4
(1889–1890): 67.
15. W. D. Howell's claim that Bellamy "virtually founded the Populist Party," quoted in
Bowman's *The Year 2000,* 134, was exaggerated. Nationalists were only a small number among the
10,000 delegates at the 1892 convention. See Martin Ridge, *Ignatius Donnelly: The Portrait of a
Politician* (Chicago: University of Chicago Press, 1962), 30.
16. See Dugald MacFadyen, *Sir Ebenezer Howard and the Town Planning Movement*
(Cambridge: M.I.T. Press, 1970), 21.
17. Henry Holiday, *Reminiscences of My Life* (London: Heinemann, 1914), 351. Holiday later
visited Bellamy in Chicopee Falls and was an enthusiastic admirer.
18. Unsigned review, "Looking Forward. . . ," *Review of Reviews* 1 (1890): 230.
19. Unsigned reviews, "Looking Backward," *The Saturday Review* 65 (24 March 1888): 356,
and 67 (27 April 1889): 508.

tion in 1895 of the "Bellamy Library" of radical publications.[20] It touched many individuals, such as Thomas Reynolds, who published his *Preface and Notes . . . to Looking Backward* in 1890, claiming to have held the same ideas himself for many years.[21] It was taken up enthusiastically by Christian Socialists, including the members of the Fellowship of the New Life; the Fellowship is interesting not only because it was the parent group of the Fabian Society, but also because William Morris appears a number of times on its lists of lecturers.[22] Various connections existed between Bellamy and the Fabians, of course, most notable among them the fact that Bellamy later wrote the introduction to an American edition of the *Fabian Essays*. The Nationalist Movement also spread to England, in the form of the Nationalization of Labour Society, with its journal, *The Nationalization News*.[23] This society, like its American counterpart, disappeared into other groups relatively quickly but its existence suggests the importance William Morris could have seen in refuting Bellamy's version of socialism.

It was in May of 1889 that Morris read *Looking Backward* and recorded his well-known reaction in a letter: "I suppose you have seen or read, or at least tried to read, *Looking Backward*. I *had* to on Saturday, having promised to lecture on it. Thank you, I wouldn't care to live in such a cockney paradise as he imagines."[24] The lecture was given to members of the Socialist League, which at this point was driving Morris out with the increasingly violent sentiments of its leaders.[25] The League's journal, *Commonweal*, had an American correspondent in Boston who kept members up to date on the Bellamy movement. A few weeks after Morris's lecture he wrote:

> A new party has been formed in Boston on socialistic principles—the Nationalist Party. Edward Bellamy, who is 'Looking Backward', and L. Gronlund, who is 'Marching Backward', are the leading spirits. The name "Socialism" is too ferocious for these gentlemen, so they prefer to style their "Socialism" as "Nationalism."[26]

The same correspondent reported that a large Boston clothing store had given

20. By Reeves, who had published the first British book edition.

21. Reynolds later wrote to Bellamy to express his "intense admiration" for *Equality*, 5 August 1897, bMs Am 1181(334), Bellamy Papers.

22. After Morris died the Fellowship's journal noted in an obituary signed J. F. O. (J. F. Onkeshott) that the Fellowship had "lost a friend," *Seed-Time* 31 (January 1897): 1. Morris's lecture on "How We Shall Live Then" was announced in *Seed-Time* 2 (October 1889): 12.

23. Bellamy wrote to support the paper and take a subscription, as well as to offer space in the *New Nation*. *Nationalization News* no. 3 (December 1890): 22.

24. *The Letters of William Morris to His Family and Friends*, ed. Philip Henderson (London: Longmans, 1950), 315.

25. *The Unpublished Lectures of William Morris*, ed. Eugene D. Le Mire (Detroit: Wayne State University Press, 1969), 278–79, 314. No text remains of this lecture on Bellamy and Grant Allen.

26. Henry F. Charles, "In The United States," *Commonweal* 5, no. 177 (1 June 1889): 174.

away thousands of copies of *Looking Backward* as a capitalist advertising gimmick. Morris had, therefore, a receptive audience for his review of *Looking Backward* in *Commonweal* in June of 1889. He criticized Bellamy's utopia for its extreme centralization, its regimentation, and for its mechanistic values. But his great fear was that socialists would read *Looking Backward* and, put off by the image of a dull utilitarian future, abandon socialism altogether. It was this, according to the recollection of his friend Andreas Scheu, which prompted Morris to begin *News from Nowhere* as a "counterblast" to *Looking Backward*.[27]

It was less a blast than a volley, however, because *News from Nowhere* appeared first serially in *The Commonweal* from January to October of 1890. Morris left the League then, saying as he went that "the success of Mr. Bellamy's book, deadly dull as it is, is a straw to show which way the wind blows."[28] Over that winter Morris revised *News from Nowhere* for its book publication, making many minor changes and adding several long passages.[29] When it appeared in March of 1891 one reviewer called it "bright as the roses and the sunshine of June."[30] Another described Morris as a member of what he might have termed the fleshly school of utopian writing:

> The *English* nation had disappeared. The race was now *Italian:* artistic, not serious; sensuous, not speculative . . . A great Nature-worship has set in; everything points to a deep joy in mere sensation, and to a deeper, vaster ignorance of what underlies it. . . . With him Beauty receives the definition of the *hareem*. Truth is a *façon de parler,* and God disappears.[31]

This illustrates a widely held view of the time, that socialism was no more than "a sublimated feast of the senses."[32] It is worth noting that this sort of charge was not leveled at *Looking Backward;* indeed, the book was endorsed by such

27. Andreas Scheu to A. R. Wallace, 3 February 1909, Additional Manuscript 46440, British Museum, London.

28. Quoted in E. P. Thompson, *William Morris: Romantic to Revolutionary,* 2d ed. (New York: Pantheon, 1977), 575.

29. Among the changes made by Morris were: addition of the passage describing the happy road-menders, perhaps in response to the objection that the utopia was too much a fairyland; addition of a section on foreign relations, perhaps to counter criticisms of insularity; many small changes and additions to "How the Change Came," indicating the seriousness with which Morris viewed the process of revolution; addition of "The Obstinate Refusers" to show more necessary work, female workers, and the political and economic freedom of the utopia; and, as if to underline Morris's attitude, addition of "and strange to say, I found that I was not so despairing" to the final page of the book. See J. Alex MacDonald, "The Revision of *News from Nowhere,*" *Journal of the William Morris Society* 3, no. 2 (Summer 1976): 8–15. See also Michael Liberman, "William Morris's *News from Nowhere:* A Critical and Annotated Edition" (Ph.D diss., University of Nebraska, 1971).

30. Unsigned review, "A Poet's Vision of a Socialist Millenium," *Review of Reviews* 3 (May 1891): 513.

31. Maurice Hewlett, "A Materialist's Paradise," *National Review* 17 (August 1891): 820–23.

32. W. Douglas Mackenzie, "The Socialist Agitation," *Westminster Review* 133 (1890): 508.

groups as the Woman's Temperance Union and named as a repository of traditional American values in the Sweet Home Family Soap Album.[33] If historian G. M. Young is correct in saying that Victorian socialism meant "everything that a respectable man saw reason to disapprove of or to fear,"[34] then a question, at least, arises about the suitability of applying the term to Bellamy and Morris both.

The comparisons of *News from Nowhere* with *Looking Backward* began almost immediately. Lionel Johnson, writing in *Academy* in May of 1891, saw Morris's vision as "virile and pleasant"; Bellamy's utopia, however, displayed "an ugliness so gross and a vulgarity so pestilent, that it deserved the bonfire."[35] They were also compared by Percival Chubb in the journal of the Fellowship of the New Life: *News from Nowhere,* he wrote,

> presents a striking contrast to Bellamy's *Looking Backward,* with which people are naturally comparing it—generally to the disadvantage of *News from Nowhere.* This fact raises the deepest question of the Socialist Movement. "What do we want?" . . . It is quite clear . . . that he that is for Bellamy's idea is against Morris's.[36]

While Morris was still revising *News from Nowhere* an edition appeared in Boston as a reprint from the serial version in *Commonweal.* Bellamy reviewed it in the *New Nation* in February of 1891. Bellamy claimed that there was no central point in Morris's utopia, that its lack of government and administrative structure rendered the kind of prosperity described there incredible. For example, Bellamy wrote, we are given no information about the railroad system, a criticism that tends to lose much of its force when we recall that there were no railroads in Morris's utopia.[37]

These are the main facts of the case. It is hardly one of history's great literary

---

33. See Bowman, *The Year 2000,* 119, and John L. Thomas, "Introduction," *Looking Backward* (1888; reprint, Cambridge: Harvard University Press, 1967), 1. Subsequent parenthetical in-text references to Bellamy's novel are to the Thomas edition.

34. G. M. Young, *Victorian England: Portrait of an Age,* 2d ed. (London: Oxford University Press, 1953), 169.

35. Lionel Johnson, "News from Nowhere," *Academy* 39 (23 May 1891): 483.

36. Percival Chubb, "Morris's Dip into the Future," *Seed-Time* 10 (October 1891): 2.

37. Bellamy, "News from Nowhere," *New Nation* 3 (14 February 1891): 47. Would Bellamy's review have been different had he seen Morris's revised version? On the whole, probably not. It is unlikely that the inclusion of the road-menders would have convinced him of the workability of Morris's society, and the obstinate refusers would be additional proof of its impracticality in economic or organizational terms. However, it is interesting to note the shifts in Bellamy's thinking between *Looking Backward* and *Equality,* among which are the admission of more violence into the transitional period and the disappearance of the large city he had glorified in *Looking Backward.* In *Equality* the city becomes a locality where population is denser than other places, not unlike the view of cities in *News from Nowhere* as places where people are apt to gather "rather thick." This shift reflects Bellamy's preference for small-town life, although it is tempting to speculate that reading Morris may have helped him revise his "official" thinking on the matter.

battles but it is interesting to note that Bellamy and Morris were themselves quite aware of the significant contrast between their ideas. Morris expressed the view that utopian visions can never be taken seriously as social blueprints but are personal to their authors, and he turned to writing romantic fantasies in his last years. Bellamy, who on the other hand did believe in the utopia as blueprint, went on to refine and expand his ideas in *Equality,* which appeared in 1896 in America, the year Morris died. A consideration of *Looking Backward* and *News from Nowhere,* with emphasis upon transformation from the old to the new societies, the political and economic structure of the new societies, and the values of the new worlds, provides further insight into the disparate utopian visions of Bellamy and Morris.

In most utopian literature there are two problems of transition to be faced: how to transform the existing society into the desired society of the future; and how to get the narrator into that future so he can report on what he sees. Both Bellamy and Morris solve these two problems—one substantive, the other literary—in interesting fashion. Bellamy's Julian West is a coupon-clipping member of the privileged class whose attitude toward strikers and reformers can be generally characterized as annoyance at the inconvenience they cause. An insomniac, he falls asleep one night in 1887 with the aid of mesmerism, and is preserved in a trance until discovered in Dr. Leete's garden in the year 2000. The destruction of West's house by fire, and his discovery, are accidental. Before he goes to sleep he has "absolutely no premonition" of what will happen. During his stay in Dr. Leete's house he admits frequently how unworthy he feels to have been selected of all his generation for this happy fate. And at the end of the book, after dreaming of going back to 1887, he wakes and knows that he may remain in the bliss of the year 2000 and in the arms of Edith, the descendant of his 1887 sweetheart.

Julian West does not have to struggle with others, nor make any hard or irrevocable choice; rather, he is carried on a wave of accident into the future, which reflects rather well the transformation of the whole society. Asked in an interview why he gave so little space to the transitional period, Bellamy replied that "when you want to induce a bachelor to enter matrimony you don't go on with a lot of particulars about the marriage license and the gloves and the ceremony—you just show him the girl and let him fall in love with her and the rest takes care of itself."[38] His argument in the novel is that society, like the reluctant bachelor, would recognize it was half in love with easeful utopia and do what was necessary to go head over heels into social bliss. The transformation of many monopolies into one great monopoly, as described by Dr. Leete, is a rapid, inevitable, nonviolent evolution of social and political structures. Near the end

---

38. Quoted in Bowman, *The Year 2000,* 118.

of the novel comes a leap of ethical consciousness as people recognize the approaching felicity, but nobody really has to do anything except cooperate with the inevitable. The notion of revolutionary action is explicitly rejected by Dr. Leete; it is, he tells Julian, simply a distraction from the main tendency. The revolutionary model did not fit well with the ethical basis of Bellamy's socialism, summed up in his essay on the "Religion of Solidarity."[39] It was also too exotic, too foreign, too inappropriate to the prosperous American context. "American Socialism" may have suffered shipwreck on "the reefs of roast beef," as one observer put it;[40] it is plain that in *Looking Backward* such individual commitments are seen as irrelevant in the face of the mighty Zeitgeist of industrial consolidation.

Think now of the transition of William Guest into the future. Here is a man actively working for the change of society, who sits in an underground railway carriage muttering "if I could but see it! if I could but see it!" His first morning in the new world he notices an inscription in the Guest-Hall, to the memory of the Hammersmith Socialists, underlining the connection between revolutionary commitment in the present world and the happiness of the future. The world visited by William Guest is only his dream world, the dream of a socialist, and at the end he must wake from the happy dream, find himself back in London, and be prepared to keep struggling for the world which he himself will never see.

And, of course, this captures the essential flavor of Morris's account of the transitional period. The description of "how the change came" is long and detailed. The struggle between owners and workers is hard, bitter, and involves considerable violence—which Morris regrets but argues the necessity for, at least for its purgative effect on the old, rotten society. Whereas Bellamy sees progress occurring along a straight, upward line, Morris's view is dialectical. It originates in that "Crusade and Holy Warfare against the age" he had learned from Carlyle and Ruskin, before he read Marx, and the process itself is revolutionary, opposed to the age and its values at every point. While Bellamy describes an evolution of the existing structures of society, Morris imagines the demolition of those structures.

These two views of social change are anticipated in two historical romances written prior to the utopias: Bellamy's *The Duke of Stockbridge* (1879) and Morris's *A Dream of John Ball* (1885). In *The Duke of Stockbridge* Bellamy describes the revolt of farmers in Shays' Rebellion of 1786. Poor economic conditions provide opportunity and motive for the "squires" to sell out the debtor-farmers, and the story consists of various clashes between the two

39. Bellamy, "The Religion of Solidarity," in *Edward Bellamy: Selected Writings on Religion and Society,* ed. Joseph Schiffman (New York: Liberal Arts Press, 1955).

40. Werner Sombart, quoted in David Herreshof, *The Origins of American Marxism* (New York: Monad, 1973), 16.

groups. The novel has been praised highly, but here we need only note the moral that Bellamy draws from the troubles: the rebellious violence of the farmers, though understandable, is not productive, and social reform is more likely achieved by legislative means.[41] Sharply contrasting with this is the conclusion Morris draws in his account of the peasants gathered around the rebel priest John Ball: they win their battle but do not change the essential character of the society, and it is clear that further struggle, along with education for revolution, is the only likely route away from a society of mastership and toward a new society of fellowship.[42]

Bellamy's view that the existing society could evolve into the better society implies a basic acceptance of the former's essential features; on the other hand, Morris's insistence upon revolution repudiates many of those features. This fact implies other major points of difference. The first of these has to do with the structure of the two utopian societies, Bellamy's being thoroughly centralized while Morris's is totally decentralized, a difference which in itself has further ramifications. To create one great capitalist—The State—out of many smaller capitalists is to centralize economic power, while in Morris's utopia the revolution does away with such elements of central power as already existed in 1890—Parliament, the railways, and others.

These opposing paradigms of sociopolitical organization are readily apparent in the two novels. *Looking Backward* describes a state that is a vast pyramid, centralized mechanically by pneumatic distribution tubes and telephone wires, and organized politically into the ranks and grades of a social army with quasi-military rewards such as merit badges.[43] The state governments have disappeared to make way for a supremely powerful national government. All these features are well known, as is Bellamy's explicit use of the image of the pyramid. Bellamy is, of course, reflecting the emergence of the centralized state, evidences of which appeared more and more rapidly in the latter part of the nineteenth century. The urbanization of society and the rise of municipal governments, the centralizing power of railways and telegraph wires, the consolidation of schools and hospitals into education and health systems—these and similar late Victorian developments underline how clearly Bellamy reflected the trend of the times.

---

41. The "Squires" see in these troubles the "first fruits of those pestilent notions of equality." *The Duke of Stockbridge: A Romance of Shays' Rebellion,* ed. Joseph Shiffman (Cambridge: Harvard University Press, 1962), 304.

42. Morris, *A Dream of John Ball,* in *The Collected Works of William Morris,* ed. May Morris, 24 vols. (London: Longmans, 1910–1915), 16:285–88; hereafter abbreviated as *CW.*

43. Another contemporary British view of the badges was that of M. D. O'Brien of the Liberty and Property Defence League: "Glory! Bits of bronze! *Esprit de corps*! Rather should we not say 'Fudge'? . . . So brilliant an idea deserves the whole lot of them, strung on a ribbon and thrown over the writer's neck." *Socialism Tested by Facts: Being An Account of Certain Experimental Attempts to Carry Out Socialistic Principles and Containing a Criticism of "Looking Backward", and the "Fabian Essays"* (London: Liberty and Property Defence League, 1892), 38–39.

Morris takes precisely the opposite course, as we know and as Bellamy complains of in his review of *News from Nowhere*. Few features of Morris's utopia reflect contemporary trends. Especially is this true of Morris's gleeful dismantling of the great cities which are, to use Walter Houghton's phrase, "the creation and symbol of liberal-industrial society."[44]

The narrative strategies of the two novels reflect this contrast between centralization and decentralization. Of course, in the technical sense both use the first-person point of view, but in a wider sense they are quite different. In *Looking Backward* Dr. Leete is virtually the sole source of information about society. His daughter Edith is allowed to take West shopping, or play music for him, but she defers to Papa on any matters of substance. Further, the story begins and ends in Dr. Leete's house, which—no doubt significantly—stands exactly where Julian West's former house had stood. At one point Dr. Leete, referring to the industrial army, tells West, "It is easier for a general up in a balloon, with a perfect survey of the field, to manoeuvre a million men to victory than for a sergeant to manage a platoon in a thicket" (p. 215). It is just this sort of view we have in *Looking Backward,* not from a balloon but from the top of Dr. Leete's house—his "favorite resort." So it is hardly surprising that Julian West's description of the city includes phrases like "colossal size," "stately piles," and "architectural grandeur," but puts no definite picture before the mind's eye.

In *News from Nowhere* the only character who comes close to Dr. Leete as "information central" is Old Hammond of the former British Museum. But he appears only for a few chapters and is left behind when the Guest travels upriver. Other characters interpret the new society to the Guest, and do not hesitate to criticize its ways. It would be stretching things to call *News from Nowhere* a hotbed of dissent but it is true that various voices are heard. Further, the long, slow upriver journey strengthens the impression of variety and individuality, which supports the anti-centralist bias. We see houses, fields, and people with a democratic attention to detail that harks back to the principles of Pre-Raphaelite paintings so familiar to Morris. There are many good examples of this attention: the careful description of the Guest House (contrasting with Bellamy's vague "piles"), the attention to nature and the seasons (it is June, but references to the corn harvest at the final feast reflect the Guest's mood before he departs), and the portraits of characters: at one point Guest observes Ellen coming out of a hay field "holding a basket in her hand"—a detail added in revision of the novel which illustrates Morris's concern that the unreal place become real to the reader.

Besides mode of transition and narrative techniques, the novels are very different in terms of values. The standards by which *Looking Backward* judges its own achievement—its values—are essentially quantitative. Throughout the

44. Walter Houghton, *The Victorian Frame of Mind* (New Haven and London: Yale University Press, 1957), 79.

book Dr. Leete's praise of the new order is almost entirely in such terms: more goods produced more efficiently, more people educated at more places, more art, more literature and science, less waste, and so forth. *Looking Backward* is an apotheosis of the values of the nineteenth-century liberal who was the intellectual descendant of Bentham. Consider the distribution system of utopian Boston, which is remarkable, according to Dr. Leete, because it illustrates "the prodigiously multiplied efficiency which perfect organization can give to labor"; it is "like a gigantic mill, into the hopper of which goods are being constantly poured" (p. 211). Such use of the word "mill" as a positive image contrasts very sharply with Morris's use of it as a term of contempt in describing the nineteenth-century education system: "no one could come out of such a mill uninjured," says Old Hammond.[45] So subtle a hint as this identifies Morris with that line of social criticism (from Blake's "Satanic" mills to D. H. Lawrence's portraits of mining country) which opposed the emerging industrial order and its effects on human beings. One such effect was the reduction of whole human beings to "hands." Perhaps Dr. Leete did not intend this sense when he said approvingly that "the machine is truer than the hand" (p. 128), but that most surely is the implication of Bellamy's system.

An interesting reflection of Bellamy's fascination with efficiency was his view that language itself is more an inconvenience than a raw material for art. His 1888 short story "To Whom This May Come" is purportedly the manuscript of a time traveler arrived at a country of mind-readers whose perfect, wordless comprehension of each other renders uncharitableness impossible and provokes an "invincible distaste for the laborious impotence of language."[46] In the less-speculative *Equality* a universal language has come into effect to make communication faster and more efficient,[47] a view completely consistent with the philosophy of *Looking Backward*. In Morris's utopia, however, people speak many languages, including local versions of Gaelic—less efficient than Bellamy's world but certainly more flavorful.[48]

The very marked difference between *Looking Backward* and *News from Nowhere* in terms of the realization of characters and settings is at least a reflection, if not a result, of what might be termed a difference in spiritual orientation between Bellamy and Morris. Although writing about a much earlier period, R. H. Tawney describes a similar distinction aptly:

45. *News from Nowhere, CW* 16:63. Subsequent parenthetical in-text references are to this edition.

46. Bellamy, "To Whom This May Come," in *Future Perfect,* ed. H. Bruce Franklin (New York: Oxford University Press, 1968), 290. The story first appeared in *Harper's.*

47. Bellamy, *Equality* (Toronto: George N. Morang, 1897), 231. The idea may have come from Zamenhof's pamphlet on "Esperanto," which appeared in 1887.

48. H. G. Wells was correct when he singled out Morris as an exception to the rule of utopian blandness, in *A Modern Utopia* (London: Thomas Nelson, 1905), 9.

Where Catholic and Anglican had caught a glimpse of the invisible, hovering like a consecration over the gross world of sense, and touching its muddy vesture with the unearthly gleam of a divine, yet familiar, beauty, the Puritan mourned for a lost Paradise and a creation sunk in sin. Where they had seen society as a mystical body, compact of members varying in order and degree, but dignified by participation in the common life of Christendom, he saw a bleak antithesis between the spirit which quickened and an alien, indifferent or hostile world. Where they had reverenced the decent order whereby past was knit to present, and man to man, and man to God, through fellowship in works of charity, in festival and fast, in the prayers and ceremonies of the Church, he turned with horror from the filthy rags of human righteousness.[49]

While the theological particulars do not strictly apply to Bellamy and Morris, there is a sense in which the two orientations to the world that Tawney describes are reflected in these authors' visions of utopia. One thinks of Bellamy's description of colonial Stockbridge, including the figure of Parson West; of the young Bellamy's immersion in the Calvinist tradition through his father's ministry; of the metaphysical dualism of "The Religion of Solidarity"; and finally of Julian West himself—a descendant of Parson West in more than name. Bellamy's narrator admits to Dr. Leete that he has been brought up a Calvinist, and he falls into a "profound depression" on the afternoon of his first Sunday in the twentieth century: "the color unaccountably faded out of all the aspects of life, and everything appeared pathetically uninteresting" (p. 286). In sum, Bellamy's outlook, a conviction that the material world of sensation and personality is merely ephemeral, unrelated to the higher or spiritual order, logically implies a disdain for that world with all of its sights, sounds, smells, and physical reality. Bellamy exemplifies that conviction in *Equality* when Mr. Barton, the preacher, observes that the "world was bound to outgrow the ceremonial side of religion . . . with its forms and symbols, its holy times and places, its sacrifices, feasts, fasts, and new moons"; Barton further claims that there now reigns a "wholly spiritual religion."[50]

In contrast with this one may think of Morris's boyhood, over which "a glimmer of Anglo-Catholic medievalism had flickered;"[51] of the influence of Romanticism and in particular the medieval revival on his early life; of his work in The Firm as a decorator of churches and maker of stained glass; of the world of John Ball which he imagined, with its rich appreciation of beauty and the expression of this in fine handwork; and finally, of Ellen in *News from Nowhere* itself: "The earth and the growth of it and the life of it! If I could but say or show

49. R. H. Tawney, *Religion and the Rise of Capitalism,* rev. ed. (1937; reprint, New York: New American Library, 1953), 190.

50. *Equality,* 231–32.

51. Graham Hough, *The Last Romantics* (1947; reprint, London: Methuen, 1961), 89.

how I love it!" (*CW,* 16:202). In this regard it may be significant that the final happy scene of the novel is set in a church:

> a simple little building with one little aisle divided from the nave by three round arches, a chancel, and a rather roomy transept for so small a building, the windows mostly of the graceful Oxford-shire fourteenth century type. There was no modern architectural decoration in it; it looked indeed, as if none had been attempted since the Puritans white-washed the mediaeval saints and histories on the wall. It was, however, gaily dressed up for this latter-day festival, with festoons of flowers from arch to arch, and great pitchers of flowers standing about on the floor. (*CW,* 16:208)

It is hardly necessary to point out that this church was a church of the fellowship of man rather than a Christian fellowship. Morris did not share John Ball's religious beliefs, but he did retain a view of the world very unlike that of the Puritans, who saw no gleam of the divine in material creation. Morris expressed this more spiritual concept of the world in his lecture, "The Arts and Crafts of To-day," in which, speaking of dining in the future, he rejected the idea of taking "some intensely concentrated pill once a year" and proposed, seriously, that "the daily meeting of the house-mates in rest and kindness for this function of eating, this restoration of the waste of life, ought to be looked on as a kind of sacrament, and should be adorned by art to the best of our powers."[52] His secular adaptation of the idea of a sacrament is reflected throughout *News from Nowhere,* in which the whole of creation is celebrated as a symbol of the new order of fellowship and its features lovingly described.

The point of these remarks about language and style is not that *News from Nowhere* is a better novel than *Looking Backward,* nor that Morris was the better writer. These are conclusions that few—least of all Bellamy himself—would deny. Bellamy admits in the preface to *Looking Backward* that the story of Julian West is no more than sugar-coating on the economic pill, and there are various statements in his notebooks reflecting a lack of interest in the art of literature, despite his initial reputation as a writer of "psychological romances."[53] The point, rather, is that style reflects content and values. Morris's careful attention to small detail, his use of a variety of speakers, reflects the individualism implicit in his political position—the tolerance for dissent, for grumbling, for obstinate refusal. His use of organic imagery (for example, the image of the garden) allies him with that Romantic anti-industrial tradition for which "organic" (linked by Coleridge with the primal power of Imagination) was a central term, a qualitative standard, something beyond the merely quantitative or

52. Morris, *CW* 22:358.
53. Bellamy wrote in a notebook, "No, to be sure I never tried my pen [at poetry] but it is not a question of pens but of souls. The poet's soul should be his in-listening ear like the oboe with musical multitudinous murmurs of song. Mine, alas, is not." Journal 4, bMs Am 1181.6(2), 9, Bellamy Papers.

mechanical (the lower order, in Coleridge's terms, of mere Fancy). Bellamy's use of language is frankly unpoetic; the extended metaphors that are used, then discarded like anecdotes in after-dinner speeches, or the frequent mechanical images, for example, reflect just as plainly the values of the utilitarian tradition out of which his social vision springs. John Stuart Mill argues in his essays on Bentham and Coleridge that they are the "seminal minds" of the century; it might be suggested that Bellamy and Morris represent a fruition of those two seeds of social and political thought. Their utopian visions may be seen as a microcosm of the Victorian debate about the need to preserve human values in a modern industrial society.[54]

They stand also on opposite sides of one of the great utopian debates about the essence of human nature. Although *Looking Backward* states that "human nature in its essential qualities is good" (p. 282), the strong central authority (represented, for example, by the ominously titled "Inspectorate," a feature added by Bellamy in revising the book) belies that optimism. Morris's more generous estimate of human nature is reflected in the freedom of his imaginary society and its belief that people would in fact cooperate and work hard because such behavior would prove intrinsically satisfying to them. Thus, *Looking Backward* and *News from Nowhere* anticipate what comes after them in our own century: the mechanized brave new world versus the "Kropotkinesque" island of Pala (in Aldous Huxley's famous work) or the emerging bureaucratic centralism of Anarres versus the Odonian ideal of an organic society of free individuals (in LeGuin's *The Dispossessed*).

If it seems that Bellamy is being unduly disparaged it is worth saying that such is not the intent. Bellamy allowed an idea to take hold of him and followed it to its conclusion sincerely and out of the best motives. Morris recognized in his review that Bellamy's criticism of nineteenth-century injustice was "forcible and fervid." It is interesting, however, that the world Bellamy created did not really reflect all his own preferences. He wasn't a man who fitted very well, or wanted to, into systems; for example, he thought independent reading a better education than that provided by school systems and colleges.[55] Indeed, in *Equality* he included the provision that people in some occupations could go on half pay and drop out of the industrial army. Perhaps Bellamy himself would have been happier in Morris's utopia than in his own, if only the place had been a little better organized.

---

54. Of course this must be qualified. Bellamy shared the values of the Benthamite position (the "liberal utopia" as Chad Walsh has called it) but, writing at the end rather than at the beginning of the century, he did not share the earlier liberal position of laissez faire. Morris shared the values of the Coleridgean position (the organic, qualitative standard which contrasted the mechanistic, quantitative values of the Benthamites) but abandoned the conservatism of that tradition as it was embodied in the authoritarian or paternalistic social visions of Carlyle and Ruskin.

55. Paul Bellamy (son of Edward) to H. W. Schneider, 2 March 1933, bMs Am 1182(49), Bellamy Papers [Morgan Papers].

DARKO SUVIN _____

Counter-Projects: William Morris and the Science Fiction of the 1880s

Historically, there is a very intimate connection between utopian fiction and other forms of what I have called science fiction in a larger sense, such as the extraordinary voyage, technological anticipation, anti-utopia and dystopia, among others. I have in fact argued that if science fiction is taken in that sense, then utopian fiction is not only, beyond a reasonable doubt, one of the historical roots of science fiction, but it can also be, logically if retroactively, subsumed into science fiction as one of its forms—that validated by and only by socio-politics. While I do not intend to deny the usefulness of studying texts in all possible ways, for example, utopian fiction in connection with utopian colonies, I have elsewhere argued that when studied as fictional literature, utopia is most usefully seen as "the sociopolitical subgenre of science fiction."[1]

I have further argued that this historical connection of utopian and science

1. Darko Suvin, *Metamorphoses of Science Fiction* (New Haven: Yale University Press, 1979), 61; see also the whole chapter leading up to this conclusion. Hereafter this work will be cited as *MOSF* and all parenthetical in-text references are to this edition. The present essay is based on that book and on my subsequent *Victorian Science Fiction in the UK* (Boston: G. K. Hall, 1983), hereafter cited as *VSF;* all parenthetical in-text references are to this text. In the first book, I argue for a theoretical definition of science fiction as a fictional genre whose necessary and sufficient conditions are the presence and interaction of estrangement and cognition. I arrive at the position that the alternate reality or possible world induced in the reader(s) by a science fiction text is not a prophecy or even extrapolation but an analogy to unrealized possibilities in the addressee's or implied reader's empirical world. Therefore, however empirically unverifiable the narrative agents, objects, or events of science fiction may be, their constellation in all significant cases shapes a parable about ourselves. It is in this position that the deep epistemological (neither simply historical nor simply technical) kinship between science fiction and utopian fiction can be based. This argument is repeated in "Science Fiction and Utopian Fiction: Degrees of Kinship," in Suvin, *Positions and Presuppositions in Science Fiction* (London and Kent: Kent State University Press, 1988). After the present essay was first given, at an MLA Session on William Morris in December 1984, I have expanded and modified my theoretical position, allowing more weight to the extrafictional connections of utopian fiction, in "Locus, Horizon, and Orientation: The Concept of Possible Worlds as a Key to Utopian Studies," *Discours social/Social Discourse* 1, no. 1 (1988): 87–108; also forthcoming in Giuseppe Saccaro del Buffa and Arthur O. Lewis, eds., *Utopia e modernità* (Rome: Gangemi).

fiction is surely neither accidental nor insignificant. Some lines of that argument may be condensed as follows: If science fiction is a fictional genre "whose main formal device is an imaginative framework alternative to the author's empirical environment," and in addition a genre which is narratively dominated by a "fictional *novum* (novelty, innovation) validated by cognitive logic" (*MOSF,* 7–8, 63), then its narrative in each case actualizes a different (though historical and not transcendental) world, with slightly or largely modified relationships and cultural norms. This "possible world" of the narrative is induced in the reader by means of a feedback oscillation between two imaginative realities. They are, on the one hand, the reader's participation in a conception of empirical reality that the collective social addressee of any text (or group of texts) possesses, and on the other hand, the narratively explicit modifications a given text supplies to that initial conception. In this light, the intimate traffic between utopian and science fiction reposes on the nearness and cultural interpenetration of the ideological categories that for the reader validate those two genres. That *validating intertextual category* is for utopian fiction sociopolitics, and for the mentioned cognate forms of science fiction it is (as the case may be) a strange otherness, technocracy, or corrupt and wrong ethics and politics.

Even more intimate (and possibly even more illuminating and lawful) is the connection of *the narrative logics* at hand. Any form of science fiction has unavoidably to explain the novum by means of a "lecture" strand, usually both masked and distributed into various narrative segments. Narratologically speaking, utopian fiction is science fiction in which that "lecture" is (still) systematically discursive. In other words, in utopian fiction the "lecture" is almost the whole plot. As Barthes has indicated, the plot of utopian fiction is a panoramic sweep conducted along the well-known, culturally current sociopolitical categories (geography, demography, religion, constitution, economics, warfare, and so on).[2]

I hope this introduction may at least sketchily indicate a context more significant than simple facticity or accident for a discussion of some not insignificant relationships between Morris and the science fiction of Victorian Britain in the decade preceding *News from Nowhere*. No doubt, this only contributes some further elements to, and, in the best case, identifies some foci of the much wider and more complex theme of "Morris and Intertextuality," within which *News from Nowhere* would deserve a monograph of its own. My essay will have two different but, I hope, complementary parts, both of them arising from data presented and works whose context is discussed at more length in my book, *Victorian Science Fiction*. I shall deal first with the image of William Morris found in two brief science fiction "alternative histories" which postulate a bad

2. Roland Barthes, *Sade, Fourier, Loyola,* trans. Richard Miller (New York: Hill and Wang, 1976), 117–20 and passim.

socialist government in a near-future U.K. Second, I shall discuss two works of science fiction, one simply dystopian and one expressly anti-utopian, elements from which were (certainly or probably) refunctioned in *News from Nowhere*. This may allow some more general conclusions about a two-way relationship between Morris and the paraliterary science fiction discourse of his time, which appears to have been more intimate than heretofore assumed.

1. Morris as a Narrative Agent in the 1880s Science Fiction

A booklet of thirty-five pages was published in London by Harrison and Sons in 1884 under the title *The Socialist Revolution of 1888, by an Eye-Witness* (*VSF* 25, 127). Two of the main investigators of the domain identify its author as "Fairfield," no first name, without giving a reason for the attribution. In all the biographical handbooks and annual lists of Victorian professions from 1848 through 1900 inclusive (*VSF* 128–35, 165), the only Fairfield to be found is Edward Denny Fairfield, a Liberal civil servant in the Foreign Office. While some internal features of the narration would not be inconsistent with both liberalism and civil service, I have been unable to confirm or disprove this attribution. The story itself belongs to the form or subgenre I have called the "alternative history." I have defined it in *VSF* as that science fiction subgenre in which an alternative locus, sharing the material and causal verisimilitude of the writer's empirical world, is used to articulate different possible solutions of such societal problems which are of sufficient importance to require an alteration in the overall history of the narrated world. After 1880, with the rise of social tensions in the whole of Britain, this form became dominant within science fiction, at the momentary expense of the Future War and the more lasting expense of the moribund Extraordinary Voyage form. More precisely, *The Socialist Revolution of 1888* is, as its title spells out, a near-future variant of this small but recognized form of social discourse. In fact, it is the best from half a dozen short-range historical alternatives that sprang up suddenly during 1884–1885, whose choice of fictional form as well as relative brevity and absence of the author's true name testifies in all cases to an urgent intervening into the suddenly sharpening British political conflicts.

The plot of the booklet is not unshrewd nor unhumorous: Socialists led by Hyndman and Burne-Jones (!) revolt through mass demonstrations and seize London, and the troops fraternize with them. After one week, they hold a plebiscite that votes in socialism as against individualism by a margin of 7.5 to 5.5 million votes. The new, clearly quite legal government repeals private property, at which—in a transposition of the Paris Commune events—all British ships flee the country with the rich and their possessions on board. Morris is appointed minister for industries in the socialist government of 1888 as the only practical person in the whole crowd who knows how to keep the expenses of production down. This is not what one might call a "Cold Civil War" text, since it gives explicit credit to the socialists for genuine good will and also implies that their mass support stems from their addressing genuine grievances. Further, the story is written from the vantage point of a high civil servant, who as secretary of the Cabinet sees the personal working out of political maneuvers. However, it has an antisocialist horizon, and it depicts how societal confusion results from the loss of affluence, international financial pressures, and increase of state meddling à la Henry George. The government therefore becomes generally detested, and in particular all the women turn unanimously against it. The passive resistance of the people, as well as of the army and police, forces Hyndman's government to call another plebiscite which abolishes socialism by a vote of 9.5 million to 100 thousand (it is unclear what happened to the some 3.4 million voters who have disappeared since the first plebiscite: presumably they are those who fled the country, rather than abstainers). The new Liberal parliament eschews vengeance against the toppled regime, and in fact keeps one important measure it enacted: the Irish Home Rule. We must today sigh at the bloodless and, except for the initial catalysis, genuinely democratic nature of all the events, shaped within a fair-minded and for this subgenre unusually even-tempered, if somewhat ironical, liberal ideology. My initial parallel to 1871 Paris (always a presupposition in such U.K. alternative histories) must be therefore amended to the effect that this is a counter-project to the Paris Commune: the English, having a genuine parliamentary tradition, would deal with such an emergency better. This brief text implies, rather than openly states, that even within the "extravagant doctrinaires" that socialists notoriously are, there is one queer (but very English) chap, namely Morris, who actually knows what production means. I will refrain from making obviously possible twentieth-century parallels, and only remark that we hear nothing else of interest about Morris: one must assume he carries on in the liberal England, suitably chastened. At any rate and at a minimum, this text establishes that the theme of a possible nonviolent change of regime was current in the social discourse prior to Morris's text.

My second text is another booklet, this one thirty-six pages, *The Next 'Ninety Three* by W. A. Watlock, published in London by Field and Tuer in 1886. It belongs to the same subgenre of near-future alternative history, and the discrepancy of having a writer's signature may be only apparent, since another fruitless search through all the Victorian biographical sources for Britain and its Empire in the British Library (*VSF,* 128–36) turned up no evidence of such a person, so that this might well be a pseudonym. The pamphlet's discursive strategy can be seen from the subtitles: . . . *or, Crown, Commune, and Colony: Told in a Citizen's Diary.* The *diary* of a *supporter* of the egalitarian regime introduced in Britain by the 1893 "Equable Distribution of Property Act" is used to present the reader with its thus doubly authenticated results: Ireland is divided into thirty-eight kingdoms, the canny Scots proceed to fuse employers and employed, but the diary naturally focuses on the woes in England. Though divided into communes, it is subjected to an all-meddling state, which introduces an equal four-hour work day for all, including the intellectuals who are obliged to do manual work. It is mentioned in passing that William Morris rebels at the iniquities of state oppression and interference, and insults the powers that be, which has, however, no particular consequence. Finally, the ground having been prepared by universal discontent, a Colonial Legion from Australia brings about the Restitution to the old regime. This is a much less fair-minded, condemnatory rather than even-tempered companion to the previous booklet, but it will serve to indicate the opposite, "Conservative" rather than "Liberal," end of the anti-socialist spectrum. It is quite interesting that the more Liberal booklet took Morris's democratism for granted and focused on his competence in production, while the Conservative view focused on his (obviously well-known) enmity toward centralized state authority. The strong-arm methods ascribed to all political factions are of a piece with the rhetorical expedient of "double nega-tion" in which a supporter of the opposed faction testifies not only to its illusions and (mis)deeds but also to the inevitable disillusionment. It is a cruder piece of work than the first booklet, but it is again not without a certain polemical, anti-revolutionary shrewdness.

2. Two Novels of the 1880s Science Fiction Refunctioned in *News from Nowhere*

It is well known that Morris wrote *News from Nowhere* among other things (to keep to the science fiction context only) as a counter-project to Bellamy's *Looking Backward,* and it has also been mentioned that he was certainly stimu-lated by Jefferies's *After London* and possibly by W. H. Hudson's *A Crystal Age* (*MOSF,* 187–88). However, it seems to me that these no doubt indispensable correlations display a one-sided emphasis on "high lit." We do not have a full overview, I believe, of what Morris read, but it is quite possible that even had he usually read no semipolitical or other (by Victorian bourgeois standards) "lower" fiction—which is a dubious assumption—the mention of his figure and behavior in these two samples of alternative history would have been pointed out to him by political comrades or opponents. The case seems much strengthened by his possible (and in the second case highly probable) use of two "farther future" science fiction works by Dering and Besant, the first of which is sufficiently obscure.

That first work, *In the Light of the Twentieth Century* by Innominatus, whom I was able to identify as Edward Heneage Dering, is less interesting. Published in

London by Hodges in 1886, it is a dream-vision of 155 pages, with a first-person narrator transferred to 1960. Dering himself (1827–1892), though son of an Anglican parson, converted in 1865 to Catholicism with his wife, novelist Lady Georgiana Chatterton, and lived the life of a recluse in a medieval country home, reputedly dressed in seventeenth-century costumes. He wrote seven novels to further his views, in addition to one book on Esoteric Buddhism, a pamphlet on philosophy, and a book of poems, and he translated from Italian books on philosophy and political science.[3] His book is accordingly an eccentric ultramontane tract or anatomy very loosely allied to a novel, which fulminates against "Corporate freedom" (that is, state control), paganism, free-love flirtation, the outlawing of caritative endeavors, and other pet Catholic horrors. There is much religious discussion on a high philosophical level, and the narrative ends in uprisings of the mob.

However unlikely a companion to Morris's radically different utopia this might be, there are two elements in it which strike me as significantly similar. First, *the framework:* at the beginning, when the *Ich-Erzähler* comes to the future, his translation is explained to him—by interlocutors who belong to those better, *ergo* unsatisfied, people who even in this soul-destroying future long for happiness—as a result of "the force of your will against the actual state of things at the time, [which] affected your own state of being *in* that time" (p. 8). He had therefore "reduce[d] the action of the heart," as the fakirs do, and slept his way to the future (p. 9). Further, at the end, as the narrator is being killed by the mob, he awakes: " 'Was it a dream? or am I delirious?' " he asks (p. 151). Second, *the skipping over of a generation:* Dering's narrator is expressly identified as being two generations into the future by the expedient of meeting the grandson of an old friend. This has no constitutive signification in his text, whereas in Morris it is meaningfully refunctioned into an enmity (as Middlebro' put it) against the generation of the fathers, and by metonymy against patriarchal authority (cf. *MOSF,* 186). Nonetheless, the fact that Morris's main narrative agents are either old men (Old Hammond and William Guest, who is in some powerful ways identified as Hammond's alternative twin) or a range of young people, from children to rather young adults, introduces a discrepancy into the supposed realistic verisimilitude of *News from Nowhere:* it amounts to an absence of fathers, or for that matter mothers too, in other words, of the whole parental or adult generation. This might be partly explained by the incomplete refunctioning of Dering in Morris, no doubt due to powerful psychological pressures in the latter. A similar situation might obtain with the fuzziness of the "dream's" validation: Morris obviously would want to use neither an esoteric "force of the

3. More elements for a characterization of E. H. Dering could be found in these books as well as in a memoir of his and another by his wife that he edited, all of which I confess to not having read; see *VSF,* 160, 227, and 238.

will" nor a fakir-type catalepsy, but he was in too much of a hurry, and probably too little interested, to supply a better motivation. Since I am in this essay not much interested in positivistic "sources," I cheerfully acknowledge that this last element is almost certainly over-determined. Besides and before Bellamy, a "long sleep" was a commonplace of fantasy arrivals into the future from Washington Irving, Edmond About, and John Macnie on (cf. *VSF passim*). Most important, Morris's affinity for this feature was probably extra-literary, since it manifested itself from his earliest prose tales and poems on. Something similar might therefore hold also for the verbal parallels describing the narrator's puzzlement upon awakening. "Was it a dream?" is an utterance to be expected in this situation. Furthermore, the famous "Was it a vision, or a waking dream?/ . . . —do I wake or sleep?" ending from Keats's "Ode to a Nightingale," Morris's great verse exemplar, would in itself have sufficed. Nonetheless, the exact semantic inversion of the second half of Dering's sentence, signaled by Morris's underline of *was*, seems more than accidental: "Or indeed *was* it a dream? If so, why was I so conscious all along that I was really seeing all that new life from the outside . . . ?" This take-off would fit well with the putative relation Morris-Dering, which I submit is in some ways analogous to the relation Morris-Bellamy: in linguistic terms, semantico-pragmatic opposition coupled with syntactic parallelism; in ideological terms, a counter-project based on the stimulating irritation supplied by some significant reusable formal elements.

My most interesting exhibit is Walter Besant's novel of 198 pages, *The Inner House,* published by Arrowsmith's as their 1888 Christmas Annual. The popular novelist, historian, and do-gooder Besant was a well-known Victorian figure so that I need not recount his biography, except to mention that I found him to be the clearest example within this genre—and possibly within Victorian fiction as a whole—of social climber as pillar of Establishment, of novelist as virulently reactionary ideologist (*VSF,* 146, 401, 406, *et passim*). The novel begins with the discovery of immortality by the Carlylean Professor Schwarzbaum from Ganz-weltweisst am Rhein in 1890. By some unexamined and perhaps burlesquely meant analogy, this discovery arrests decay in all domains, so that from the second chapter on the plot moves within an ironic "perfect Socialism" (p. 103). In it there is no property and little work, people all live and dine together and dress uniformly (the famous ant heap of petty-bourgeois antisocialism), births are allowed only to compensate for a mortal accident, and finally all emotions—religion, art, love, suffering, and competition (!)—are suppressed, so that life carries on in calm stupor. In a narratively clumsy move (perfectly consonant with the other aspects of this clumsy book), the story is told in first person by the arch-villain, an ex-servant and—horrors!—scientific egalitarian, the mainstay of the ruling College of Physicians. Of course, this alone would not establish a sufficient parallel between Besant's and Morris's texts, since the whole tradition of future alternative history (for example, Bellamy and the four texts discussed here) used a first-person narrator for obvious reasons of giving the reader an anchor of familiarity to counteract strangeness.

However, a second element suggests that this story is the source of another refunctioning by Morris. Almost all the oldsters were liquidated in a Great Slaughter at the beginning of Besant's "socialist" epoch. One of the few oldsters left is "the Curator of the Museum" in the new capital, who lives with his granddaughter Christine. Perusing old books in the museum, she rediscovers love, honor in battle (*sic!*), and the dignity of Death. With the help of a sailor "curiously unable to forget the old times" (p. 88), she revives the discontent of the quondam "gentle class" (p. 89); it is unclear why that class survived the Great Slaughter of the propertied, but Besant is above such petty consistencies since he wants to have both a horrible warning and a happy ending. This class revolts to regain leadership, land, wealth, and for good measure arts, amusement, and love. The "Inner House" of the title is where the Secret of Life is kept; the rebels, not being able to bring the people over to their side, secede from the College of Physicians' rule. I think it is beyond doubt that Old Hammond and Clara as well as their location at the country's central museum, the only source of a historical memory otherwise absent from the new society, are a refunctioning of the old curator and his granddaughter. The museum—which is from a forgotten anterior epoch that is not coincidentally the time of the story's author and original readers, and which exists to be visited by the traveler into the future—will be taken over from Morris in Wells's *Time Machine* and thence become a staple of much modern science fiction. Possibly, a few other touches in *News from Nowhere* may also be counter-projects to Besant's; for example, his emphasis on revival of love and jealousy may have suggested Morris's throwback murderer in chapter 24, as well as the backsliding due to book-reading by the grumbling *laudator temporis acti* in chapter 22 who is so eloquently put down by Clara in favor of the Book of Nature.

3. Some Concluding Indications on Morris and on Counter-Projects

I hope to have indicated the possibility, and perhaps the probability or the near-certainty, of a few matters that might fruitfully engage further attention by the community of Morris critics. First, it is by now accepted that Morris used some elements from the More-to-Bellamy utopian panoramas and the Jefferies-cum-Hudson devolutionary anticipations. However, the two works discussed in part I here do not only allow us to glean some testimonies as to Morris's image. Beyond that, they suggest the possibility of Morris's having been alerted through them (if in no other ways) to the existence of paraliterary forms such as the alternative history or the science fiction genre as a whole (of which alone I have found 182 new book-size titles published in the U.K. from 1848 through 1890). The discussion in part 2 here suggests, second, that Morris indeed knew at least the very "middlebrow" work of Besant and probably that of Dering. Further, it shows that Morris found ways to use at least Besant's "keeper of past knowledge" motif in the same way he used the "sleeping into the future" frame of Bellamy's, and possibly also of Dering's and some other writers: in a "contrary" proceeding of subversion and inversion to which I have applied the term of *counter-project*. Finally, he may also have in the same manner reused the evacuation of the adult generation from Dering's text.

Of course, Morris not only ideologically stood on their heads the elements he had (entirely or incompletely) refunctioned from Dering and Besant, but also, and just as important, he made triumphant sense of most of them. But this does not prevent us from using the insights obtained from the existence of such refunctionings for two purposes: first, to explain some minor but not uninteresting discrepancies in *News from Nowhere;* and second, to follow Morris's very process of refunctioning. That process is instructive on its own as the work of an artist who refuses the fetish of individualist originality. He proceeded, in my opinion quite rightly too, as all the great creators have done: he made lion-flesh of digested mutton. With Molière, he could have exclaimed: *Je prends mon bien où je le trouve.*

Morris's stance is also, last but not at all least, instructive as a formal procedure originating in the ethos and attitude of dialectical negation and sublation that seems common to consistent socialists, from Marx to Brecht (from whose playwriting practice I borrowed the term of counter-project), and which includes William Morris as one of its best practitioners. I would like to end this chapter—appropriately enough for one on Morris—with a pointer to possible general discussions about this procedure. A counter-project can, I think, be provisionally defined as the use of some significant aspects or relationships from one universe of discourse for contrary axiological conclusions in and by means of another universe of discourse, the induced value-judgments being intended to shape the reader's pragmatic orientation. As a rule, the discursive aspects will be narrative agents and/or narrative space-time—in this case, a grandfather-grand-daughter pair in a future country's only museum and repository of information about the past. However, the notion of universe of discourse or (in more familiar semiotic fashion) of a Possible World, is not limited to fictional "possible worlds," but comprises also nonfictional (doxological) "possible worlds." As suggested, this will be particularly clear in the case of writers strongly committed to a salvational doctrine or belief about human relationships in everyday "reality"—socialists. The counter-project is obviously always some kind of inversion, and I would further speculate that it has an affinity with the rhetorical trope of *chiasmus,* or Marx's *Poverty of Philosophy* as counter-project to (rebuttal of) Proudhon's *Philosophy of Poverty.* It must be added, nonetheless, first that we are here entering into extremely complex philosophical debates about Possible Worlds, and second that I know of no sustained discussion of the discursive form of counter-project. These first notes of mine are thus mainly a call for such a discussion, in an informed feedback with social history. In any such discussion, the whole opus of William Morris, and in particular *News from Nowhere,* will be a fulcrum.

MICHAEL HOLZMAN

The Encouragement and Warning of History
William Morris's *A Dream of John Ball*

In the spring of 1886, William Morris, with his colleague in the Socialist League, E. Belfort Bax, began to publish in the League's newspaper, *Commonweal,* a series of historical and explanatory articles about socialism under the general title of "Socialism from the Root Up." These were later collected and published as a thick volume, *Socialism: Its Growth and Outcome.*[1] Midway in this serialization Morris inserted another series, a historical romance entitled *A Dream of John Ball.*[2] Appearing as it did in the pages of *Commonweal,* the romance can be seen as a set of illustrations, as it were, for "Socialism from the Root Up," a fairly scholarly animation of history "co-opting" history itself for the socialist cause. This chapter will trace the sources for *A Dream of John Ball,* note the changes Morris introduced into the traditional story, and make some observations about Morris's purposes.

The motto Morris had given the Socialist League was "Educate, Agitate, Organise," and the function of *Commonweal* was to help accomplish all three of these aims. In general, the materials published in *Commonweal* were commentaries on the news of the day, reports on socialist activities, and accounts of socialism and economics. Some articles were technical explanations of socialist theory; many were historical, following the example of H. M. Hyndman in seeking the roots of English socialism in peculiarly English traditions; and others followed the more internationalist line of Engels with news of the "movement" from all over the world and accounts of such crucial events as the Paris Commune and the Haymarket Riot. *Commonweal* also published literary works, most but not all of which were by Morris himself.

A common misinterpretation of Morris's relationship to socialism, particu-

1. Ernest Belfort Bax and William Morris, *Socialism: Its Growth and Outcome* (London: Swan Sonnenschein, 1893).
2. William Morris, *The Collected Works of William Morris,* ed. May Morris, 24 vols. (London: Longmans, 1910–1915); *A Dream of John Ball* appears in vol. 16, and all parenthetical in-text page references are to this volume and edition.

larly as regards his literary work, was that Morris was "naturally" an aesthete, whose interest in socialism is to be regretted. We no longer see his socialism as an aberration, an interlude between periods of exquisite aestheticism, but we have not yet arrived at a full understanding of the transition from *The Earthly Paradise* to *The Pilgrims of Hope,* that is, the transition from an art which enunciates its critique of everyday life by denial and that which carries an explicit critical burden. That transition was accomplished in the small group of literary works that were serialized in *Commonweal,* each of which was solidly enmeshed in Morris's work as a revolutionary socialist. Just as much of *News from Nowhere* was written as part of a debate within socialism—presenting Morris's arguments against anarchism—so *A Dream of John Ball,* the earlier piece, was clearly an effort to teach the value of history to socialists, in opposition to the position of historical inevitability taken by their opponents.

Morris and Bax were following Engels and Marx in the genre of polemical historical narrative with the articles of "Socialism from the Root Up." In their first installment Morris and Bax claimed that history is on the side of socialism:

> Our adversaries are sometimes forward to remind us that the present system with which we are so discontented, has been made up by the growth of ages, and that our wills are impotent to change it; they do not see that in stating this fact they are condemning their own position. Our business is to recognise the coming change, to clear away obstacles to it, to accept it, and to be ready to organise it in detail. Our opponents, on the contrary, are trying consciously to stay that very evolution at the point which it has reached today; they are attempting to turn the transient into the eternal; therefore, for them history has no lessons, while to us it gives both encouragement and warning which we cannot afford to disregard.[3]

"Socialism from the Root Up" was an agitational as well as an educational document.[4] Accounts of historical events can be a way in which the victors of historical struggles claim the support of reality itself for their arrangements, or a way in which their challengers seek to undermine those claims. Morris and Bax sought by retelling the history of England to change the conception of that history in the minds of their readers, to make the possibility of alternative interpretations of the past vivid, and thus to make the possibility of alternative futures vivid, also.

The second installment of "Socialism from the Root Up" included a description of the fourteenth-century English Peasants' Rebellion.

---

3. "Socialism from the Root Up," "Chapter I—Ancient Society," *Commonweal,* 15 May 1886, 53.
4. "I think the duty of the League is educational entirely at present; and that that duty is all the more important since the SDF has entirely given up that side of things." William Morris to Joseph Lane, 30 March 1887, *The Collected Letters of William Morris,* ed. Norman Kelvin (Princeton: Princeton University Press, 1987), 2:631.

By this time serfdom generally was beginning to yield to the change introduced by the gilds and free towns: the field serfs partly drifted into the towns and became affiliated to the gilds, and partly became free men, though living on lands whose tenure was unfree—copyholders, we should call them. This movement towards the break-up of serfdom is marked by the peasants' war in England led by Wat Tyler and John Ball in Kent, and John Lister (dyer) in East Anglia, which was the answer of the combined yoemen, emancipated and unemancipated serfs, to the attempt of the nobles to check the movement.[5]

It may have been this simple statement which set off Morris's imagination, drawing him back in another way to his favorite historical period, an epoch of history that he had already brought to life in hundreds of pages of more or less idealized poetry and prose, in scores of drawings and other designs.

"Socialism from the Root Up" would continue to appear regularly through its thirteenth chapter in the 30 October 1886 issue of *Commonweal*, approximately one chapter every other week, a rhythm broken only by the appearance of Morris's "An Old Story Retold," in the 18 September 1886 issue. The first episode of *A Dream of John Ball* then ran on the front page of the 13 November 1886 issue. Like "Socialism from the Root Up," it thereafter appeared on the interior pages of the newspaper, frequently the third. *A Dream of John Ball* occupied that position continuously without interruption by other serializations to its final episode on 22 January 1887. "Socialism from the Root Up" resumed immediately in the *Commonweal* issue for 5 February 1887. The serialized parts of *A Dream of John Ball* were, then, physically interchangeable with those of "Socialism from the Root Up" as pages in *Commonweal*. For a year its readers could open their paper knowing that they would find either the historical and technical work on socialism written by Morris and Bax, or, in the same place, the imaginative expansion of this material in Morris's *A Dream of John Ball*. There is more to education than the enumeration of facts and the marshaling of arguments. Particularly for the task that Morris had set himself, the overwhelming claims of the system which he opposed were such that simply to imagine vividly a world in which the nineteenth-century given was not necessarily the real was as much a contribution to knowledge as Bax's economic expertise. Much writing about contemporary conditions attributed them to some iron law of necessity. Morris attempted to show in his socialist prose romances that those conditions were not inevitable.

John Ball is a figure in Froissart's *Chronicles,* which includes an account of the origins of the rebellion. Froissart began with an explanation of serfdom

5. "Socialism from the Root Up," "Chapter II—Mediaeval Society," *Commonweal,* 22 May 1886, 61. Morris's reference to John Lister (dyer), who joined the rebellion with his arms still stained with woad, would, of course, have a personal meaning to Morris himself, whose dyeing experiments had often left him in a similar condition.

itself: "Ther was an usage in England, and yet is in diverse countreys, that the noble men hath great fraunches over the comons, and kepeth them in servage." This statement is then expanded and the nature of serfdom made specific: "That is to say, their tenauntes ought by costome to laboure the lordes landes, to gather and bring home theyr cornes, and some to threshe and to fanne, and by servage to make theyr hey, and to heaw their wood and bring it home." Froissart states that serfdom was more common in England than elsewhere, especially in the counties of Kent, Essex, Sussex, and Bedford. It was there that the rebellion began, with a complaint against serfdom and an appeal to natural law, as it were:

> These unhappy people of these sayd countreys began to styrre, bycause they sayde they were kept in great servage; and in the begynning of the worlde they sayd ther were no bonde men. Wherefore they maynteyned that none ought to be bonde, without he dyd treason to his lorde, as Lucifer dyde to God.

Therefore, the serfs argued that as they were not criminals or rebels, they ought to receive wages for their work:

> Saying, why shuld they than be kept so undre lyke bestes, the which they sayd they wold no lengar suffre, for they wolde be all one; and if they labored or dyd any thyng for theyr lordes, they wold have wages therfor as well as other.[6]

Froissart says that the English peasants were required to farm the lands of their feudal lords; harvest and store their grain; thresh it and make hay; hew and cart their lords' wood. He acknowledges that these feudal burdens were greater for them than those of peasants elsewhere. He then lays out their appeal to be paid for their labor, an appeal based on the common nature of humanity and the unnaturalness of class society.

After giving these causes of the rebellion and sketching the previous career of John Ball—a habitual agitator and troublemaker—Froissart follows a tradition dating back to the Greek historians by repeating the reasons for the rebellion in the guise of giving a sample of Ball's preaching. I will quote this, as Morris had read it, for Froissart's style in this dramatization is carried over into Morris's accounts of John Ball's speeches.

> A ye good people, the maters gothe nat well to passe in Englande, nor shall nat do tyll every thyng be common; and that there be no villayns or gentlymen, but that we

6. John Froissart, *The Chronicle of Froissart,* trans. Sir John Bourchiers, Lord Berners (New York: AMS Press, 1967), 2:223–25. This use of Froissart was a habit of Morris from his earliest period, that of *The Defence of Guenevere*. As Carole Silver has noted, "Morris is fond of developing hints and implications from his source into major incidents or motifs in his own poems"; *The Romance of William Morris* (Athens: Ohio University Press, 1982), 18.

may be all unyed toguyder, and that the lordes be no greatter maisters than we be.
What have we deserved, or why shulde we be kept thus in servage? We be all come
fro one father and one mother, Adam and Eve: wherby can they say or shewe that
they be gretter lordes than we be? Savynge by that they cause us to wyn and labour
for that they dispende. They ar clothed in velvet and chamlet furred with grise, and
we be vestured with pore clothe; they have their wynes, spyces, and good breed, and
we have the drawyng out of the chaffe, and drinke water; they dwell in fayre houses,
and we have the payne and traveyle, rayne, and wynde in the feldes; and by that that
cometh of our labours they kepe and maynteyne their estates: we be called their
bondmen, and without we do redilye them servyce, we be beaten; and we have no
soverayne to whom we may complayne, nor that wyll here us nor do us right. Lette
us go to the kyng, he is yonge, and shewe hym what servage we be in, and shewe
hym howe we wyll have it otherwyse, or els we wyll provyde us of some remedy.
And if we go togyder, all maner of people that be nowe in any bondage wyll folowe
us, to the intent to be made fre; and whan the kyng seyth us, we shall have some
remedy, other by fayrnesse or otherwyse.

Froissart's version of John Ball's speech again begins with the assertion that only
a return to the natural order—abolishing feudal relations—is just. This is
followed by a list of comparisons between the lives of the lords and those of the
serfs: in clothing, drink, food, and housing. He points out that the wealth of the
lords is derived from the poverty of the serfs, and he urges his listeners to go
with him to the king to petition for an end to serfdom. Morris took these
materials, which he had been familiar with since childhood, and formed them
into a narrative to complement the drier historical account given in "Socialism
from the Root Up."[7]

As Carole Silver reminds us, Morris was at pains to inform himself concerning the historical background of the events he recounted.[8] He (and Bax) were
working a vein that saw much activity in those years. Thorold Rogers and
Engels, primarily, but many others also in England and on the Continent were
attempting what we would now call revisionary history. (Kautsky's work on the
Peasants' War in Germany was an extended historical narrative that closely
parallels Morris's fictionalized history of the earlier English equivalent.) The
English Peasants' Rebellion of 1381 was a dramatic, and particularly well

7. Another potential source for the figure of John Ball was Raphaell Holinshed, *Chronicles,
beginning at Duke William the Norman, Commonlie Called the Conqueror and Descending by
Degrees of Yeers to all the Kings and Queenes of England in their Orderlie Successions* (New York:
AMS Press, 1965), 2:740.
8. "Morris carefully bases his fictional versions of events on the medieval and contemporary
works of English historians. Supplementing Froissart's account of the rebellion with such sources as
Holinshed's *Chronicles* and *The Chronicle of John Hardying*, he turns to nineteenth-century historians for analysis and interpretation. He derives materials from Sir Henry Maine, Bishop Stubbs,
Edward Freeman, John Richard Green, and Thorold Rogers, as well as from the more popular
writings of Southey, Macaulay, and Cobbett." Carole Silver, *Romance of William Morris*, 124.

documented, instance of peasant resistance to medieval social relations. Wat Tyler's march on London, the confrontation with the young king, Richard II, the extensive nature of the rebellion and its sudden collapse, all served to give it emblematic status in such popular accounts as Froissart and Holinshed, and later in a rich literary and historical tradition. The formation of the rebellion—its causes and its failure—were all timely matters for consideration at the end of the nineteenth century when the social and labor relations that had succeeded feudalism were in their turn in crisis.

A Dream of John Ball animates the textual sources that Morris had at hand and turns them to his own purpose. In the first scene, the Dreamer—and it is important to keep in mind that this narrator is a persona for Morris himself, a vehicle for his dialectic—meets a group of villagers, one of whom, Will Green, takes the Dreamer/Morris persona to be an itinerant story-teller and like himself a member of John Ball's revolutionary Fellowship. This is confirmed for Will Green when the Dreamer "leant forward and whispered in my ear: '*John the Miller, that ground small, small, small,*' and stopped and winked at me, and from between my lips without my mind forming any meaning came the words, '*The king's son of heaven shall pay for all*'" (p. 220). This seems at first rather peculiar. What is the meaning of these spells? Now, in Thomas Walsingham's *Historia Anglicana* we find a copy of the letter that the historical John Ball circulated to incite and direct the fourteenth-century rebellion against feudalism. The fragment of English which is embedded in Walsingham's Latin chronicle begins with a paragraph of salutation and advice:

> John Schep, som tyme Seynt Marie prest of Yorke, and now of Colchestre, greteth welle John Nameless, and Johan the Mullere, and Johan Cartere, and biddeth hem that thei ware of gyle in borugh, and standeth togiddir in Goddis name, and biddeth Peres Plouyman go to his werke, and chastise well Hobbe the robber, and taketh with you Johan Trewman, and all his fellows, and no mo (and loke seharpe you to on heued, and no mo).

The country folk—the laborers, the millers, the teamsters, the plowmen—are to unite against the "gyle" of the town, its lawyers and privileges. These instructions are followed by what even Holinshed found to be "dark" verses:

> Johan the Muller hathe ygrowude smal, smal, smal;
> The Kyngis sone of hevene shall pay for alle.
> Be ware or ye be wo,
> Knoweth your frende fro youre foo,
> Haveth ynowe, and seythe 'Hoo:'
> And so welle and bettre, and fleth synne,

And sekth pees, and holde therynne.
'And so biddeth Johan Trewman and all his felawes.'[9]

Perhaps John Ball's remarkable letter was in fact what Morris took it to be, a set of instructions for the revolutionaries, including a sign and countersign so they might recognize one another. Morris's use of fourteenth-century documents at the beginning of a romance serialized in a newspaper intended for a mixed audience is a significant indication of his attitudes toward his politicized literary work of this period. Morris thought of *A Dream of John Ball* as serving an educational function for the readers of *Commonweal.* Giving them this piece of authentic historical information was at once a sign of and part of his duty as a revolutionary party leader.[10] This is the context for a characteristic journalistic comment by Morris on the official festivities of Lord Mayor's Day that year: "When the poor begin to know that they are poor not by irremediable accident, but because they are robbed by a useless class who can be got rid of, the beginning of the end is at hand."[11] This was precisely the function of *A Dream of John Ball, Commonweal,* and the Socialist League itself: to bring knowledge about their situation and its history to "the poor." Part of that knowledge was information about the history of such educational and agitational work. Ball's verses were the fourteenth-century equivalent of Morris's own "Chants for Socialists," the slogans and sermons forerunners of *Commonweal.* A revolution, Morris was informing his readers, has a literary aspect—or at least an ideological one. Ball's function in Wat Tyler's Rebellion paralleled, and justified, Morris's own work as a propagandist, street corner orator, poet.[12]

Morris uses a fairly long interior scene in a tavern in chapter 2 of *A Dream of John Ball* as a device for conveying background information about the Fellowship, the wrongs of the people, and their resolve to bear it no longer. The tavern setting for this is particularly pleasing: "The walls were panelled roughly enough with oak boards to about six feet from the floor, and about three feet of plaster above that was wrought in a pattern of a rose stem running all round the room" (p. 221). It is an interior courtesy of Morris and Company. The narrator

9. Thomas Walsingham, *Historia Anglicana* (London: Longman, Green, Longman, Roberts, and Green, 1864), 2:33-34.
10. "The rebellion of 1381 had become an important event in the work of historians contemporary with Morris, particularly those whom he admired. . . . Talking of the system of slogans and catchwords [J. R. Green, in his *History of the English People,* 1878] writes: In the rude jingle of these lines began for England the literature of political controversy: they are the first predecessors of the pamphlets of Milton and Burke.'. . . Thus it was an *articulate* uprising with real possibilities of victory." John Goode, "William Morris and the Dream of Revolution," in *Literature and Politics in the Nineteenth Century,* ed. John Lukacs (London: Methuen, 1971), 247.
11. "The Moral of Last Lord Mayor's Day," *Commonweal,* 20 November 1886, 265.
12. For other parts of his audience, the exchange of old English phrases brought the gratification of recognition of old texts, a verbal window, as it were, into something quite near the world of Malory so loved by the Pre-Raphaelites.

tells the villagers that he is from Essex, the center of the rebellion. They react with "a great shout . . . For I must tell you that I knew somehow, but I know not how, that . . . ," whereupon Morris inserts the background of Wat Tyler's Rebellion: how the landowners had sought to tighten their hold on the peasants, how the peasants had risen against them, and how "at St. Albans they were wellnigh at blows with the Lord Abbot's soldiers."[13] During dinner, the narrator's (read "Morris's") clumsiness with the medieval utensils is taken as a sign that he is an Oxford scholar (and not a countryman), which he acknowledges, and then it is more or less natural for him to pay for his supper by telling a story, in this case an Icelandic tale.

We are not told which tale the "Oxford Clerk" relates in the tavern—some fierce Saga fragment, no doubt—but Morris gives some details of the "stave of Robin Hood" which is sung as a return:

> It was concerning the struggle against tyranny for the freedom of life, how that the wild wood and the heath, despite of wind and weather, were better for a free man than the court and the cheaping-town; of the taking from the rich to give to the poor; of the life of a man doing his own will and not the will of another man commanding him for the commandment's sake. (p. 224)

This nineteenth-century urban glorification of the outdoor life contrasts strongly with the historical John Ball's complaints about agricultural working conditions. Where in the fourteenth century the progressive position was the tendency toward urbanization, Morris, in more than one of his roles, saw progress in de-urbanization, that glorification of country life best seen in his *News from Nowhere*.

Morris works another piece of authentic material from the rebellion into his romance by having the villagers sing John Ball's verses, including the catch about the Miller grinding "smal, smal, smal," ending with a choral shout that "John Ball hath rung our bell!" as the village church's bells summon them to the cross. Here again Morris takes a strange phrase from John Ball's letter, drama-tizes it, and makes it meaningful. John Ball's speech at the cross stands alone as the third installment of the serial and the fourth chapter of the book. Morris recasts Froissart's set-piece as a nineteenth-century interpretation of Ball's doctrines. It begins with a summary of the rebellion to that moment (the day before the march on London), a summary largely taken from Froissart. Ball tells how he had been held prisoner by the archbishop and how the rebels had freed him and burned the archbishop's palace, then begins a decidedly Morrisian critique of orthodox morality:

13. Walsingham had kept his *Chronicle* at St. Albans. There was an "ancient building" at St. Albans, the cathedral, on behalf of which Morris had written a letter to the chapter in 1878.

for I say to you that earth and heaven are not two but one; and this one is that which ye know, and are each one of you a part of, to wit, the Holy Church, and in each one of you dwelleth the life of the Church, unless ye slay it. Ah, my brothers, what an evil doom is this, to be an outcast from the Church, to have none to love you and to speak with you, to be without fellowship! (p. 230)

One difficult task for a socialist organizer in the 1880s was dealing with the hold of the chapel over the working class. The aggressive atheism of international Marxism did not go over well with many of the coal miners, for example. Morris approaches this problem by claiming that socialism itself is the truly religious force in society. Thus the burden of the next part of Ball's sermon becomes an equation of socialist fellowship and Christian morality:

Forsooth, brothers, fellowship is heaven and lack of fellowship is hell: fellowship is life, and lack of fellowship is death: and the deeds that ye do upon the earth, it is for fellowship's sake that ye do them, and the life that is in it, that shall live on and on for ever, and each one of you part of it, while many a man's life upon the earth from the earth shall wane. (p. 230)

Morris invents a late medieval heresy, claiming that earth itself is heaven and that hell is found in the hearts of the rich. "Therefore, I tell you that the proud, despiteous rich man, though he knoweth it not, is in hell already, because he hath no fellow" (p. 231). Already, barely into his story, Morris makes its point explicit in an aside: the tale is about "how men fight and lose the battle, and the thing that they fought for comes about in spite of their defeat, and when it comes turns out not to be what they meant, and other men have to fight for what they meant under another name" (pp. 231–32). This dialectical moral will be the subject of the final dialogues in the church.

The priest confesses that while in prison he had momentarily regretted not having taken the Christian path of prayer and help for individuals instead of the socialist path of sacrifice for the good of all. It is not charity, for Morris's priest, that is the good; it is fellowship. If fellowship is that which is good, domination is clearly evil: "Yea, forsooth, once again I say as of old, the great treading down the little, and the strong beating down the weak, and cruel men fearing not, and kind men daring not, and wise men caring not" (p. 233). (Froissart had written: "We be called their bondmen, and without we do redilye them servyce, we be beaten; and we have no soverayne to whom we may complayne, nor that wyll here us nor do us right.") The speech of Morris's John Ball modulates from an ecstatic vision of fellowship to a savage indictment of the rich:

Forsooth, in the belly of every rich man dwelleth a devil of hell and when the man would give his goods to the poor, the devil within him gainsayeth it, . . . Forsooth, too many rich men there are in this realm; and yet if there were but one, there would be one too many, . . . and ye shall lay their heads in the dust. (p. 234)

John Ball completes his condemnation of present evils with a vision of future bliss.

What else shall ye lack when ye lack masters? Ye shall not lack for the fields ye have tilled, not the houses ye have built, nor the cloth ye have woven; all these shall be yours, and whatso ye will of all that the earth beareth; then shall no man mow the deep grass for another, while his own kine lack cow-meat; and he that soweth shall reap, and the reaper shall eat in the fellowship the harvest that in fellowship he hath won; and he that buildeth a house shall dwell in it with those that he biddeth of his free will; and the tithe barn shall garner the wheat for all men to eat of when the seasons are untoward and the rain-drift hideth the sheaves in August; and all shall be without money and without price. Faithfully and merrily then shall all men keep the holidays of the Church in peace of body and joy of heart. And man shall help man, and the saints in heaven shall be glad, because men no more fear each other; and the churl shall be ashamed, and shall hide his churlishness till it be gone, and he be no more a churl; and fellowship shall be established in heaven and on earth. (p. 237)

Morris's John Ball follows Froissart's in his listing of the tasks of labor and its rewards: fields tilled, hay mowed, housing and clothing provided for. And Morris adds a list of benefits to be expected from fellowship that are the reverse of the evils noted by Froissart's rebel priest. There are, however, two differences between the presentations: the centrality of the category of fellowship, introduced by Morris's character—surely a medievalization of the essence of socialism itself—and, oddly enough, the Christianity of the nineteenth-century phrasing, too obvious to be stated, perhaps, by the older chronicle, or perhaps needed for period color by the newer.

Here, within the essentially negative vision of *A Dream of John Ball*, we already see the essence of the positive dream that was not written out in full until 1890 in *News from Nowhere*. Morris's changes in Froissart's account of Ball's sermons are directed to the *Commonweal* audience. Where Froissart's John Ball complains about scarcity in the categories of food, shelter, and clothing, Morris's proclaims the possibility of abundance in each of these same categories. Froissart's John Ball asserts the unity of the peasants, a political unity for the achievement of political ends; Morris's priest calls for "fellowship" as a way to achieve economic liberation. If fellowship is the solution to the problems of medieval domination, clearly, for Morris, it was also the solution to the agony of nineteenth-century capitalist domination. The work of uniting the working class as an answer to the evils of the modern world was a task that Morris thought necessary from the time of his involvement in the Eastern Question Association in his pre-socialist days.[14] His writings in *Commonweal,* including his romances, were instrumental to that work.

Morris's careful handling of the historical materials is further illustrated in his description of a battle in chapters 5 and 6.[15] The battle is with a group of local knights and, it is emphasized, their lawyers.[16] One of the demands of the rebellion had been the execution of all lawyers. The labor shortage after the Great Plague had caused a loosening of feudal duties and a general rise in the wage levels. Lawyers, then, were used by the landowners to return wages and obligations to their pre-plague levels—thus the hatred of the peasantry for lawyers and legal records. The Edenic dream of a world that is transparently meaningful often finds expression in complaints about the opposite condition, a world whose meaning is obscured by such arrangements, for which lawyers are responsible. How satisfying, even retrospectively, to envision such an easy solution to the problem as simply killing the lawyers! Morris was much belittled by the Fabian socialists, as if he did not understand their goals; perhaps he understood them better than did the Fabians themselves, understood that bureaucratic solutions to economic problems become political problems, and thus thought it would be better, in a utopian way, to be free of all such folks and their works.

The chapter entitled "Betwixt The Living & The Dead" takes place, as do all the succeeding chapters, inside the village church. The Dreamer and the priest arrive there, look around, and settle themselves in for the long night ahead. They begin by talking of the battle's dead, viewing the bodies, and expressing their opinions about death itself. John Ball voices fairly conventional ideas about a judgmental afterlife, while the Dreamer expresses a materialist philosophy. After this discussion the Dreamer attempts to leave the church to return to Will Green's, but the priest restrains him: "For once more I deem of thee that thou has seen things which I have not seen, and could not have seen" (p. 267). This repeated expression by the priest is one of the centers of the text: rather than John Ball himself going into the future in order to learn the consequences of his rebellion, or the Dreamer simply visiting the past in order to learn the secrets of the origins of nineteenth-century conditions, John Ball receives a visit from "Morris," so that the past might have the secrets of the future communicated to

14. J. W. Mackail, *The Life of William Morris* (London: Oxford University Press, 1950), 1:357–60. See also E. P. Thompson, *William Morris: Romantic to Revolutionary,* 2d ed. (New York: Pantheon, 1977), ch. 5.

15. These constitute the fourth and fifth episodes of the *Commonweal* serialization, which appeared 4 and 11 December 1886.

16. There is another historical touch in this episode. Froissart mentions prominently in his account a knight, Sir John Newton, taken prisoner at Rochester by the rebels, who is used as an intermediary with the nobles. In Froissart the knight is an unwilling tool of the rebels. Morris makes him a collaborator, paralleling Morris's own position as a gentleman who has cast his lot in with that of the workers.

it, and the present might learn its similarities and differences from the past. The Morris persona "finds" that the fourteenth-century physical environment, including its man-made features, compares quite favorably with the degraded landscape of the late nineteenth century, but he also "finds," and communicates to the readers of *Commonweal*, that the past was as socially damaged as their own time. Somehow, the romantic and medievalizing Morris has become to some degree a historical realist. What Morris has seen that John Ball could not have seen is precisely the historical development of the forces against which Ball was struggling. That knowledge was not merely the gift of living in the nineteenth rather than in the fourteenth century, but it was also the consequence of the studies that had brought him to the point of writing tales such as *A Dream of John Ball* in his socialist newspaper.

"When I wrote my little book," Morris said, "I did it with the intention of bringing in the socialistic dialogues at the end rather than dealing with the literary and dramatic side of the story."[17] Chapter 10, "Those Two Talk of the Days to Come," containing the first part of those "socialist dialogues," begins with a declaration from John Ball that his visitor is qualified to judge, not "if thou thinkest we are right to play the play like men, but whether playing like men we shall fail like men," qualified because Ball takes the visitor for "a scholar who hast read books; and withal, in some way that I cannot name, thou knowest more than we; as though with thee the world had lived longer than with us" (pp. 267–68). The reason for Ball's sense that the Dreamer is a visitor from the future—the fact that his guest is a scholar—is one more indication of Morris's faith in education as a form of revolutionary action. He presents himself to the members of the Socialist League, to the readers of *Commonweal*, as an educator, "a scholar," a possessor of essential information, chiefly historical. Ball's sense of the visitor's origins—his perception of the guest's extended perspective—is an essential device of the plot.

The conversation resumes (the socialistic dialogues begin) with John Ball asking the Dreamer about the outcome of the rebellion which the priest is about to lead. (Later, in *News from Nowhere*, similar material is handled with the same device in "How The Change Came," where a different Morris persona asks old Hammond to describe the process of the successful revolution which had destroyed capitalism. In chapter 10 of *A Dream of John Ball* the fact of the historical act is known to the questioner, but not its consequence; in chapter 17 of *News from Nowhere*, the result is known, but not the act of which it is a consequence.) Following this question by John Ball and until nearly the end of the story, we have no "literary and dramatic" apparatus, only "socialistic dialogues."

After John Ball guesses that the Dreamer is a messenger from the future or

17. Thompson, *William Morris*, 837.

from "the Master of the Fellowship and the King's Son of Heaven," the Morris persona acknowledges that he knows what will happen to the rebellion, but says, modestly, "if I know more than thou, I do far less; therefore thou art my captain and I thy minstrel"—a statement of mere fact, at least insofar as Morris was the teller of John Ball's tale in the pages of *Commonweal*. This does not keep him from quickly revealing the priest's fate: "Surely thou goest to thy death." The visitor further informs John Ball that his rebellion will succeed at first, but then has to add that it will be eventually defeated through trickery and lack of leadership. This see-saw of encouraging and disappointing news from the future continues as the Dreamer assures John Ball that the goals of the rebellion nonetheless will be achieved: slavery and villeinage will end. This is a major victory, The Victory, from John Ball's point of view. That which now exists, almost always seems inevitable and eternal. To struggle against it takes courage; to win must seem miraculous. Morris reminds his readers that if the waning of feudalism seems "natural" to us, it was not so at the time.[18] No sooner has Ball rejoiced at the prospect of the end of feudalism than the Morris persona tells him of the rise of commercial capitalism and of how "few shall be the free men that shall hold a rood of land whom the word of their lord may not turn adrift straightway" (p. 271). When John Ball cannot at first grasp this and thinks that he has been told that villeinage will be replaced by universal slavery, Morris uses Ball's confusion as the occasion to explain the difference between legal and "wage-slavery." John Ball does not think much of this difference: "The man may well do what thou sayest and live, but he may not do it and live a free man." The Morris persona agrees: " 'Thou sayest sooth,' said I" (p. 273). The problem that John Ball has difficulty in grasping is that the movement of history, as conceived by Morris, is not unilinear. The ending of feudalism does not bring economic liberation: it brings capitalism.[19] Engels, writing about medieval peasant rebellions in general, had stated:

This sally beyond both the present and even the future could be nothing but violent and fantastic, and of necessity fell back into the narrow limits set by the contemporary situation. The attack on private property, the demand for common ownership was bound to resolve into a primitive organisation of charity; vague Christian equality could at best resolve into civic "equality before the law"; elimination of all authorities finally culminates in the establishment of republican governments

18. "Nor could the English tenantry of the 1370s be as certain as ourselves that villeinage would eventually 'wither away.' " R. B. Dobson, "Introduction," in *The Peasants' Revolt of 1381,* 2d ed. (London: Macmillan, 1983), lxi.

19. According to Goode, in this Morris was following Marx's teaching. John Goode, "William Morris and the Dream of Revolution," in *Literature and Politics in the Nineteenth Century,* ed. John Lukacs (London: Methuen, 1971), 249.

elected by the people. The anticipation of communism nurtured by fantasy became in reality an anticipation of modern bourgeois conditions.[20]

The priest's speculations about wage-slavery continue into chapter II, "Hard It Is For The Old World To See The New." He thinks that police power will be necessary to make people work under such a system:

> And there again shall ye need more soldiers and more constables till the land is eaten up by them; nor shall the lords and masters even be able to bear the burden of it; nor will their gains be so great, since that which each man may do in a day is not right great when all is said. (p. 274)

The visitor replies by raising the specter of the "police power" of starvation, stating that the commercial system will cause famine in the midst of plenty so that the workers will fight one another in order to secure inadequately paid work.[21] The honest priest sees this as a paradox, and takes comfort in the hope of depopulation, but the narrator must take that consolation from him also.

> "Alas, poor man!" I said; "nor mayst thou imagine how foul and wretched it may be for many of the folk; and yet I tell thee that men shall increase and multiply, till where there is one man in the land now, there shall be twenty in those days—yea, in some places ten times twenty." (pp. 275–76)

As this was not exactly the result that John Ball had expected from his efforts, the Dreamer asks him if he thinks that the rebellion is worthwhile in the light of such a future. Their dialogue has now extended into the darkest part of the night. The priest tells the Dreamer that he believes his efforts justified if in the distant future people will once more follow his example and rebel against domination. The Dreamer is able to assure Ball that although the people will be so oppressed that

20. F. Engels, *The Peasant War in Germany* (1850; Moscow, 1956), 60, quoted in R. B. Dobson, *The Peasants' Revolt of 1381*, 2d ed. (London: Macmillan, 1983), 402.

21. There is a footnote to the text of the romance at this point which underlines its relationship to "Socialism from the Root Up": "Forestaller, one who buys up goods when they are cheap, and so raises the price for his own benefit: forestalls the due and real demand and supply; regrater, one who both buys and sells in the same market, or within five miles thereof, buys, say a ton of cheese at 10 a.m. and sells it at 5 p.m. a penny a pound dearer without moving from his chair. For us Socialists the word monopolist will cover both species of thief.—Ed." These terms had already been explained for regular readers of *Commonweal* in the 12 June 1886 issue, where Morris and Bax regret that the old England is gone: "Medieval England is gone, the manners and ways of thought of the people are utterly changed; they are called English, but they are another people from that which dwelt in England when forestalling and regratting were misdemeanors." Morris apparently realized in the six months that elapsed between the reference and its dramatization that the terms needed some explanation. Nonetheless, this repetition is a significant indication of the close relationship between the two texts.

they will not be able to rebel for a long time, he trusts that eventually that moment will come.

The final chapter of the book merges two installments from the *Commonweal* serialization, those of 15 and 22 January 1887. It begins with another question from John Ball: How can there be many rich people as well as many poor people in the society of his future (that of the Dreamer's present)? The Dreamer/Morris explains to him, and the *Commonweal* audience (and to later-day critics who would believe Morris naive about such things), the wonders of automation and modern nineteenth-century transportation technology. John Ball grows hopeful once more: "There should be all plenty in the land, and not one poor man therein, unless of his own free will he choose to lack and be poor, as a man in religion or such like" (p. 281). John Ball's socialism, *unlike Morris's own,* is utopian, not scientific. Morris's narrator therefore disabuses Ball of this particular illusion, pointing out that men who own nothing but their own labor power cannot be rich, and that all the surplus value of their work will be appropriated by those who do not work, at which point the next to the last installment in the serial ends with the priest appealing to the utopia of technology: " 'Yea,' he said; 'but how could I deem that such things could be when those days should become wherein men could make things work for them?' " (p. 282). The next week *Commonweal* carried the Dreamer's disheartening reply: "Many men shall be as poor and wretched always, year by year, as they are with thee when there is a famine in the land; nor shall any have plenty and surety of livelihood save those that shall sit by and look on while others labour; and these, I tell thee, shall be a many" (p. 282). And what is more, he says, the poor will not rebel because the sheer numbers of idle that the system will be able to float will allow a limited upward mobility that will bribe some and delude others into thinking they might be able to become one of the robbers rather then remain among the robbed. (This is probably a reference to the nineteenth-century ideology of hard work and just rewards.)

By this point in the story the symbolic dawn is advancing in the church, "the colours coming into the pictures on wall and in window" (p. 284). John Ball asks, finally, the question for which the entire story was written: Is there a remedy to class domination, and if so, "what that remedy shall be?" The Dreamer realizes that the dream is ebbing with the dawn, so he speaks quickly. He takes the progress of the light itself as a figure of the future of class conflict (the Morris who was writing the story having become convinced that "class antagonism is really the key to the solution of the social question");[22] the Dreamer compares John Ball's revolt to the light of the moon, the oppression of industrial capitalism to the dark before the dawn, and the cold light of early morning to the realization of the truth of class oppression and the moment when, at its worst, that oppression can at last be remedied:

22. Kelvin, ed., *Letters,* 2:766.

> The time shall come, John Ball, when that dream of thine that this shall one day be, shall be a thing that men shall talk of soberly, and as a thing soon to come about, as even with thee they talk of the villeins becoming tenants paying their lord quit-rent; therefore, hast thou done well to hope it; and, if thou heedest this also, as I suppose thou heedest it little, thy name shall abide by thy hope in those days to come, and thou shalt not be forgotten. (p. 285.)

When the priest presses him for details, all that the Dreamer can tell him is that at first there will be difficulties and confusion, but at last "the Day will come." At that moment full daylight reaches the church, and John Ball and the Dreamer fade from one another: "Thou hast been a dream to me as I to thee," says John Ball, and then "Farewell, friend" (p. 286).

In the final scene of the romance, which mirrors the first, the Dreamer is lying in bed, "the south-westerly gale rattling the Venetian blinds and making their hold-fasts squeak" (p. 287). It is dawn not in fourteenth-century Kent but in nineteenth-century London. The dreamer, now awakened, goes to the window and looks at the degraded landscape, thinking of escaping to the countryside, where "I might of my own will carry on a day-dream of the friends I had made in the dream of night and against my will" (p. 288). But then he hears the factory whistles calling the workmen to the factories; that momentary reversion to Pre-Raphaelite ideals fades, and the Dreamer dresses, ready for his "day's 'work' as I call it, but which many a man besides John Ruskin (though not many in his position) would call 'play'" (p. 288).

The sufficiency of the Dreamer's answer to John Ball's plea for historical justification is vital to the relationship of the story to Morris's own historical context at the time it was written. Thus, E. P. Thompson sees that:

> the problem . . . is whether "John Ball's" struggle and death is not a mockery in the light of the centuries of capitalism to come. The answer is twofold: first, "John Ball," symbol of the oppressed struggling for objectives incompatible with the necessities of history, has no alternatives; he can only achieve the dignity of manhood by rebellion—"to strive was my pleasure and my life." Second, his life is given deeper meaning by its foreshadowed consummation in "The Change Beyond The Change," in which his aspirations, and those of the nameless millions he represents, will be at length fulfilled.[23]

In Thompson's view, then, the Dreamer's answer to John Ball's plea for historical justification is sufficient, and in the story itself John Ball seems to accept that answer. It is nothing to him if he must die, and although it is disappointing that the rebellion will not end domination, the promise that eventually "the Day will come" is enough to make the effort worthwhile. But what is it, exactly, that the Dreamer tells John Ball about the future? He is explicit enough about the

23. Thompson, *William Morris*, 837.

disadvantages of capitalism, but all he actually says about the end of that system is that it "shall be a thing that men shall talk of soberly, and as a thing soon to come about."

By the time Morris wrote *A Dream of John Ball,* on the one hand a large trade union movement was determined to win as many economic gains as possible, and on the other a small number of workers and middle-class intellectuals were intent on more radical change.[24] Morris, as a leader of the Socialist League, saw the power of the economic system of his time, believed in the necessity for an end to that system, and hoped that he and his fellows would be able to accomplish something toward that end. Part of his efforts in that direction were expended in writing the articles of "Socialism from the Root Up" for *Commonweal,* narrating the history of the working class, and analyzing that history for his readers. This technical exposition was supplemented by the dramatizations of history in his romance about the Peasants' Rebellion. Politically, Morris was working with hardly anything to offer except hope itself; that is what he offered to the readers of *Commonweal* in *A Dream of John Ball,* and therefore that was all the Dreamer had to offer John Ball within the story.

The story Morris chose to tell in order to illustrate the history and economics of "Socialism from the Root Up" was the story of a failed rebellion. The wider historical context of *A Dream of John Ball* as a didactic work was that of an era of stillborn rebellions, failed revolutions, preeminently the Paris Commune, but certainly going back as far as the Continental revolutions of 1848 and the English Chartist rebellion. When Morris wrote *A Dream of John Ball,* the propaganda of the Socialist League was "Utopian in form, but in actual effect and tone defeatist."[25] It was "utopian" in that it offered a refusal of the reality of the times, but "defeatist" in that all that it had to offer was that refusal.

But *A Dream of John Ball* is utopian in another sense, and I will conclude this chapter with some reflections on that aspect of the romance. The narrative structure of *A Dream of John Ball* is elegantly complicated throughout the fourteenth-century sequences by the ambiguity of the dream motif. At times it seems clear that "Morris" is dreaming of John Ball, but at other times it almost appears to be the case that John Ball himself is having a typically fourteenth-century "vision" of this conversation with a visitor from the future. The two between them produce a historical analysis of the rebellion not limited to the historicism to which the form of the narrative might otherwise have been subject. These intricacies are summed up in the romance's title, a dream *about* John Ball, a dream *of* John Ball, *the* dream of John Ball and of all visionaries.[26] Carole Silver writes of Morris that:

24. A. L. Morton and George Tate, *The British Labour Movement* (London: Lawrence and Wishart, 1956), "The Revival of Socialism," 155–84.

25. Thompson, *William Morris,* 515.

26. Goode, "William Morris and the Dream of Revolution," 251.

Because he feels that ameliorating the evils of his society is not enough, but that his world must be entirely reconstructed, Morris does not propose concrete solutions to Victorian social problems or pragmatic alternatives to its way of life. Instead, drawing upon history and myth, he creates worlds that are criticisms of his own. Even those works based on history, like *A Dream of John Ball*, are intended to be mythic. Going beyond the realm of conscious ideology, they depict ideal worlds which appeal to the universal, nonrational desire for the rebuilding of a lost terrestrial Eden and the restoration of a golden age.[27]

The dream is always a moment antithetical to social reality; it is the not-real and thus tied to the real as utopia was the twin of Henry VIII's England. The passages of *A Dream of John Ball* that establish this antithesis are those which frame the story, the beginning and end in Morris's own nineteenth-century England. This dream form matters. It is in dreams that we refuse those parts of reality that we dislike, constructing, each one of us, a utopia of gratification. The dream is the last defense of the individual against a social world that is threatening, punishing, or merely insufficiently rewarding. Morris begins *A Dream of John Ball* with the comment that "Sometimes I am rewarded for fretting myself so much about present matters by a quite unasked for pleasant dream. I mean when I am asleep. This dream is as it were a present of an architectural peep-show. . . . I have seen in the dreams of night clearer than I can force myself to see . . . in dreams of the day" (pp. 215–16).

Morris set out in *A Dream of John Ball* to bring to the readers of *Commonweal* "the encouragement and warning of history," to give an account of the Peasants' Rebellion—a failed revolt against feudalism—in order to give hope for what he wished to be an eventually successful transformation of capitalism. His use of historical materials, particularly Froissart's dramatization of John Ball's speeches, took those materials out of the realm of traditional history and placed them in his own time, as a call for that better world which he would see in the "pleasant" future of *News from Nowhere*. This very effort introduced a fragment of that world into the pages of *Commonweal* as an artistic vision, *A Dream of John Ball*. The aesthetic dimension is the manifestation of utopia in the waking world. A literary utopia makes a private dream public and by doing so acts to change the public world in two ways: it provides a gratifying world of the imagination, and it provides a critique of those aspects of the "real" world which superfluously deny gratification.

On the literal level of the narrative of *A Dream of John Ball*, Morris played on general notions about dreams and uses our suspension of disbelief—anything can happen in a dream—to make the transition from nineteenth-century London to fourteenth-century Kent: "the unhedged tillage and a certain unwonted trimness

27. Silver, *Romance of William Morris*, 109.

and handiness abut the enclosures of the garden and orchards, puzzled me for a minute or two . . . I was of course used to the hedged tillage and tumble-down bankrupt-looking surroundings of our modern agriculture" (p. 217). We might pause here, at the end of these considerations, over that initial comparison of hedged and unhedged tillage, apparently simply a statement of historical fact, but reverberating from Morris's literary work to his artistic style. Morris's characteristic artistic production, in whatever medium, was the border or frame, a boundary between art and life, perhaps a wall to keep the world of industrialism away from the delicate designs of Burne-Jones. The unhedged fourteenth-century fields proclaim their utopian nature by this absence of boundaries. Protected within the frames of dream and art, the earthly paradise of fourteenth-century Kent glows in the dulling pages of a nineteenth-century radical newspaper: an escape from those "six counties covered with smoke," and a promise.

CAROLE G. SILVER

Socialism Internalized
The Last Romances of William Morris

In 1892, after reading an ingenious if fanciful *Spectator* review of *The Wood beyond the World* which analyzed that romance as an allegory of Capital and Labor, Morris wrote the journal a rebuttal in which he announced: "I had not the least intention of thrusting an allegory into 'The Wood beyond the World'; it is meant for a tale pure and simple, with nothing didactic about it."[1] Commenting that when he wrote on social problems, he tried to be as direct and clear as possible, Morris indicated that this romance—and, by implication, all his others—was not intended as either socialist or allegorical.

Since the 1890s, scholars and critics have been trying to prove that Morris did not mean what he said. The list of romances written between 1890 and 1896 is lengthy: *The Story of the Glittering Plain, The Wood beyond the World, Child Christopher and Goldilind the Fair, The Well at the World's End, The Water of the Wondrous Isles,* and *The Sundering Flood;* most scholars now agree that these are not allegories as Morris would have defined the term. Unlike *Pilgrim's Progress,* they do not utilize narrative primarily to promote a thesis nor do they incarnate abstract ideas as characters and settings. Instead, critics suggest that Morris's romances are parabolic, or romances of types or, at the least, obliquely symbolic.[2]

The political orientation of the romances is not as immediately apparent, however, for Marxist doctrines and historical interpretations are less overt in them than in *The House of the Wolfings* and *The Roots of the Mountains,* written in the late 1880s when Morris was most active in the English Marxist movement. Yet they are subtly but richly colored by socialism; Marxism is implicit as an

---

1. May Morris, *The Introductions to the Collected Works of William Morris,* ed. Joseph Riggs Dunlap, 2 vols. (New York: Oriole Editions, 1973), 2:499.

2. See, for example, Carole Silver, *The Romance of William Morris* (Athens: Ohio University Press, 1982); Richard Mathews, *Worlds Beyond the World: The Fantastic Vision of William Morris* (San Bernardino, Calif.: Borgo Press, 1978); and Charlotte H. Oberg, *A Pagan Prophet: William Morris* (Charlottesville: University Press of Virginia, 1978).

assimilated system of values. Morris's socialist sensibility is revealed by his rejection of Victorian realist and naturalist fiction and his choice of an alternative genre, that of romance, as well as by his selection or avoidance of certain conventional contents and the ideology they imply. The genre, setting, characters, and plot structure of his last six prose fictions demonstrate socialism internalized.

As a "scientific socialist," Morris believed that the art and literature of a given society were integrally related to its economic structure. His repudiation of the most significant form of his era—the Victorian realist novel—was itself a challenge to bourgeois aesthetics. Form is ideology, and Morris, in writing romances, deliberately created works that one commentator has called "anti-novels."[3] Moreover, the few Marxist and Anarchist pronouncements that were available to Morris regarding the appropriate form, content, and function of socialist literature coalesced with his own taste in determining his choice of genre.

Contrary to popular belief, Morris's socialist mentors did not particularly espouse aesthetic realism. As Terry Eagleton has demonstrated, Marx and Engels were not the fathers of the "socialist realism" of the 1920s and '30s.[4] They praised individual nineteenth-century novels; Marx, for example, admired Balzac and applauded "the English realists"—including Thackeray, Charlotte Bronte, and Gaskell—as revealers of social and political truths.[5] Yet, what he and Engels really valued was not the realist mode but the sense of contemporary history, the "typicality," and the attack on middle-class behavior and on social conventions the works of such novelists contained. Not coincidentally, Marx and Morris shared many of the same literary tastes; both loved folk ballads and tales, Greek drama, ancient epic, and the heightened fiction of the Dumas (père et fils), Scott, and Dickens. Engels and Morris shared an interest in medieval German literature. Most important, Peter Kropotkin, Morris's closest colleague among the theorists of "scientific socialism" and the only one with whom he had more than minimal contact, was actively antagonistic to the realist and naturalist literary movements of the time.

In *An Appeal to the Young,* translated and published in 1885 by H. M. Hyndman, Morris's close associate in the Social Democratic Federation, Kropotkin explained his position. Appealing to artists, he argued that the art of the

3. The term is used by Patrick Brantlinger to describe *News from Nowhere* in "*News from Nowhere:* Morris's Socialist Anti-Novel," *Victorian Studies* 19 (1974): 35.

4. See the discussion in *Marxism and Literary Criticism* (Berkeley: University of California Press, 1976), 37–48, in which Eagleton demonstrates that "socialist realism" was derived from nineteenth-century Russian "revolutionary democratic" critics and received its support from Lenin.

5. Karl Marx, "The English Middle Class," *New York Tribune,* 1 August 1854, in *Literature and Art, by Karl Marx and Frederick Engels: Selections from Their Writings* (New York: International, [1947]), 133.

present era "is commonplace . . . mediocrity reigns supreme." The revolutionary ideal has vanished and been replaced by the false idol of realism:

> failing an ideal, our art fancies that it has found one in realism when it painfully
> photographs in colors the dewdrop on the leaf of a plant, imitates the muscles in the
> leg of a cow, or describes minutely in prose and in verse the suffocating filth of a
> sewer, the boudoir of a whore of high degree.[6]

Kropotkin objected to realism as a mere reproduction of surfaces and as trivial
and inhumane in content. He disliked naturalism, as did Engels,[7] not only
because he found it sordid but also because it assumed that proletarians, the hope
of humanity, were social and hereditary victims rather than heroes. Naturalism
doomed them to the sewer of Zola's *Germinal* or the decadent career of Nana.

Agreeing with Kropotkin, Morris takes the argument a step further. He views
realism itself as antiproletarian. In *News from Nowhere,* he describes even works
in which "radical cobblers" have a part (a reference to Charles Kingsley's *Alton
Locke*) as "silly old novels"; he remarks that nineteenth-century fiction despised
"everybody who *could* use his hands."[8] When Ellen, one of Morris's alter-egos
in *News from Nowhere,* speaks of "something loathsome" about Victorian novels
despite their "cleverness, vigor, and capacity for story-telling" (*CW,* 16:151),
she approaches the heart of the matter. That "something loathsome" is the
bourgeois nature of conventional realism, its preoccupation with the chiefly self-
created problems, excessive introspection, and foolish aspirations of a non-
productive middle-class hero and heroine. To Morris, the core of the realist
novel is unsound; its subject is "the troubles of a middle class couple in their
struggle toward social uselessness," and its method is the pointless study of
social "anomalies and futilities."[9] Morris objects, as well, to something beyond
the content, method, and class bias of realist fiction. Old Hammond, another of
the Morris alter-egos in *News,* announces what it is:

6. Kropotkin's *Appeal* was first published in *De Revolte* in 1880; the Hyndman translation was
published in London by the Modern Press in 1885 and republished by the Freedom Press in 1889. My
citation is from *The Essential Kropotkin,* ed. Emile Capouya and Keitha Tompkins (New York:
Liveright, 1975), 19.

7. See Engels's letter to Margaret Harkness, quoted in Peter Demetz, *Marx, Engels, and the
Poets: Origins of Marxist Literary Criticism* (Chicago: University of Chicago Press, 1959), 97.

8. *The Collected Works of William Morris,* ed. May Morris, 24 vols. (London: Longmans,
1910–1915), 16:17, 20; hereafter cited as *CW,* and all parenthetical in-text references are to this
edition.

9. "The Society of the Future," in *Political Writings of William Morris,* ed. A. L. Morton (New
York: International, 1973), 200; E. Belfort Bax and William Morris, *Socialism: Its Growth and
Outcome* (London: Swan Sonnenschein, 1893), 308. In the latter work, Morris states his belief that
"as to literature, fiction as it is called, when a peaceful and happy society has been sometime afoot,
will probably die out for want of material" (308).

there was a theory that art and imaginative literature ought to deal with contemporary life; but they never did so; for, if there was any pretense of it, the author always
took care . . . to disguise or exaggerate, or idealise . . . so that, for all the
verisimilitude there was, he might just as well have dealt with the times of the
Pharaohs. (*CW,* 16:102)

In effect, Morris finds Victorian realism essentially unrealistic.

Yet, among the five "literary men" who constitute *News from Nowhere*'s
community of authors,[10] two are writing works which resemble Victorian
novels. Robert the weaver's "sort of antiquarian book about the peaceable and
private history . . . of the end of the nineteenth century" (*CW,* 16:20) is
justified, in part, by the fact that his primary intention is to give his audience a
picture of England before the revolution. But what of Boffin, the Golden
Dustman, who, according to Dick (Nowhere's cultured but anti-intellectual
"non-literary man" [*CW,* 16:206]), "will spend his time in writing reactionary
novels, and is very proud of getting the local colour right" (*CW,* 16:22)? Boffin's
novels and the Nowherians' discussions of literature suggest that the debate
about the value of realism is still very much alive in the society of the future.
Clara wonders why the people of her society still "find the dreadful times of the
past so interesting" (*CW,* 16:102) as subject matter for the arts; Ellen's grandfather, Nowhere's official grumbler, complains that in his world, a "good old
book like Thackerary's 'Vanity Fair' " (*CW,* 16:158) can no longer be produced.

Vanity Fair is paradigmatic of the flaws of realist fiction and Morris's attack on
Thackeray's novel is part of his explanation of what is wrong with its genre.[11]
Morris sees realism as grounded in competition, as requiring unhappiness, and
as necessitating the use of the language of conventional sentiment. Novels like
Thackeray's demand "good solid unlimited competition . . . [as] the condition
under which they were written" (*CW,* 16:149); they are the products of societies
in which "most people are thoroughly unhappy" (*CW,* 16:152). Boffin's realist
novels (parallels to Thackeray's) depend for their accurate "local colour" upon
his using as models figures from forgotten and reactionary places "where people
are unhappy, and consequently interesting to a story-teller" (*CW,* 16:22). Both
Boffin's and Thackeray's works center on emotions that the people of Nowhere
perceive as destructive and antisocial. In the world of the future, people are no
longer "conventionally sensitive or sentimental"(*CW,* 16:58) and "whatever

10. The five are Robert, Boffin, Old Hammond, William Guest, and a nameless figure encoun-
tered on the journey up the Thames. When Guest and his friends come ashore at Bisham, they find
most of its people haymaking; however, among the few remaining inside the communal house is a
man who has chosen to stay at home to get on with some literary work.

11. In her *Introductions,* May Morris notes that, unlike such other authors as Swinburne, Morris
did not include Thackeray's *Vanity Fair* in his list of great books published by the *Pall Mall Gazette*
(2:653–54). She also cites an early letter of Morris's in which he refers to Thackeray's style as
"precious bad" (1:115).

sentiment there is is . . . real and general," rather than confined to persons who are "very specially refined" (*CW,* 16:59). Thus, there is little place in life or literature for the "sham sorrow[s]" nursed by "the ridiculous characters in . . . queer old novels" (*CW,* 16:198).

This does not mean that literature has died. It has merely changed its form. Nowherians have selected genres that are accessible to all, graceful, pleasant, full of incident, and appropriate in mood to their function in communal life. The people of the future prefer "tales" to realist novels. Painted on the walls of the Hall at Bloomsbury are scenes from the folk tales of the Brothers Grimm "which in yesterday's world only about a half a dozen people in the country knew anything about." In Nowhere, "everybody knows the tales" (*CW,* 16:100) and enjoys them. Even children who do not read much else, read "story books" (*CW,* 16:31), while adults too spend evenings "telling stories" (*CW,* 16:140). While the oral tradition has been reborn, written tales still survive and flourish. Nowhere's "popular culture" is truly popular, for it comprises tales from folklore, myth, legend, and primary epic as well as romances that derive from these sources.

Thus, bypassing Victorian bourgeois realism, Morris himself writes romances that Nowherians would enjoy. He chooses a "truthful" genre that is popular, rooted in folklore, "typical" in content, rich in incident, and free of middle-class conventions and ideologies. Morris's natural predilection for non-realism in general and romance in particular may have been reinforced by Kropotkin's plea to writers: "Tell us what a rational life would be, if it did not encounter at every step the follies and ignominies of our present social order."[12]

Morris's method is to demonstrate "rational life" in realms and eras outside those of the "present social order" of Victorian England, and to present figures who have not been damaged, as he believed he was, by "sham societies." Thus, he depicts the future reborn after revolution in *News from Nowhere,* the heroic age of "upper barbarism" and primary epic[13] in *The House of the Wolfings* and *The Roots of the Mountains,* and the later Middle Ages in the last romances. The world Morris portrays in these final works is virtually modeled on the medieval England he described in his lecture on "The Hopes of Civilization." It is composed of:

the many chases and great woods, the stretches of common tillage and common pasture quite unenclosed; . . . the little towns, well bechurched, often walled; the villages just where they are now . . . but better and more populous . . . the beautiful manor-houses, some of them castles once and survivals from an earlier period;

12. *Essential Kropotkin,* 23.
13. For a discussion of "upper barbarism" see Silver, *Romance of William Morris,* 128–32; Morris associates that period of social development with the creation of primary or folk epic.

some new and elegant; some out of all proportion small for the importance of their lords.[14]

A preindustrial world, it is one in which the alienation caused by capitalism has not yet occurred. Even the archaic language of the romances serves a socialist purpose. Engels had praised Carlyle's style as "a direct and violent reaction against the modern bourgeois English Pecksniff variety,"[15] and might well have said the same of Morris's language. Morris's compounds, archaisms, and neologisms are akin, in their Germanic roots, to Carlyle's. Like the settings of the later romances, their language removes the reader from the sights and sounds of Victorian commercial society.

Depicting medieval commerce, the romances do not shun the middle class of the Middle Ages, though they deny or obliquely criticize Victorian political, economic, and social values. The lust for lordship or imperial power, the drive toward profit-seeking and unfair competition, the prevalence of selfish individualism and non-cooperation, all are traits Morris equates with capitalism and either banishes from or punishes in the worlds he creates.

In terms of theme and subject matter, however, Morris's omissions are as significant as his inclusions. For example, although the romances are quests, their objects are not the pursuit of treasure, land, or dominion over others. Instead, these novels are accounts of the human quest for maturity, love, and a just social order. *The Glittering Plain* depicts Hallblithe's search, through realms of guile and false promise, for his kidnapped bride, the Hostage. *The Wood beyond the World* describes Golden Walter's misguided pursuit of the wrong lover, the Lady, his rescue by a more appropriate woman, the Maid, and their adventures in founding a new and better realm. *Child Christopher and Goldilind the Fair,* a version of the medieval English romance, *Havelok the Dane,* explores the adventures of the two figures named in its title as they strive to regain their rightful inheritances and to redeem and unite their lands. *The Well at the World's End* chronicles the journey of Ralph and Ursula to the source of the water of life and the use of the power they gain for social liberation. *The Water of the Wondrous Isles* traces Birdalone's voyage to personal freedom and her struggles to free others, while the unfinished tale of *The Sundering Flood* outlines Osberne and Elfhild's search for each other and movement toward personal union and communal action.

Significantly, only Morris's villains waste their time getting and spending; unlike traditional heroes of romance, Morris's protagonists are prone to refuse kingship and power. Ralph, in *The Well at the World's End,* rejects the chance of kingship in Goldburg, refuses to rule in Utterbol, and accepts only titular

14. "The Hopes of Civilization," in Morton, *Political Writings of William Morris,* 162.
15. In a book review for *Model,* London, 1850. See *Literature and Art,* 118.

lordship in the Land of Abundance. Osberne, in *The Sundering Flood,* twice refuses to permit his grateful allies to elevate him to knighthood. Child Christopher, whose kingdom has been usurped, accepts rule only after his restoration has been ratified by a folkmote. Walter, in *The Wood beyond the World,* wins his kingdom by passing a ritualized, proto-socialist test; he chooses the tokens of battle for his people instead of the emblems of pride and luxury. Both Christopher and Walter devote their kingly power to freeing prisoners and thralls, aiding the poor, and battling the forces of guile and greed.

Although Morris describes evil societies in considerable detail, he seldom portrays workers or peasants as ignoble figures. While medieval merchants and their communities—commercial centers called "cheaping towns"—are sometimes depicted as negative forces, Morris's "ordinary folk" are hearty, loyal, and natively intelligent—the "rough-handed and bold set of good fellows" of his lecture on "The Hopes of Civilization."[16] Faced with evil societies, they may choose to become outlaws, an act Morris views as a legitimate response to tyranny. The Men of the Dry Tree (in the *Well*) steal from the rich to give to the poor; Jack O' the Tufts and his seven sons (in *Child Christopher*) are the forces of social justice. To be Robin Hoods in a fellowship of merry men is an admirable alternative to serving an unjust state. Other "ordinary folk" may be debased by thralldom—a condition Morris had long considered analogous to the state of the English working class; yet, like the people of Utterbol (in the *Well*), once they free themselves they cease to practice the unhealthy guile that had marked them as slaves. Unlike equivalent figures in medieval romances and Victorian realist novels, Morris's proletarians share the same culture, speak the same language, and express the same ideas as virtuous middle-class and aristocratic figures. The romances do depict class oppression, but the great social gap that Morris believed made a Victorian worker and his master differ in all respects does not exist.[17]

Moreover, the individualism that Marxism considers excessive—a preoccupation with self that is manifested in deliberate isolation or extensive introspection—is either obliquely absent from or openly criticized by the romances. Life is naturally communal and, in the good societies Morris depicts, homesteads, villages, manors, and free towns, mutual aid and almost instinctive cooperation are the norm. In *The Sundering Flood,* Osberne and his fellow Dalesmen choose to help the knights who serve a free town against a despotic baron both because the cause is just and because the knights request neighborly aid.

However, the conventions of romance require that a hero leave the group and

16. Morton, *Political Writings of William Morris,* 161.

17. See, for example, Morris's comments on class alienation in "Of the Origins of Ornamental Art," in *The Unpublished Lectures of William Morris,* ed. Eugene D. Le Mire (Detroit: Wayne State University Press, 1969), 153.

undergo a period of painful and solitary initiation. Even during this period or during the alienation from fellowship caused by personal grief, Morris's heroes do not brood or nurse the "sham sorrow" Morris condemned as a convention of the realist novel. The death of a lover or beloved is accompanied by grief, pain, and the desire for solitude—factors clearly visible in the accounts of Ralph's agony over the slaying of the Lady of Abundance (in the *Well*) and Aurea's misery about the death of Baudoin, her Golden Knight, in *The Water of the Wondrous Isles*. There are no sentimental or conventional death scenes. Indeed, excessive grief is seen as destructive, and survivors usually live to love again. The only Morris hero who rejects society because he suffers from love is Arthur in the *Water*. He is punished for his self-involvement by physical and mental illness. For the other Morris heroes, solitude is merely a preparation for fellowship to come.

Eliminating concepts antithetical to socialism, ridding romance of bourgeois realist conventions, Morris emphasizes instead the drama of the class struggle and the triumph of such values as work, love, and fellowship. For Morris, history, of which romance is a transmutation, is the history of class conflict, and Kropotkin's admonition to "figure forth to us the heroic struggles of the people against their oppressors"[18] is to be followed. Morris's two most striking examples of class warfare in the last romances concern the oppression of the proletariat by powerful, predominantly middle-class groups. In the City of the Sundering Flood (in the romance of the same name), the Lesser Craft Guilds and ordinary workers, helped by outside forces from the free towns, rise against and overthrow a powerful oligarchy composed of the rich merchants of the Greater Guilds, the barons, and an idle king. The City is metamorphosed into a free town of the variety that Morris, Engels, and Kropotkin considered the great achievement of the medieval communal spirit. Social change purifies Utterhay (in the *Water*) and Utterbol (in the *Well*). The only place Morris deems unreclaimable is The Burg of the Four Friths (in the *Well*), where a middle-class despotism prevails. An ugly, militaristic city-state that exploits its female thralls and murders their men, the Burg is overthrown by open revolution. Its inhabitants are ejected and a new society, composed of the freed slaves and their allies, is created within its walls.

The class struggle is central to *The Well at the World's End* and *The Sundering Flood,* providing each romance with much of its incident and structuring its form. In other romances it is more obliquely depicted through accounts of the rebellions of thralls against their evil masters (as seen, for example, in the behavior of the Maid in *The Wood beyond the World*) and Birdalone and the three captive maidens in *The Water of the Wondrous Isles*) or in the battles of outlaws against tyrants and oppressors (as in *Child Christopher*).

In all the romances work is a prime virtue, and willingness and skill in labor

18. *Essential Kropotkin*, 23.

are the traits of characters portrayed as "good." Communities unsustained by labor such as the Glittering Plain (in the romance of the same name) or the Isle of Increase Unsought (in the *Water*) are devoid of virtue. When Morris's heroes are not questing or struggling with oppressors, they are hunting, building, or making useful things. His own skillful work rescues Hallblithe of *The Glittering Plain*. He escapes a false paradise of sloth only because he has the ability and perseverance to build a boat. Osberne of *The Sundering Flood* learns courage through his labor as a herdsman and, through the tutelage of his guardian spirit, becomes a skillful craftsman. Birdalone, the female hero of the *Water*, grows and prospers in her self-imposed exile by becoming a superb craftswoman—the head or Master of the Guild of Embroiderers. Unlike Victorian realist novels, Morris's romances venerate rather than despise all those who *can* "use their hands."

Moreover, the romances repeatedly demonstrate the value of association and equality, stressing the importance of fellowship and of the unselfish spirit that brings it to fruition. Morris had attacked the Victorian realist novel for its emphasis on selfish erotic passion; thus, the lovers in his romances never follow that pattern denounced in *News* of living "happily in an island of bliss on other people's troubles" (*CW*, 16:151). Each romance takes the lovers it depicts beyond private passion into fellowship. After all their trials, Hallblithe and the Hostage (of the *Glittering Plain*) do not return alone to Cleveland by the Sea. Instead, they bring with them a new member for the *gens* and ten maidens whom they have freed from thralldom. Walter and the Maid, the heroes of the *Wood*, rebuild a kingdom and help create a new society of fellowship. For Ralph and Ursula, in the *Well*, the end of personal love is the cleansing of corrupt communities and a successful battle against the invaders of Ralph's homeland. When Birdalone and Arthur are finally united (in the *Water*), they share only a brief period of unwedded bliss before seeking their friends in order to "knit up the links of the fellowship once more" (20:364). Their aim is the reformation of Utterhay, and their companions, Viridis and the Green Knight, give up a kingdom to join them in making the free town free.

In Morris's final romances erotic passion is itself informed by socialist thought. Relationships are interclass and free of economic considerations. Golden Walter, the son of a great merchant, weds the Maid, a thrall of unknown parentage. Ursula, the yeoman's daughter, is the bride of Ralph, son of a minor king. Birdalone, the child of a widow reduced to beggary, unites with a noble knight, Arthur, while her friend, Aurea, a "lady of high degree," finds happiness with Robert Gerardson, a freeman's son. Only ignorant or evil characters question lineage and they are always silenced.[19] When marriage occurs, it is

19. In the *Wood beyond the World*, two middle-class inhabitants of Stark Wall question the Maid's lineage when Walter becomes their king. A wiser inhabitant of the town rebukes them by saying that the Maid will found a line whose descendants will bless her name. In *The Well at the World's End*,

often a voluntary private union that does not need the sanction of religion or law. Never is it the bourgeois institution that Engels condemned as an "official cloak of prostitution" and Morris denigrated as an arrangement designed to protect individual property and to resist such external forces as fellowship.[20]

Since love is not tied to property and women ideally are not tokens of exchange, "free unions" among lovers meet with approval. In a conventional Victorian novel, the love of Ralph and the Lady of Abundance would be treated as adultery; in the terms established in a Morrisian romance, the relationship is acceptable because it is loving. Birdalone and Arthur simply make love to "wed" each other, while the nature of the union of Osberne and Elfhild, in *The Sundering Flood,* is never even discussed. Lovers love and unite and for Morris that union is enough.

In effect, Morris's last romances simply and undidactically praise lovers, workers, outlaws, and all who practice association and equality. Without overtly preaching, these works clearly proclaim the worth of joyful labor, cooperation, and mutual aid, and the possibility of harmonizing personal and communal needs. At the same time, they repudiate capitalist ideology and the literary form that bears it. Like the works of literature Morris praised in his lecture on "The Society of the Future," his final prose fictions "tell their tales to our senses and leave them alone to moralize the tale so told."[21] Through their internalized Marxism and direct sensory appeal, they constitute a new literary genre, the socialist romance.

Ralph's brother, Hugh, himself a failure, snobbishly questions Ursula's background and is soundly reprimanded.

20. Frederick Engels, *Socialism: Utopian and Scientific* (New York: International, n.d.), 35; Bax and Morris, *Socialism,* 3.

21. *Political Writings of William Morris,* 200.

CHRISTOPHER WATERS

Morris's "Chants" and the
Problems of Socialist Culture

In January 1878, Henry Broadhurst, the "Lib-Lab" secretary of the Labour Representation League, organized a "Workmen's Neutrality Demonstration." It was sponsored by the Eastern Question Association, of which William Morris was the treasurer. The event took place in the Exeter Hall in London, and it demonstrated the strength of opposition to British involvement in the Near East. Morris had been persuaded to write a song for the occasion, to be performed by a working-class choir as a prelude to the main address. The five verses of the work, sung to the tune of "The Hardy Norseman's Home of Yore," called on workers to voice their displeasure at government intervention in the crisis:

> Wake, London Lads, wake, bold and free!
>   Arise and fall to work,
> Lest England's glory come to be
>   Bond servant to the Turk!

In his autobiography, Broadhurst commented on the success of Morris's contribution, and on the importance of song in the work of political propaganda in general. He also claimed that "this was the first occasion on which music and singing were introduced to while away the time of waiting at a political meeting," and that "since then the practice has grown rapidly into favour, until it has now become practically universal."[1] Broadhurst was mistaken when he suggested that the use of Morris's rousing song by the Eastern Question Association was the "first occasion" on which song had been used to generate enthusiasm at a political meeting: Owenites and Chartists had realized just how effective song could be in their own propaganda work earlier in the century. Nonetheless, by

---

1. Henry Broadhurst, *The Story of His Life from a Stonemason's Bench to the Treasury* (London: Hutchinson and Co., 1901), 83. For Morris and the Eastern Question Association, see E. P. Thompson, *William Morris: Romantic to Revolutionary,* 2d ed. (New York: Pantheon, 1976), esp. 214–19.

127

1878 most of their songs had been forgotten, although in the following decade—in part due to the efforts of William Morris—the socialist movement would become interested in them once again. Despite Broadhurst's ignorance of earlier radical song traditions, however, the late 1870s did mark a revival of interest in the relationship between music and politics. It also marked a period when Morris began to realize that his own literary skills could be valuable in the work of political propaganda.

It was through his connection with the Eastern Question Association that Morris began to become involved in various political crusades. In the 1880s, after severing his ties with the Liberal Party, Morris joined H. M. Hyndman's Democratic Federation—later the Social Democratic Federation (SDF)—which he soon left in order to establish the Socialist League. From the mid-1880s to the early 1890s he also wrote a number of "chants" for the movement to which he now devoted his energies. Rather than refer to his contributions as "songs," he preferred to speak of his "chants," hoping they would be recited, rather than sung, to the accompaniment of a harp or a lute, as was the case with the works of medieval minstrels. The earliest of the chants appeared in the SDF's weekly, *Justice,* in 1884. Some were published in the journal of the Socialist League, *Commonweal,* and a good number of them were issued by the league in pamphlet form as *Chants for Socialists.* Most of them were later collected and published in *Poems By the Way* (1896), *Pilgrims of Hope and Chants for Socialists* (1915), and in Morris's *Collected Works,* edited by his daughter, May.[2]

Little has been written about Morris's chants and the role they played in the socialist movement. E. P. Thompson, who devoted a few pages to them in his biography of Morris, suggested that they were largely ephemeral, written for the day-to-day needs of the movement. Thompson also claimed they were popular insofar as they relied on familiar symbols, metaphors, and images that had been cultivated by the romantic movement. Because of these specific intellectual debts, Thompson concluded, the chants cannot be viewed as representative of a poetry of "revolutionary realism."[3] Indeed, Morris's chants were similar to the songs of the Chartists, which were also indebted to the poetry of the romantic movement for their models, particularly to the work of Byron and Shelley. Another critic, however, has suggested that while the earlier romantic radicals addressed their work *to* the working class, the hero of Morris's chants was the working class itself. Because of this their success was guaranteed, and they "directly influenced the labour movement of his day. . . ."[4] But how wide-

2. For the publication history of the *Chants,* see the appendix to this chapter. See also Eugene D. Le Mire, "The Socialist League Leaflets and Manifestoes: An Annotated Checklist," *International Review of Social History* 22 (1977): 26–27.

3. Thompson, *William Morris,* 637–39.

4. Jessie Kocmanova, *The Poetic Maturing of William Morris* (Prague: Státní Pedagogické Nakladatelství, 1964), 188–94. See also John Miller, "Songs of the British Radical and Labour Movement," *Marxism Today* 7 (June 1963): 180–86.

CHANTS for SOCIALISTS

BY

WILLIAM MORRIS.

CONTENTS:

LONDON:

Socialist League Office,

13 FARRINGDON ROAD, HOLBORN VIADUCT, E.C.

1885.

PRICE ONE PENNY.

Title page, *Chants for Socialists*, by William Morris (London: Socialist League, 1885).

spread was that influence, and to what extent can we refer to the chants as part of an alternative, socialist culture that Morris and his comrades were attempting to establish in Britain?

Socialism and Song

Many Victorian social critics considered music to be of central importance in their various programs of moral reform, and the role played by music in the socialist movement can only be understood in this context. In 1871, seven years before Broadhurst's "Workmen's Neutrality Demonstration," the High Church theologian Hugh Haweis published his influential book, *Music and Morals.* In its twentieth edition by 1903, the work soon became a key text for those who believed that music could be used in the struggle to reform working-class morals. Moreover, Haweis's book was also mentioned by socialists when they discussed the relationship between music, politics, and social change.

Born in 1838, Haweis later recalled how he had become interested in the "elevating" power of music while working in the slums of Bethnal Green. After noting that most slum dwellers "were leading dull lives . . . with little refreshment or variety," he decided "to try the effect of music, and good music, upon their narrow, busy, overburdened lives."[5] Enthusiastic about the results, he wrote about the relationship between musical harmony and social harmony in *Music and Morals,* and managed to convince various philanthropists to sponsor free concerts where workers might develop a taste for edifying music. His thoughts on the subject of music and social reform influenced the development of numerous organizations, such as the Kyrle Society, the People's Entertainment Society, and the People's Concert Society, as well as the movement to provide workers with temperance music halls. Taken together, such organizations were dedicated to conferring a "great good" on the population by destroying workers' ties to "lower forms of amusement" and by training them to a "very high standard of taste." The result of such efforts, claimed one reformer, would be a strengthening of working-class commitment to the dominant social order.[6]

Music played a prominent role in the various attempts to promote what was known as "rational recreation" because, as one historian has noted, it touched the emotions as well as the intellect; while rational, it was also inspirational.[7] This fact was not wasted on activists in the socialist movement; they also recognized that music could generate strong emotional responses among those who heard it. Herbert Burrows, for example, a member of the SDF and one of

5. H. R. Haweis, *My Musical Life,* 2d ed. (London: W. H. Allen and Co., 1886), 116–18.
6. Florence A. Marshall, "The People's Concert Society," *Macmillan's Magazine* 43 (April 1881): 437.
7. Hugh Cunningham, *Leisure in the Industrial Revolution* (London: Croom Helm, 1980), 102–4.

the organizers of the match girls' strike, once recounted the visit by a group of poor street musicians to a London slum:

> The music died out in soft sweetness,
>   Entwined with a pathos of pain,
> And the struggle for crust and for garret
>   Claimed the lives of the toilers again.
> But their hearts had been softened and strengthened.[8]

The key to Burrows's own song is its emphasis on the extent to which the "toilers" had been "softened and strengthened" by the music of these street performers. By temporarily releasing them from the hardships of daily life, music had strengthened their resolve to struggle for a better world in which such suffering would not exist. For Burrows, music could transport the listener to an imaginary realm of beauty, which, when contrasted with present miseries, would intensify the resolve to struggle for the advent of a new, socialist society.

Socialists like Burrows seemed to be interested in music because of all the arts it appeared to them to be the least corrupted by capitalism. As Morris noted on numerous occasions, paintings and works of literature had become mere commodities, sold in the market like any other goods. But despite the growing prevalence of music-hall fare, music remained relatively immune from intensive commercial exploitation and could be practiced and enjoyed by all, including those without any formal training. Moreover, music had strong roots in working-class life, and for centuries it had been an important part of a genuinely popular, working-class culture. While most workers did not write poetry or paint, they could—and often did—sing. In particular, music played a major role in the lives of workers from nonconformist backgrounds, and socialists hoped to harness this form of popular creativity for their own movement. Thus they encouraged the use of music at political rallies. As one correspondent claimed in *Justice:* "The one reproach to our movement is that we neglect music. Apart from the pleasure and refining influence of music, it is generally admitted that it would be, if practiced, a great aid to us in our propagandist work."[9]

Of all the late Victorian socialists to write about music, John Bruce Glasier was perhaps the most important. A disciple of Morris and the author of an "appreciation" of Morris's *Chants,* Glasier believed that poetry and song could play a major role in the struggle for socialism. According to Glasier, while various "popular leisure-hour attractions" only reached the "emotional centres" of the "weaklings of the nation," music was "a purer and more imaginative" art which could exert a "potent and lasting influence" on the populace. Like other

8. Reproduced in James Leatham, *Songs for Socialists,* 3d ed. (Aberdeen: James Leatham, 1890), 19.

9. *Justice,* 25 June 1910, 3.

socialists, Glasier believed that the first stirring of idealism and enthusiasm that had so influenced the socialist movement came from Blake, Burns, Keats, Ruskin, Shelley, Whitman, and Wordsworth. Together, he wrote, their poems "still bear our souls company, keeping glorious our thoughts and inspiring our youth with a mystic urge towards all that makes for the redress and nobler achievement of mankind."[10] Not only did Glasier wish to harness the work of these poets to the socialist cause, but he also wanted socialists to follow in their footsteps. He wrote several socialist songs of his own, including the anarchist-inspired pieces, "When the Revolution Comes" and "We'll Turn Things Upside Down."

Unfortunately, Morris seldom wrote about the relationship between his poetry and the socialist movement, and he rarely commented on the uses the movement made of his own chants. But the purpose of the Socialist League—indeed, Morris's lifelong goal—was "to make more socialists," and this entailed a process of conversion in which music, given the nineteenth-century emphasis on its social utility, could play an important role. Morris was friendly with several musicians and composers, including Gustav Holst, and he valued their commitment to the socialist cause. Moreover, as early as 1884, when the Democratic Federation established a band to perform at various open-air gatherings, Morris supported the idea and took charge of the band fund.[11] While others discussed the relationship between music and socialism at a more theoretical level, it was Morris who contributed some of the most important songs to the movement.

Morris and the Chants

Morris was not the only socialist to write songs for the labor movement. Edward Carpenter's "England, Arise!" became the banner of the socialist cause, while songs by Herbert Burrows, Jim Connell, John Bruce Glasier, Fred Henderson, Tom Maguire, and a number of lesser-known figures were sung at various socialist gatherings. The importance of their songs to the movement is attested to by the number of songbooks that various socialists compiled. Some of the more prominent anthologies included Carpenter's *Chants of Labour* (1888), the work that served as a model for later works; *The Labour Songbook* (1888?), published by the Bristol Socialist Society; the *Socialist Songs* (1889) of the Aberdeen Branch of Morris's Socialist League; *Songs for Socialists* (3d edition, 1890), compiled by Morris's colleague, James Leatham; John Trevor's *Labour Church Hymnbook* (1892); Glasier's *Socialist Songs* (1893); Robert Blatchford's

10. J. Bruce Glasier, *Socialism in Song: An Appreciation of William Morris's "Chants for Socialists"* (Manchester: National Labour Press Ltd., 1919), vii-viii. Glasier's sister made similar claims about her brother's poetry. See Elizabeth Glasier Foster, *Bruce Glasier and His Poetry* (privately printed, n.d.), esp. 42.

11. "Music for the People," *Justice,* 24 May 1884, 1.

Clarion Songbook (1906); *The SDF Songbook* (1910?); and the Fabian Society's *Songs for Socialists* (1912).

These songbooks shared the goal of fashioning a literary and musical culture for the socialist movement. While each collection had its own particular emphasis, overall they were similar both in their contents and in the themes they stressed. It is important to note that the songbooks did not merely consist of material written by late nineteenth-century socialists, for all of them acknowledged the importance of earlier romantic and radical traditions for the socialist cause. The compilers of the Fabian anthology, for example, claimed that their work was not solely a "lyrical expression of Fabian Socialism" (at which point one reviewer caustically remarked: "We should think not—and what the 'lyrical expression of Fabian Socialism' would be like is truly tantalizing to the imagination").[12] Rather, the editors appropriated material from earlier intellectual traditions that could be used both in constructing and in legitimating a new, socialist culture.

Of the 532 titles in the nine songbooks just cited, 15 percent were songs written by the prominent romantic poets (almost 29 percent in the Fabian anthology). Indeed, works by Blake, Burns, Kingsley, Lowell, Shelley, Whitman, and Whittier were pervasive in the anthologies. Apart from Carpenter's "England Arise!," Lowell's "True Freedom" was the only work to appear in all nine anthologies. But most of all it was Shelley who remained of paramount importance for late Victorian socialists. Several of them wrote pamphlets suggesting the enormous debt they owed to him, while Shelley's poem, "Men of England," appeared in two-thirds of the songbooks. Moreover, the songbooks also included a number of pieces written by various Chartists. These included the vaguely utopian pieces, "Sons of Labour" by John Mackay Peacock and "Truth is Growing" by Thomas Cooper, as well as the more explicitly radical poem by Ernest Jones, "The Song of the Lower Classes."

Despite the prominence of such pieces, some 40 percent of all the songs that appeared in these anthologies were written by activists in the late nineteenth-century socialist and labor movements. And of the writers of those songs, William Morris stands out as the most prominent—and the most prolific. Responsible for some 8 percent of the titles in these collections, Morris towered above his comrades as a poet of socialism. Virtually all the songbooks included at least one piece by Morris, and most of them included several. "The March of the Workers," written for *Commonweal* in 1885, appeared in eight of the books; "The Voice of Toil," written for *Justice* in 1884, appeared in seven; "All for the Cause," also written for *Justice,* appeared in six, as did his "Come, Comrades, Come."

What strikes one in reading these works is Morris's lack of originality in terms

---

12. *Daily Herald,* 26 August 1912, 4.

Title page, *Chants of Labour,* edited by Edward Carpenter with two designs by Walter Crane (London: Swan Sonnenschein, 1905).

Illustration by Walter Crane from Carpenter's *Chants*.

of the themes and imagery he chose to develop, but just as apparent is his ability to work with this material in a more sophisticated manner than most of his contemporaries. Morris succeeded, where many of his comrades failed, in developing a powerful mode of expression that stayed clear of the sentimentalism that characterized a large number of socialist songs. Take, for example, "The Day is Coming." Hardly original in its content, it is merely one example of a whole genre of optimistic, "coming day" songs that were popular with socialists. Charles Mackay, the editor of the *Illustrated London News,* had written a similar song in the 1850s, an enormously popular work that sold more than 400,000 copies. It was reprinted in several socialist anthologies because it appealed to those who sensed the importance of utopian imagery and optimistic sentiment in converting workers to their cause:

> There's a good time coming, boys,
>   A good time coming;
> We may not live to see the day,
>   But earth shall glisten in the ray
> Of the good time coming.[13]

Mackay's poem lacks any clear understanding of the forces that prevented the "good time" about which he wrote from being realized. Nonetheless, it foreshadowed a whole genre of socialist songs that also spoke of the ideal society of the future. Utopian sentiment in the socialist movement was widespread, and it was cultivated because it was supposed to generate the desire for a new society. According to one writer, that desire could be stimulated by expressing utopian sentiments through music and song. "Music," he wrote, "must represent an aspiration after the ideal beauty, an attempt to express in a tone-picture something beyond the rays of verbal description or realistic experience."[14]

Like Mackay's poem, Morris's chant, "The Day is Coming," offers a vision of well-being in the society of the future:

> Come hither lads, and hearken, for a tale there is to tell,
> Of the wonderful days a-coming when all shall be better than
>   well.

But unlike Mackay's work—and unlike similar pieces written by other socialists (such as Montague Blatchford's "Hark! A New Song Ringing," H. H. Sparling's "When the People Have Their Own Again," and W. D. Tait's "The Time is Coming")—Morris's picture of the socialist millennium is full of concrete

13. Reproduced in *The Labour Church Hymnbook* (Manchester: Labour Church Institute, 1892), 47.
14. "How Commercialism Affects Our Music," *Justice,* 26 October 1895, 2.

details of the socialist future. It is full of references to better housing and the joys of work, leisure, shared wealth, security, and communal well-being. In fact, "The Day is Coming" is a poetic synopsis of the vision of the future that Morris would elaborate several years later in *News from Nowhere*.

"The Day is Coming" also stands apart from other works of the genre because in it Morris makes an attempt to contrast his vision of an idyllic future with his understanding of the dismal realities of the present. This is what differentiates the piece more than anything else from works that, at least superficially, share a similar theme:

> Ah! Such are the days that shall be! But what
> are the deeds of to-day,
> In the days of the years we dwell in, that wear
> our lives away?

For Morris, a vision of the future was worth cultivating because it could breed working-class discontent with the present and thus inspire the struggle for the socialist society of the future. He thus took great pains in his poetry to juxtapose past and present in order to encourage the kind of activity that would bring about "the change" he so ardently longed for:

> Oh why and for what are we waiting, while our brothers
> droop and die,
> And on every wind of the heavens a wasted life goes by?
> How long shall they reproach us where crowd on crowd they
> dwell,
> Poor ghosts of the wicked city, the gold-crushed hungry hell?
> Through squalid life they laboured, in sordid grief they died,
> Those sons of a mighty mother, those props of England's pride.

According to Glasier, "The Day is Coming" was "almost the most beautiful socialist utterance," condensing the essence of the "whole call" of socialism.[15] To be more specific, the chant transcends the vague utopian yearning that characterizes the majority of the songs of the "coming day" genre by offering an analysis of oppression and a corresponding call for revolutionary action.

"All for the Cause" is another of Morris's chants that depicts the socialist society of the future. More than "The Day is Coming," it focuses on the struggle that will be necessary to bring that society about. Glasier referred to it as a socialist communion hymn: "Here we feel in full glow that inner sense of benediction—of worship . . . which is the final assurance and strength of all self-

---

15. Glasier, *Socialism in Song*, 8.

renunciation for human weal. . . ."[16] According to Morris, it was through self-renunciation for the Cause that true comradeship was born. "All for the Cause" called on individuals to march forward with the banner of socialism, to experience new forms of intense comradeship, and to identify with those who had already suffered in the battle:

> Hear a word, a word in season, for the day is drawing nigh,
> When the Cause shall call upon us, some to live, and
> some to die!

While "All for the Cause" speaks of sacrifice, it also speaks of courage. Indeed, it is from those who have sacrificed themselves in the past that socialists can gain the courage and strength that will assist them in their present struggle:

> Mourn not therefore, nor lament it that the world
> outlives their life;
> Voice and vision yet they give us, making strong
> our hands for strife.

The theme of martyrdom also characterizes Morris's "A Death Song," written in December 1887 for the funeral of Alfred Linnell, the agitator who had died from injuries inflicted by the police at the Trafalgar Square demonstration on "Bloody Sunday," November 13.[17] Police brutality on that occasion outraged Morris, and the funeral of Linnell was an extraordinary event which hardened the conviction and resolve of socialists:

> What cometh here from west to east awending?
> And who are these, the marchers stern and slow?
> We bear the message that the rich are sending
> Aback to those who bade them wake and know.
> *Not one, not one, nor thousands must they slay,*
> *But one and all if they would dusk the day.*

Not only does the song develop an image of working-class unity and determination in the wake of Linnell's death, but it also depicts Morris's own bitterness at the refusal of the ruling class to listen to the arguments workers like Linnell had been making:

> They will not learn; they have no ears to hearken.
> They turn their faces from the eyes of fate;

16. Ibid., see 17–20.
17. William Morris, *Alfred Linnell. A Death Song* (London, 1887). The song was written too late in Morris's career to appear in the various editions of the *Chants* published by the Socialist League.

SOLD FOR THE BENEFIT OF LINNELL'S ORPHANS.

ALFRED LINNELL

Killed in Trafalgar Square,
NOVEMBER 20, 1887.

A DEATH SONG,
BY MR. W. MORRIS.
Memorial Design by Mr. Walter Crane.

PRICE ONE PENNY.

Title page, William Morris, *Alfred Linnell. A Death Song* (1887). Illustration by Walter Crane.

> Their gay-lit halls shut out the skies that darken.
> But, lo, this dead man knocking at the gate.
> *Not one, not one. . . .*

If "A Death Song" represents Morris at his most pessimistic, "The Voice of Toil" encourages workers to gain strength from martyrs like Linnell. Pessimism is discouraged:

> I heard men saying, leave hope and praying,
>   All days shall be as all have been;
> To-day and to-morrow bring fear and sorrow,
>   The never-ending toil between.

At the same time, workers are told to pay attention to the history of popular struggles, to learn from them and gain sustenance from them:

> When Earth was younger 'midst toil and hunger
>   In hope we strove, and our hands were strong;
> Then great men led us, with words they fed us,
>   And bade us right the earthly wrong.
> Go read in story their deeds and glory,
>   Their names amidst the nameless dead;
> Turn then from lying to us slow dying
>   In that good world to which they led.

The heroes Morris refers to in "The Voice of Toil"—Glasier claimed he meant them to be Wat Tyler and John Ball[18]—were invoked to give strength to those engaged in the current struggle by indicating the continuities between the popular movements of the past and the present. But most of all it was the promise of victory that charged the movement with the energy necessary to sustain it, hence the popularity of Morris's "March of the Workers." Published in virtually all of the anthologies, it was perhaps the most frequently sung of the chants, and along with Carpenter's "England, Arise!" became one of the principal marching songs of the movement. Not only does it speak of the "good time coming," but it also holds out the promise of that good time to everybody—even the rich are invited to share in its joys: "Then be ye of us, let your hope be our desire." More than this, victory is also guaranteed because of the devotion and commitment of the people to the struggle:

> What is this the sound and rumour? What is this
>   that all men hear,
> Like the wind in hollow valleys when the storm

18. Glasier, *Socialism in Song*, see 12–14.

            is drawing near,
    Like the rolling on of ocean in the eventide of fear?
    'Tis the people marching on.

The Chants and Socialist Culture

Despite the familiar romantic imagery that permeates Morris's chants, the abstractions which characterize many of the works of the romantic movement and which socialists reproduced are largely absent. While Morris's earlier works often spoke in general terms of "anguish," "tyranny," and "slavery," and while they also spoke of the desire for a world of "freedom" and "justice," in his later works Morris abandoned many of these abstractions. In their place he substituted an emphasis on the importance of the concrete struggles of real people. The stress Morris placed on *activity* in his chants differentiates them from many of the romantic antecedents to which he was indebted. As Glasier wrote, Morris's songs spoke "*of* the people" not "*to* or *in behalf* of the people." For example, Shelley, in "Men of England," directed his thoughts *to* the oppressed: "The seed *ye* sow, another reaps." By contrast, Morris, in "All for the Cause," speaks as *one* of the oppressed: "*We* who were once fools and dreamers, then shall be the brave and wise." This, Glasier believed, is what distinguished Morris's chants from the work of Burns and Shelley in particular.[19]

It also differentiates them from many of the songs written by other socialists at the end of the century, writers who persisted in using vague generalities rather than speaking in a language of a shared and popular struggle. Morris attempted to break with the past, and by making use of the first person plural he tried to voice the aspirations of the people. One critic has suggested that the use of "we" in such works is an "empty dramatic device" that too often masquerades a lack of real identification between the poet and his or her audience.[20] Nonetheless, Morris used it with some success, generating a sense of common purpose and shared identity among those who sang his songs. In "No Master," for example, Morris asks:

            And we, shall we too, crouch and quail,
                Ashamed, afraid of strife,
            And lest our lives ultimately fail
                Embrace the Death in Life?

19. Ibid., 5.
20. Ian Watson, *Song and Democratic Culture in Britain* (London: Croom Helm, 1983), 41. For the role played by Chartism in shifting the content of radical poetry away from a vague, romantic idealism, see Horst Roessler and Ian Watson, "In Defence of Ernest Jones," *Gulliver: Deutsch-Englische Jahrbücher* 12 (1983): 136.

For many of those who were familiar with Morris's songs, the answer was a resounding no, and it was this sense of camaraderie between those who struggled together, captured in such songs as "No Master," that made Morris's chants appealing to so many socialists.

The extent of that appeal is often hard to measure, but it can be gauged from several impressionistic sources, such as this description of the activities of the Bristol Socialist Society:

> It still lingers in my memory as some Enchanted Hall of Dreams. There was music and song and dance. . . . Night after night bands of socialists, young and old, would meet for study and debate, and terribly practical work, too, for the unemployed and unskilled workers. . . . Never did our meetings break up without our singing one of Morris's songs to a crooning Irish melody—I think "The Message of the March Wind" to the tune of "Teddy O'Neill" was the favourite.[21]

The chants were also popular with individuals who did not belong to Morris's Socialist League or related bodies such as the Bristol Socialist Society. Christian Socialists, for example, often extolled the virtues of the chants. In the early 1880s, the *Christian Socialist* urged its readers to acquire a copy of "The Day is Coming," claiming that "it ought to stir the blood of any Englishman that hears it."[22] In the United States, Morris's chants also accompanied the struggle for socialism. In Omaha, Nebraska, the Women's Socialist Union opened its meetings with the singing of a socialist song, often one written by Morris. Likewise, Morris's "March of the Workers" was especially popular with the Knights of Labour, and at one time or another most of the chants appeared in the newspapers published by radical and socialist organizations in the United States, including the *Workmen's Advocate, People, The Coming Nation,* and *The Appeal to Reason.* They were also published by Charles Kerr, the influential Chicago socialist who established a press that made available the works of many British and continental socialists to the American public.[23]

Despite the widespread popularity of Morris's chants among those already converted to the cause of socialism, the attempt made by Morris and his contemporaries to write songs *for* the socialist movement was fraught with contradictions. On the one hand, socialists—Morris in particular—wanted to see the revival of popular artistic creativity. But, on the other hand, they offered their own songs to the very people whose creativity they wished to encourage.

21. Samson Bryher, *An Account of the Labour and Socialist Movement in Bristol* (Bristol: Bristol Labour Weekly, 1931), 22.

22. *Christian Socialist,* October 1883, 66.

23. Mari Jo Buhle, *Women and American Socialism, 1870–1920* (Urbana: University of Illinois Press, 1983), III; Philip S. Foner, *American Labor Songs of the Nineteenth Century* (Urbana: University of Illinois Press, 1975), 289, 294, 321–23.

Montague Blatchford was one individual who, while praising Morris's chants, also encouraged the re-emergence of a genuinely "popular" popular culture. Blatchford was founder of the Clarion Vocal Union, a radical working-class choral organization associated with the readers of a widely read socialist weekly, *The Clarion,* for whose pages he once wrote, "formal classical coldness . . . and involved metaphysical art" were of no use to the working class. Instead, workers required "an art of their own, art that is built upon their lives."[24]

Blatchford was not alone in this belief. Edgar Bainton, a socialist, a composer, and a professor of composition in Newcastle Upon Tyne, once delivered a lecture to the local branch of the Independent Labour Party in which he discussed the relationship between music and socialism. Echoing Morris's writings on art, Bainton claimed that music had once been an expression of the aspirations of the people, but in the late middle ages wandering minstrels began to professionalize musical production; in so doing, they undermined the importance of music created by the people themselves. As was the case in so much of the cultural criticism developed by late Victorian socialists, the robust popular culture of an earlier Merrie England was contrasted with the barrenness of its nineteenth-century counterpart. For Bainton, the solution to the problem was to be found in returning music to the people, encouraging people to make their own music again.[25]

But what did it mean to call on the "people" to create their own music, holding up to them a picture of their musical creativity in the middle ages? Bainton, along with Blatchford and many of the socialists who compiled various anthologies of socialist songs, often spoke of the need for the people to make their own culture. Nonetheless, underneath the rhetoric many of the socialists seemed to think they knew best what the workers really desired. Some of them were even under the illusion that the material in their socialist anthologies was representative of a genuinely popular culture. As Carpenter claimed in the preface to his own collection, the works he had selected were for, and mostly *by,* "the people." But in making this suggestion Carpenter merely romanticized "the people" and confused a tradition that developed *from* the people with one manufactured *for* them by middle-class socialists.

Other activists were slightly more aware of the problem. For example, H. W. Hobart, a member of the Social Democratic Federation and a writer on cultural affairs for *Justice,* reviewed Carpenter's anthology: "Few people can decide better what the workers want in the way of labour chants . . . than the toilers themselves," but he added, somewhat parenthetically, "or, at any rate, those who have an affinity with the working classes."[26] On many occasions, Morris

---

24. "Old English Music," *Clarion,* 7 July 1905, 3.
25. Edgar L. Bainton, *Music and Socialism* (Manchester: Fellowship Press, 1910?).
26. *Justice,* 19 May 1888, 2.

himself felt the kind of affinity with the working class that Hobart spoke of, despite his own middle-class background. But there were times when he didn't. Referring to a talk he gave in Stepney in 1885, he once said, "I don't seem to have got at them yet—you see this great class gulf lies between us."[27]

When Edgar Bainton called on the "people" to make their own art, he had taken his cue from Morris, who was appalled at the extent to which capitalism had robbed workers of their creativity. But despite Morris's call for a revival of popular art, his chants were anything but popular in his sense of the term. Although they often made use of the first person plural, thus giving the appearance of emanating from the working class, they were quite distinct from forms of working-class cultural production. As A. L. Lloyd, the historian of the folk song movement, has suggested, the songs of the Chartist and socialist movements "had little influence on the sort of thing the singing miners, mill hands and foundry workers made for themselves."[28]

Industrial folk songs were part of a culture of the people—the kind of culture that Morris himself called for, but could not, of course, provide. They were also expressions of local occupational experience, rooted in the work places and communities in which they were written. Socialist songs needed to transcend these geographical boundaries in order to assist in the construction of a national—even international—movement, a movement with a culture that could bind together the diverse social groups that were attracted to socialism. This they achieved by keeping alive the aspirations of the romantic movement, wedded, in the case of Morris's chants, to a more radical analysis of capitalist exploitation. They were manufactured and imposed from above, but the best of them—particularly those written by Morris—could help inspire the struggle for the new society socialists desired.

If the society Morris dreamed of is ever realized, then a genuinely popular culture might flourish once again. In the meantime, both industrial folk songs written by workers and songs written by middle-class socialists might work together, inspiring the movement to which Morris devoted a good deal of energy. It is interesting to note that many of the varied traditions socialists drew upon when compiling their songbooks a century ago are still being invoked in popular struggles today. Following the miners' strike of 1984–1985, workers in the coal fields of the North East recorded an album, "Which Side Are You On?"[29] Not only does it include songs of struggle written by miners themselves—songs that represent a "flowering of creativity amongst the mining communities," as the album put it—but it offers the listener a number of nineteenth-century ballads

27. Quoted in J. W. Mackail, *The Life of William Morris* (London: Longmans, 1899), 2:153.
28. A. L. Lloyd, *Folk Song in England* (London: Lawrence and Wishart, 1967), 318.
29. "Which Side Are You On?" (Music for the miners from the North East.) Available from Which Side Records, 23 Brighton Grove, Newcastle Upon Tyne NE4 5N5, England.

and pieces written for workers by more recent middle-class sympathizers such as Bertolt Brecht. No doubt William Morris would heartily approve of such a combination, for he never intended his own chants to become detached from the very real struggles for which they were written.

Appendix: Morris's Socialist Songs—Publication History

Abbreviations Used in the Listings

Song sources

Chants #1: Chants for Socialists [1 song] (London: Reeves, 1884).
Chants #2: Chants for Socialists [6 songs] (London: Socialist League, February-May 1885).
Chants #3: Chants for Socialists [7 songs] (London: Socialist League, 1885 and 1892).
Poems: William Morris, *Poems By the Way and Love is Enough* (London: Longmans, 1896).
Pilgrims: William Morris, *Pilgrims of Hope and Chants for Socialists* (London: Longmans, 1915).
CW: The Collected Works of William Morris, introduced by May Morris, 24 vols. (London: Longmans, 1910–1915).
Peck: *Chants for Socialists,* introduced by Walter Edwin Peck [*Library of Social Justice #1*] (New York: New Horizon Press, 1935).

Selected socialist songbooks in which Morris's songs appeared

EC: Edward Carpenter, *Chants of Labour* (1888).
BSS: Bristol Socialist Society, *The Labour Songbook* (1888?).
SLA: Socialist League (Aberdeen), *Socialist Songs* (1889).
JL: James Leatham, *Songs for Socialists* (1890).
JBG: John Bruce Glasier, *Socialist Songs* (1893).
GP: Georgia Pearce, *The Clarion Songbook* (1906).
SDF: *The SDF Songbook* (1910?).
FS: Fabian Society, *Songs for Socialists* (1912).

"ALL FOR THE CAUSE"

Justice, 19 April 1884; *Chants #2 & #3; Poems; Pilgrims;*
CW, vol. 9; Peck; EC; SLA; JL; JBG; SDF; FS.

"THE DAY IS COMING"

Justice, 29 March 1884; *Chants #1, #2 and #3; Poems; Pilgrims; CW,* vol. 9; Peck; BSS; SLA; JL; JBG.

"THE DAY OF DAYS"

Time, November 1890, p. 1178; *Poems; CW,* vol. 9; GP.

"A DEATH SONG"

Pamphlet, December 1887; *Poems; CW,* vol. 9; JBG; SDF.

"DOWN AMONG THE DEAD MEN" ("COME, COMRADES, COME")

Chants #3; Pilgrims; CW, vol. 24; Peck; EC; JL; JBG; GP; SDF; FS.

"DRAWING NEAR THE LIGHT" ("LO, WHEN WE WADE THE TANGLED WOOD")

Commonweal, April 1888; *CW,* vol. 9; JBG; GP; SDF.

"THE MARCH OF THE WORKERS"

Commonweal, February 1885; *Chants #2* and *#3; Pilgrims; CW,* vol. 24; Peck; EC; BSS; SLA; JL; JBG; GP; SDF; FS.

"MAY DAY" (2 poems)

Justice, May Day 1891 and 1894; *CW,* vol. 24; JBG.

"THE MESSAGE OF THE MARCH WIND" (FROM "THE PILGRIMS OF HOPE")

Commonweal, March 1885; *Chants #2* and *#3; Poems; Pilgrims; CW,* vol. 24; Peck.

"NO MASTER"

Justice, 7 June 1884; *Commonweal,* March 1889; *Chants #2* and *#3; Pilgrims; CW,* vol. 24; Peck; EC; BSS; SLA; JBG; SDF.

"THE VOICE OF TOIL"

Justice, 5 April 1884; *Chants #2* and *#3; Poems; Pilgrims; CW,* vol. 9; Peck; EC; SLA; JL; JBG; GP; SDF; FS.

FLORENCE S. BOOS───────────────────────────

Narrative Design in *The Pilgrims of Hope*

The Pilgrims of Hope (1885) was Morris's last poetic narrative, his first major
socialist work, and the only one of his romances with a contemporary setting.
Was he well-advised to abandon an art form he had practiced for thirty years?
Did he later conclude that narrative verse was ill-suited to his evolving social and
literary purposes, or that his romances required more remote historical or
utopian settings? There is no doubt that Morris's imagination sought more
congenial environments in the remote past and projected future. Two years
before his death, in the 1894 essay, "How I Became A Socialist," he bluntly
remarked that "Apart from the desire to produce beautiful things, the leading
passion of my life has been and is hatred of modern civilization,"[1] and *Pilgrims*
clearly resonates with this "hatred." Does this mean that the work is somehow
transitional, a forced and unstable attempt to honor failed revolution in archaic
verse?

I will argue that it does not—that Morris's "modern" communist poem holds
up well. Its superposition of style and content reflects (among other things) his
refusal to write a tidily didactic work, and its unusual mixture of wry humor and
impassioned advocacy, pastoral romance and urban realism, effectively heighten
the sense that an immensely desirable expression of the human spirit has been
crushed. Even the poem's subdominant and conflicted love plot obliquely witnesses the hero's dedication to other lives besides his own. *Pilgrims* is also more
amenable to feminist readings than many of Morris's earlier works, and the
development of the character of Richard, his self-conscious hero, is one of
Morris's fullest analyses of the sources of creativity and revolutionary
commitment.

Unfortunately, he is also Morris's only working-class hero. Later Morrisian
heroes tend to be leaders of one sort or another (the gifted priest John Ball, the
various tribal figures of the German romances); intellectuals or "scholars" (the
transmutations of Morris in *Ball* and *Nowhere*); or children of the long-achieved

───────────

1. William Morris, *The Collected Works of William Morris,* ed. May Morris, 24 vols. (London:
Longmans, 1910–1915), 23:279; hereafter cited as *CW.*

revolution (in *Nowhere*). Even one exception to the pattern is worth noting, for no other major Victorian poetic hero belongs to the urban poor. Tennyson's Enoch Arden, for example, is a fisherman; Rossetti managed one protagonist who was an Italian revolutionary (though also a murderer); Browning's fondness for monks, artists, and literati is well known; and Swinburne's theoretically revolutionary sentiments in *Songs before Sunrise* are most often addressed to fellow writers. It is even hard to find a contemporary *socialist* poem of any length with a working-class hero.

Morris's choice of the topic itself was thoroughly natural, for many emigré revolutionaries were drawn to the newly formed Socialist League, and Morris's London joiner and Paris Communard was a hero with whom most readers of *Commonweal* would wish to identify. Other unassuming examples of rank-and-file heroism in the poem also provided clear socialist models. The protagonist's wife, for example, is also a devoted Communard who dies on the ramparts, the first of Morris's tributes to an active if still-secondary role for women in "the Social-Revolution."

Morris lectured on the Commune several times, and the joint work *Socialism: Its Growth and Outcome* devotes more pages to it than to any other event of the century.[2] Morris's personal response was complex, and tinged with a kind of revolutionary stoicism. In his March 1887 *Commonweal* article, "Why We Celebrate the Commune of Paris," he notes warily that socialists may "take both warning and encouragement from its events," but responds to an assertion that we should not celebrate our defeats with the argument that

> this means looking not at this event only, but at all history in too narrow a way. . . . For I say solemnly and deliberately that if it happens to those of us now living to take part in such another tragedy it will be rather well for them than ill for them. Truly it is harder to live for a cause than to die for it. . . . It is for boldly seizing the opportunity offered for thus elevating the mass of the workers into heroism that we now celebrate the men of the Commune of Paris. . . . This was why the fall of the Commune was celebrated by such hecatombs sacrificed to the bourgeois god, Mammon; by such a riot of blood and cruelty on the part of the conquerors as quite literally has no parallel in modern times [an observation long since sadly super-seded]. And it is by that same token that we honour them as the foundation-stone of the new world that is to be.[3]

In *The Pilgrims of Hope,* Morris undertook to examine poetically the tragic as well as heroic implications of such "exemplary" actions. The result blends

2. Ernest Belfort Bax and William Morris, *Socialism: Its Growth and Outcome* (London: Swan Sonnenschein, 1893), ch. 16.
3. *Commonweal,* 19 March 1887, p. 89.

romantic pastoralism and aggrieved realism in ways that create the internal energy and emergent meaning of his work.

The poem's prefatory lyric, "The Message of the March Wind," provides a frame and vantage point for much of what follows. "The Message" may have been conceived originally as a separate poem, for Morris often designed parallel poetic structures in large and miniature, the latter inset in the former; "The Message" appeared alone in the March 1885 *Commonweal,* and the first installment of the main text the next month announced its author's intention to follow the fortunes of the lovers who in "The Message of the March Wind" were already touched by sympathy with the cause of the people.

Like the prefatory Singer of *The Earthly Paradise,* the "Message"'s speaker evokes a scene of apparent tranquility and natural beauty, but his carefully counterpointed images and quietly alternating rhythms subtly suggest tension, incompletion, and anticipation.

> Love mingles with love, and no evil is weighing
> On thy heart or mine, where all sorrow is healed. . . .
> There is wind in the twilight; in the white road before us
> The straw from the ox-road is blowing about;
> The moon's rim is rising, a star glitters o'er us,
> And the vane on the spire-top is swinging in doubt.
> Down there dips the highway toward the bridge crossing over
> The brook that runs on to the Thames and the sea.
> Draw closer, my sweet, we are lover and lover;
> This eve art thou given to gladness and me.

The March wind has been an emblem of hope since Shelley's great ode, but the poem's allusions to "healed" sorrow here are implicitly elegiac: the poem's unnamed lovers are secure for the moment ("this eve"), but they "draw closer," as the twilight, rising wind, blowing straw, doubtful vane, and darkened river create a sudden chill. Like Ecclesiastes' rivers (and the Thames near Kelmscott), the brook also "runs on to . . . the sea," and "the wind in the elm boughs" blows in fact from London, where

> . . . the March wind again of a people is telling;
> Of the life that they live there, so haggard and grim,
> That if we and our love amidst them had been dwelling
> My fondness had faltered, thy beauty grown dim.
> This land we have loved in our love and our leisure
> For them hangs in heaven, high out of their reach;
>
> . . . .
> The singers have sung and the builders have builded,
> The painters have fashioned their tales of delight;

> For what and for whom hath the world's book been gilded,
>   When all is for these but the blackness of night?

An image of Kelmscott manor may hover here, as an exemplar of what "the builders have builded," and comfortable refuge in which "[t]he painters have fashioned their tales of delight." Morris was well aware of his privileges. His impoverished protagonist Richard later remarks with bitter accuracy that

> . . . he who is rebel and rich may live safe for many a year,
>   While he warms his heart with pictures of all the glory
>   to come.
> There's the storm of the press and the critics maybe, but
>   sweet is his home, . . .
>   All is fair and orderly there as the rising and setting
>   sun.

In "The Society of the Future" (1887), a contemporary essay, Morris remarked in his own voice that

> I have always belonged to the well-to-do classes, and was born into luxury, so that necessarily I ask much more of the future than many of you do; and the first of all my visions, and that which colours all my others, is of a day when the words poor and rich . . . will have lost their old meaning.[4]

"The March Wind" here concludes with the wind's exhortations:

> It biddeth us learn all the wisdom it knoweth;
>   It hath found us and held us, and biddeth us hear:
> For it beareth the message: "Rise up on the morrow
>   And go on your ways toward the doubt and the strife;
> Join hope to our hope and blend sorrow with sorrow,
>   And seek for men's love in the short days of life."

Section 2, "The Bridge and the Street," describes the removal of the hero and his wife to London, and refracts Morris's personal anger and alienation through a darkened glass of romantic imagery.

> In the midst of the bridge there we stopped and we wondered
>   In London at last, and the moon going down,
> All sullied and red where the mast-wood was sundered
>   By the void of the night-mist, the breath of the town.

4. May Morris, *William Morris: Artist, Writer, Socialist,* 2 vols. (Oxford: Basil Blackwell, 1936), 2:445–56.

> On each side lay the City, and Thames ran between it
> > Dark, struggling, unheard 'neath the wheels and the feet.
> A strange dream it was that we ever had seen it,
> > And strange was the hope we had wandered to meet.

Compare Engels's description of London in *The Condition of the Working Class in England* (1844):

> Hundreds of thousands of men and women drawn from all classes and ranks of society pack the streets of London. Are they not all human beings with the same innate characteristics and potentialities? . . . Yet they rush past each other as if they had nothing in common. . . . We know well enough that this isolation of the individual—this narrow-minded egotism—is everywhere the fundamental principle of modern society. . . . The disintegration of society into individuals, each guided by his private principles and each pursuing his own aims, has been pushed to its furthest limits in London. Here indeed human society has been split into its component atoms.[5]

Richard's only consolations are his "grey-eyed" companion, and the rebellious hopes which she shares.

> From us from henceforth no fair words shall be hiding
> > The nights of the wretched, the days of the poor.
> . . . Let us grieve then—and help every soul in our sorrow;
> > Let us fear—and press forward where few dare to go;
> Let us falter in hope—and plan deeds for the morrow,
> > The world crowned with freedom, the fall of the foe.

In section 3, "Sending to the War," the two of them watch a dreary mock-heroic spectacle: a military parade in the streets of London ("the flag of an ancient people to the little breeze unfurled").

> We two stood in the street in the midst of a mighty
> > crowd, . . .
> While all about and around them the street flood ebbed and
> > flowed,
> Worn feet, grey anxious faces, grey backs bowed 'neath the
> > load.
> Lo the sons of an ancient people!
> . . . Who shall bear our name triumphant o'er every land and
> > sea,

5. Frederich Engels, *The Condition of the Working Class in England* (Stanford: Stanford University Press, 1972), 30–31.

> Read ye their souls in their faces, and what shall help you
>   there?
> Joyless, hopeless, shameless, angerless, set is their stare.

Once again, only solidarity and shared "dream[s] of . . . deliverance" give consolation:

> Sick unto death was my hope, and I turned and looked on my
>   dear,
> And beheld her frightened wonder, and her grief without a
>   tear,
> And knew how her thought was mine—when . . . somehow, I knew
>   not why,
> A dream came into my heart of deliverance drawing anigh.
> . . . my dream was become a picture of the deeds of another
>   day. . . .
> Far and far was I borne, away o'er the years to come,
> . . . Where then in my dream were the poor and the wall of
>   faces wan?
> Here and here by my side, shoulder to shoulder of man,
> Hope in the simple folk, hope in the hearts of the wise,
> For the happy life to follow, or death and the ending of lies.

Morris's hope for a "people's war" and "new peace" contrasts pointedly with the sentiments of Tennyson's *Maud* (1855), an early favorite of Morris's youth, whose superpatriotic speaker is an enthusiast for exactly the sort of imperial adventure that made the older Morris "sick unto death." Chauvinism was alien to the adult Morris, and it is impossible to imagine his writing the jingoist doggerel (say) of Tennyson's "Riflemen, form!"

The dramatic monologues of the poem's next two sections are spoken by the narrator's wife, and give expression to the poem's central exhortation that political action end as well as begin in love. Morris's two chief protagonists are pointedly egalitarian ("My wife is my servant, and I am the servant of my wife/ And we make no work for each other"), and they are also almost allegorical in their anonymity: the wife is a "country maiden" who is never named, and the husband is not actually identified as "Richard" until section 6. In section 4 ("Mother and Son"), the wife, who will later die in Paris when her child is six, addresses her young infant son. Often in Victorian poetry the birth of a male infant forecasts social change ("A Drama of Exile," "In Memoriam"): here, the mother's tone is more intimate and elegiac:

> . . . while yet thou art little and hast no thought of thine
>   own,
> I will tell thee a word of the world, of the hope whence thou
>   has grown,

> Of the love that once begat thee, of the sorrow that hath made
> Thy little heart of hunger, and thy hands on my bosom laid.
> Then mayst thou remember hereafter . . . this tale of thy
>   mother's voice,
> As oft in the calm of dawning I have heard the birds rejoice,
> As oft I have heard the storm-wind go moaning through the
>   wood,
> And I knew that earth was speaking, and the mother's voice was
>   good.

She is proud of her integrity ("I am true") and acuity ("All things I saw at a glance"), and comments with unabashed pleasure on the physical presence which her "firstling" will never really know:

> . . . to thee alone will I tell it that thy mother's body is
>   fair,
> In the guise of the country maidens who play with the sun and
>   the air,
> Yea, I am fair, my firstling, if thou couldst but remember
>   me? . . .
> I am true, but my face is a snare; soft and deep are my eyes,
> And they seem for men's beguiling fulfilled with the dreams of
>   the wise.
> Kind are my lips, and they look as though my soul had learned
> Deep things I have never heard of. My face and my hands are
>   burned
> By the lovely sun of the acres. . . .

She also remembers fondly her husband's youthful gaze, full of hope and an inchoate "wisdom" of its own:

> . . . fair and fierce is thy father, and soft and strange are
>   his eyes
> That look on the days that shall be with the hope of the brave
>   and the wise.
> It was many a day that we longed, and we lingered late at eve
> Ere speech from speech was sundered, and my hand his hand
>   could leave.

In a reciprocal tribute which appears in the following section, the husband later expresses gratitude for her admiration, and acknowledges indirectly that his eyes, also "soft," may also have suggested "deep things . . . [he] never heard of:"

> . . . I met the woman I love, and she asked, as folk ask of
>   the wise,
> Of the root and meaning of things that she saw in the world of
>   lies.
> I told her all I knew, and the tale told lifted the load
> That made me less than a man; and she set my feet on the road.

The wife's lonely monologue to her uncomprehending son manifests the tenderness and beauty of language which Morris infused into his most interesting poetic women (Aslaug, Guenevere, Psyche, and to some extent Gudrun), but also the separate emotional sphere in which they were supposed to dwell. Like Guenevere, the wife of *Pilgrims* is proud of her beauty, but the beauty is a sturdy rural comeliness ("My face and my hands are burned"), her pride in it is wryer and more muted, and she dissociates herself from the male projections her beauty evokes. Guenevere's impassioned "defence" sometimes achieves a kind of heroic stature, but the "defence" of the "country maiden" is a different sort, more appropriate to a woman who dies on the barricades:

> Such is thy mother, O firstling, yet strong as the maidens of
>   old,
> Whose spears and whose swords were the warders of homestead,
>   of field and of fold.[6]

Also included in her soliloquy to the child is a proud socialist's denunciation of "petit-bourgeois" marriage, and its pathetic proletarian imitations:

> Many a child of woman tonight is born in the town, . . .
> Many and many an one of want and use is born; . . .
> Prudence begets her thousands: "Good is a housekeeper's life,
> So shall I sell my body that I may be matron and wife."
> . . . But thou, O son, O son, of very love wert born.

Ultimately, though, her monologue is overshadowed by the sadness and lonely apprehension of someone whose deepest thoughts and hopes remain unfulfilled.

> Now waneth the night and the moon—ah, son, it is piteous
> That never again in my life shall I dare to speak to thee
>   thus.
> But sure from the wise and the simple shall the mighty come to
>   birth;

6. For the historical origins in Tacitus and Gibbon of Morris's view of Germanic women, see my "Morris' German Romances as Socialist History," *Victorian Studies* 27, no. 3 (Spring 1984): 321–42.

> And fair were my fate, beloved, if I be yet on the earth
> When the world is awakened at last. . . .

It is perhaps fitting that, like many of Morris's more significant male heroes, the wife herself was parentless ("No mother of me, the foundling"), and her deepest sense of personal and social identity mingles memories of "the lovely sun of the eves" with a projective hope that her son will somehow fulfill his parents' aspirations, in ways that she will not know:

> When . . . [o]n the eve of the toil and the battle all sorrow
>   and grief we weighed,
> We hoped and we were not ashamed, we knew and we were not
>   afraid.

Sections 5 and 6 retrace the protagonists' early efforts to survive in London, and the events and decisions which lead to their thoroughgoing conversion to "communism." It is already clear that both derive much of their Morrisian strength of character from early communion with nature. Richard is illegitimate; his father, a "rich man . . . who skulked," gave his "mother money, but left her life to scorn; . . . we dwelt alone in our village: I knew not my mother's 'shame.'" The original class-marginality of *Pilgrim*'s hero gives some plausibility to his tendency to see what he encounters through middle-class eyes (compare Jack London's *The Abyss,* and Orwell's *Down and Out in Paris and London*); he has not always been inured to the poverty he suffers as an adult, and he reacts with the sensitivity and stubborn idealism of someone who knows there are alternatives. Again, one should probably compare this situation with Morris's own, as the legitimate firstborn son and heir of a real "rich man," who may nevertheless have seemed to Morris almost as distant as Richard's absent father in the poem. Natural comparisons also arise between some aspects of Morris's upbringing (his father's early death, the idyllically pastoral life at Walthamstow, remembered for the rest of his life with great fondness, and his boyhood rambles near Marlborough College) and *Pilgrim*'s semi-idyllic descriptions of Richard's rural childhood.

> Then a lawyer paid me money, and I lived awhile at a school,
> And learned the lore of the ancients, and how the knave and
>   the fool
> Have been mostly the masters of earth: yet the earth seemed
>   fair and good
> With the wealth of field and homestead, and garden and river
>   and wood;
> And I was glad amidst it, and little of evil I knew. . . .

At the time of the Paris Commune Morris was only thirty-six, and the descriptions and life-history of Richard and his wife sometimes suggest idealized, counterfactual projections of a fringe-proletarian life Morris might have led, but did not, and a companion ("sturdy as the maidens of old") he might have had, but did not. Richard is also granted one experience Morris *seems* not to have had: friendship with "our Frenchman," also unnamed, who proudly narrates to him his part in the failed revolution of 1848 ("telling me chapters of the tale that never ends"). From London, despair at the condition of their fellow workers prompts Richard and his wife to write the Frenchman for advice ("to ask if he would be our master, and set the learners their task"), but the letter is returned marked "dead," and they know that "all that we saw henceforward with our own eyes must we see." Richard sets to work with his only physical skill, that of a joiner, and "worked as other men worked. . . . The life of the poor we learned, and to me there was nothing new/ In their day of little deeds that ever deathward drew." Quick to resist, he also has little patience with the half-measures of the more pious sorts of reformers, who "wrought me-seems as those who should make a bargain with hell,/ That it grow a little cooler, and thus forever to dwell"; so that when a workmate inevitably invites him to join him at "our Radical spouting-place" to hear "one of those Communist chaps," he readily comes. Richard is now about twenty-five, elsewhere in Morris's writings a symbolic age of maturity, and is stirred by the deepest experience of his life when a "grizzled man" rises, and speaks "as though a message he bore, . . . / Bitter to many." Unlike Richard, but like Morris himself, and rather like his descriptions of John Ball and Guest in *News from Nowhere,* the unnamed speaker is "partly shy" and physically unimpressive ("thickset and short," and "dressed in shabby blue"); but his message quickly moves Richard to "follow . . . end to end . . . the tale of the new-told gospel" (no reluctance to acknowledge that Marxism is an "alternate religion" here), and inspires intense spiritual kinship with someone whose "words were my very thoughts," who "spoke like a friend long known." Richard is disappointed only when the audience tepidly applauds, and fails afterward to "rise up with one cry/ And bid him straight enroll them":

> . . . *my* hope full well he answered . . .
> In fear lest he should escape me, I rose ere the meeting was
> done,
> And gave him my name and my faith—*and I was the only one.*
> (Emphases mine)

Richard's intense joy is again expressed in religious language ("now the streets seem gay and the high stars glittering bright/ And for me, I sing amongst them . . . I was born once long ago: I am born again tonight"), and should be compared to Morris's less poetic memories of the decision to join the Democratic

Federation in 1884: "I can only say that I did not measure my hope, nor the joy that it brought me at the time."[7] The millenarian hopes, and the sense that "even as he began it seemed as though I knew/ The thing he was going to say, though I never heard it before," were very likely Morris's own.

The section that follows (number 4, "The New Proletarian") beautifully invokes the equally intense hope and frustration of visionary hopes that remain unfulfilled. The question is put in plain but suggestive terms: "How near to the goal are we now, and what shall we have to behold" (cf., "How long, oh Lord, how long . . . ?" and "What is to be done?"). Similar biblical cadences underlie the wind's question in section 1:

> How long and for what is their patience abiding?
>   How oft and how oft shall their story be told,
> While the hope that none seeketh in darkness is hiding
>   And in grief and in sorrow the world groweth old?

Again in the language of Hebrew prophets, Richard evokes

> . . . loving kindness seared by love from our anguish torn
> Till our hope grow a wrathful fire, and the light of the
>   second birth
> Be a flame to burn up the weeds from the lean impoverished
>   earth.

His newfound "faith" is quickly tested when a corrupt lawyer defrauds the couple of a small patrimony that provided one "middle-class" pleasure, a tiny rented house near the outskirts of the city. His employer gleefully drives home the point: "Well, sir, you have got your wish. . . . And are now no thief of labour, but an honest working man," and orders him to "make an end of your [rebellious] talk/ At once and for ever henceforth, or out of my shop you walk." At this point Richard makes the remark quoted earlier that he and his wife are each other's servants, and adds that

> . . . country folk we were
> And she sickened sore for the grass and the breath of the
>   fragrant air
> That had made her lovely and strong.

For both their sakes, then, he enjoins himself to silence at least at work, but of course he has

---

7. Morris, *CW,* 23:277.

> . . . read day after day
> Whatever books I could handle, and heard about and about
> What talk was going amongst them; and I burned up doubt after
>   doubt,
> Until it befell at last that to others I needs must
>   speak. . . .

Soon afterwards, a shopmate reports his "next night's speech on the street," and his few days of forced silence come to an end.

In section 7 ("In Prison—And at Home"), the still-unnamed wife narrates subsequent events which have since led to Richard's two-month prison sentence: a "well-dressed reptile" has "screeched . . . infamies" at Richard as he spoke, and caned his wife when she angrily protested; Richard then attacked him, and was dragged away by the police. Like Richard (and Morris), she is deeply depressed by the apathy of (most of) the people socialists struggled to convince:

> . . . dull they most of them stood
> As though they heeded nothing, nor thought of bad or of good,
> While some (O the hearts of slaves!) although they might
>   understand,
> When they heard their masters and feeders called thieves of
>   wealth and of land,
> Were as angry as though *they* were cursed. Withal there were
>   some that heard. . . .

Compare Morris's sad lines of 1883:

> But the loss of the people; how are we to measure that?
> That they should have great men living and working amongst
> them, and be ignorant of the very existence of their work,
> and incapable of knowing what it means if they could see it![8]

The wife's description of the trial resembles *Commonweal* accounts: the police swear to a false testimony, whereupon a patronizing "white-haired fool" at the bench sentences Richard to two months, and advises him to become the "good" petit-bourgeois his education would permit:

> What have you got to do to preach such perilous stuff? . . .
> If you needs must preach or lecture, then hire a chapel or
>   hall;

8. Ibid., p. 168.

> Though indeed . . . you seem clever; who knows but you might
>   rise.
> And become a little builder should you condescend to be wise?

The wife broods over her husband's imprisonment, and again echoes Revelations, this time verbatim: "How long, O Lord! how long?" At section's end, the two lovers are united against a hostile world, the consolation promised by "The Message of the March Wind."

An abrupt chronological shift occurs in section 8, "The Half of Life Gone." Richard has now survived the Commune's fall with a now-motherless son, and watches in a field as "men and maids, . . . wives and gaffers grey" work to make hay:

> . . . little changed are they
> Since I was . . . amongst them. . . .
> Strange are they grown unto me; yea, I to myself am strange.

At length, he struggles to submerge his lonely resignation in one of the poem's longer lyrical celebrations of natural beauty:

> . . . though high over [the clouds], are the wings of the
>   wandering herne;
> In measureless depths about him doth the fair sky quiver and
>   burn;
> The dear sun floods the land as the morning falls toward noon,
> And a little wind is awake in the best of the latter June.

As he watches "the woman that stoops and kisses the face of the lad," he yields for a moment to illusion, and evokes his wife's lost presence, in a lingering fantasy that she has returned to the fields:

> Whose is the voice that laughs in the old familiar place?
> Whose should it be but my love's, if my love were yet on the
>   earth? . . .
>   . . . let me look and believe that all these will vanish away,
> At least when the night has fallen, and that she will be there
>   mid the hay,
> Happy and weary with work, waiting and longing for love.
> There will she be, as of old. . . .
>   . . . thus, only thus shall I see her, in dreams of the day
>   or the night, ...
> She was and she is not; there is no such thing on the earth.

His mourning is made even more painful by an estrangement that is obliquely described in the sections that follow.

In the retrospective section 9 ("A New Friend"), a middle-class socialist named Arthur (whose name, like Richard's, suggests a heroic British past) comes

> . . . to our workmen meetings some knowledge of men to learn.
> He kindled afresh at my words, although to try him I spake
> For what it was really worth. . . .

He becomes Richard's closest male comrade, in both senses of the word, encourages Richard to write, finds him commissions for political articles, and helps the couple in every way he can. Unfortunately, to everyone's mutual dismay, he falls in love with Richard's wife, and she is also drawn to him in turn, before both die on the barricades. Throughout all of this, Richard struggles to preserve his original idealistic respect for his friend, who remains for him in some senses "like a perfect knight of old time as the poets would have them to be":

> He loved me; he grieved my soul: now the love and the grief
>   are past;
> He is gone with his eager learning, his sadness and his mirth,
> His hope and his fond desire. There is no such thing on the
>   earth. . . .

The cadence of the last sentence repeats Richard's earlier, twice-repeated lament for his wife, and the section ends with a quiet valediction:

> He died not unbefriended—nor unbeloved maybe.
> Betwixt my life and his longing there rolls a boundless sea.
> And what are those memories now to all that I have to do.
> The deeds to be done so many, the days of my life so few?

Section 10, "Ready to Depart," describes the sober preparations of Richard, his wife, and Arthur to join the last Paris Communard defenses against the armies of the bourgeoisie. Just before departure, they sit together in the "fire-lit room," and talk of "Betrayers and betrayed in . . . France":

> As I spoke the word "betrayed," my eyes met his in a glance,
> And swiftly he turned away; then back with a steady gaze . . .
> I knew though he looked on me, he saw not me, but my wife:
> And he reddened up to the brow. . . .

The wife's response—affectionate pity, unmixed with contrition—confirms his fears:

> "O Richard, Richard!" she said, and her arms about me came,
> And her tears and the lips that I loved were on my face once
>   more.
> A while I clung to her body . . . then we sundered and sore she
>   wept, . . . we sat apart again,
> Not speaking, while between us was the sharp and bitter
>   pain. . . .

This obvious estrangement is tempered by a paradoxical solidarity: they face this alienation together, as a *common* problem:

> We were gentle and kind together, and if any had seen us so,
> They had said, "These two are one in the face of all trouble
>   and woe."
> But indeed as a wedded couple we shrank from the eyes of men,
> As we dwelt together and pondered on the days that come not
>   again.

The scene's psychological awkwardness is oddly plausible, and Richard's responses may reflect Morris's to Jane Morris's liaison with Rossetti in the early 1870s, conveyed in letters and veiled autobiographical descriptions at the time. Richard compares himself to those whose lives have been

> . . . so empty and bare
> That they have no words of complaining; nor so happy have they
>   been,
> That they may measure sorrow or tell what grief may mean . . .

In a letter of 25 November 1872, Morris wrote:

> One thing wanting ought not to go for so much. . . . to have real friends and some sort of an aim in life is so much, that I might still think myself lucky: and often in my better moods I wonder what it is in me that throws me into rage and despair at other times.[9]

In the same letter, he remarks that Jane is "very good and kind to me," notes "her company is always pleasant," and regrets her absence.

9. Norman Kelvin, ed., *The Letters of William Morris,* 2 vols. (Princeton: Princeton University Press, 1984), 1:172.

When Arthur brings the news that the siege of Paris is reaching its climax, the couple listen keenly, and Richard suggests that it might be appropriate to go

> ". . . we three together, and there to die like men."
> "Nay," [Arthur] said, "to live and be happy like men." Then
>   he flushed up red
> And she no less. . . .
> I reached out my hand unto him, and I kissed her once on the
>   brow,
> But no word craving forgiveness, and no word of pardon e'en
>   now.

The triangle in *Pilgrims of Hope* is an unresolved narrative complication, but it also provides Morris with a model instance of sublimation for the larger political cause. A less oblique account of the estrangement might have seemed more realistic (compare the wife's memory of the doomed deputy's affairs in *Z*), but it would also have diminished the tone of political empathy with which Morris wished to end the poem.

Michael Holzman has argued that the triangular subplot is especially prominent in *The Pilgrims of Hope* because the dates of the Paris Commune corresponded to the period of Morris's own greatest marital stress;[10] but such configurations appear also in Morris's work as early as the juvenilia of the 1850s—the early poem "Fame," for example, and the 1856 prose romance "Gertha's Lovers"—as well as in *The Defence* and—most strikingly—in one of the best *Earthly Paradise* tales, "The Lovers of Gudrun," written in June 1869. Here, the configuration recapitulates not only (some poetic counterpart of) Morris's response to Jane Morris's rejection, but also a time-lapsed version of his more gradual progression (*after* the period of the Commune) toward socialism, in a series of related motifs: disappointment, loneliness, and renunciation of sexual rivalry; inward struggle to retain and deepen an ethic of generosity; and transference of private hopes to strenuous public activity and revolutionary socialism ("my soul was cleared of confusion, as nigher the deed-time drew," section 10).

Broader ethical imperatives are also present in Morris's earlier uses of the triangular love motif: the rejected suitor in "Gertha's Lovers" serves his successful rival, King Olaf, and the unloved Bodli of "The Lovers of Gudrun" struggles (and fails) to balance his deepest loyalties, to his lifelong friend and his wife; similar imperatives reappear later in *The Roots of the Mountains, News from Nowhere,* and *Water of the Wondrous Isles.* Rossetti caricatured Morris

10. Michael Holzman, "Propaganda, Passion, and Literary Art in William Morris's *The Pilgrims of Hope*," *Texas Studies in Literature and Language* 24, no. 4 (Winter 1982): 377.

several times, verbally as well as visually, but Morris never complained directly in any extant correspondence about Rossetti's behavior, or that of his wife.

In sections 11, 12, and 13—"A Glimpse of the Coming Day," "Meeting the War Machine," and "The Story's Ending," appear some of Morris's finest lyrical invocations of the beauty of earth and hope for its betterment. The three English revolutionaries arrive in Paris, and witness the people's joyful celebrations of liberation by the Communards. The youthful Wordsworth's earlier exultation at the French Revolution, "Good was it in that day to be alive/ But to be young was very heaven"[11] echoes not only in Richard's more plain-spoken certainty that "that day at last of all days I knew what life was worth,/ I say that I saw [the coming day] now, real, solid and at hand," but also in the pain of pastoral remembrance and kindred hopes for his beloved land which follow.

All three characters work to exhaustion: Richard's wife "wears the brancard of the ambulence-women," and Arthur "as in all he did,/ Showed a cheerful ready talent that nowise might be hid; And . . . hurt the pride of no man." Inevitably, however, the narration approaches the Commune's final fall:

> . . . many a thing we learned, but we learned not how to
>   prevail
> O'er the brutal war-machine, the ruthless grinder of
>   bale; . . . .
> It drew on nearer and nearer, and we 'gan to look to the end—
> We three, at least—and our lives began with death to blend;
> Though we were long a-dying. . . .

In one characteristic skirmish, his wife suddenly turns to him with an unexpectedly deep, intimate look:

> . . . straight she looked upon me with such lovely, friendly
>   eyes
> Of the days gone by and remembered, that up from my heart 'gan
>   rise
> The choking sobbing passion. . . .

It is her last gaze, for she suddenly turns with him in shocked horror to see "a man who was running and crouching, stagger and fall." As they both run to the dying Arthur, Richard is wounded and his wife is killed.

> . . . thereafter as [Arthur and Richard's wife] lay
> Both dead on the litter together, . . . folk who knew not us,

---

11. William Wordsworth, *The Prelude,* ed. Carlos Baker (New York: Holt, Rinehart, and Winston, 1954), 392.

> But were moved by seeing the twain so fair and so piteous,
> Took them for husband and wife who were fated there to die,
> Or, it may be lover and lover indeed—but what know I?

Richard thus preserves his empathy and respect into death, a pattern reminiscent of earlier Morris narratives such as the 1856 "Story of the Unknown Church" and the 1858 "Concerning Geoffray Teste Noire." The deaths of Arthur and Richard's wife here are part of a general hecatomb, of course, and the wounded Richard is extraordinarily fortunate that he later survives the Commune's fall. Well aware of this, Richard pleads with a nurturant Earth to remember these unrecognized heroes "of the latter days," as he returns to England to raise his son, whom he will try to infuse with his own ideals, and prepare for the new revolution to come. Like the "old Frenchman" of his youth, he will now preserve the Communards' memory, and that of his friends—"Their life was thy deliverance, O Earth, and for thee they fought—... and we were a part of it all, the beginning of the end." In the poem's final section, "The Story's Ending," Morris pleads with the poem's *Commonweal* audience to revere the memory of the Communards in their turn, and reenact their deeds:

> Amid them shall spring up the story. . . .
> Year after year shall men meet with the red flag over head,
> And shall call on the help of the vanquished and the kindness
>   of the dead.

The Pilgrims of Hope thus provides a stoic as well as millenarian response to obvious questions of catastrophic failure and loss. Morris was well aware that socialism could not survive many moral "victories" such as the crushing of the Paris Commune, and he disdained palliation. In "L'Envoi" to *The Earthly Paradise* he had defended the poem's confessional honesty as a faithful rendition of his own weaknesses, and in the early 1870s, he turned away from an enormous potential audience for his narratives when he no longer felt himself able to express his deepest preoccupations honestly in his poetry.[12] His answer to the question "How long?" mixed fatalism about our personal and collective inadequacies with belief in communal ideals that make it possible, for a time at least, to transcend them. Recurrent estrangements between men and women, in particular, seemed to Morris part of the natural order: in a familiar passage in *News from Nowhere,* Hammond notes that in the new society "We do not deceive ourselves, indeed, or believe that we can get rid of all the trouble that besets the dealings between the sexes."[13] In a 1886 letter to Burne-Jones, the fifty-two-

    12. See my *The Design of 'The Earthly Paradise'* (Lewiston, N.Y.: Edwin Mellen Press, 1989), 383–84.
    13. *CW,* 16:57.

year-old Morris expressed briefly a desire to be "twenty years younger," so that he could serve more vigorously the cause of socialism, but added that then "there would be the Female complication somewhere. Best as it is after all."[14]

Morris thus blended personal and psychological acceptance of loss with his utopian communism: our private lives are troubled by inevitable forms of personal alienation, but we are all the more urgently advised therefore to seek new social orders to mitigate them. Salvation may recede before us, but our deepest glimpses of it are communal. To Freud's claim that "civilization" ("Kultur") is founded on repression of pleasurable instincts, Morris would have countered that what needs sublimation are not "instincts," especially sexual ones, but the possessiveness of destructive self-pity. In the language of *Socialism: Its Growth and Outcome:* "socialistic religion would be that higher form of conscience that would impel us to actions on behalf of a future of the race, such as no man [*sic*] could command in his ordinary moods."[15]

Another familiar tenet of the "socialistic religion" that Morris tried sincerely to live was the injunction, expressed in *Socialism: Its Growth and Outcome,* that marriage be based on "mutual inclination and affection, an association terminable at the will of either party. It is easy to see how great the gain would be to morality and sentiment in this change. . . . There would be no vestige of reprobation weighing on the dissolution of one tie and the forming of another."[16] Richard, the narrator of *Pilgrims,* did not "own" his wife's attachment, and could not blame her therefore for its loss. Threats of death had not been easy for either of them to face—"no hatred of life, thou knowest, O Earth mid the bullets I bore—" but adherence to this sexual ethic may have been for Richard an even more difficult test. He passed both, and survived with his integrity and idealism intact.

Richard's personal struggles thus recapitulate the poem's basic theme—that revolutionary commitment is deepened by tragic loss. A more psychologically detailed examination of the hero's struggle for emotional equilibrium would be desirable, but might have seemed inappropriate for a poem designed to illustrate political themes for a *Commonweal* audience. As it is, Richard's clear-sighted response to marital loss reinforces his stature as a poetic hero who achieves that tenuous equilibrium in his personal as well as political life, despite his personal inadequacies, (relative) poverty, and vulnerability to political oppression.

In an essay on "The Lesser Arts," Morris advised artists to seek instruction in both "Nature and History," and *Pilgrims of Hope,* like his other socialist writings, conveys an equal sense of both these poles of human experience.

14. Philip Henderson, ed., *The Letters of William Morris to His Family and Friends* (London: Longmans, 1950), 248.

15. Bax and Morris, *Socialism: Its Growth and Outcome,* 298–99.

16. Ibid., 299–300.

Morris's socialist writings are not simplistically didactic, and they seldom employ the detailed characterization of realistic fiction, but they do explore recurrent psychological and historical cycles of utopian and tragic experience. Their primary aim is usually not detailed analysis of an unjust system or advocacy of revolutionary doctrine, but re-creation of the underlying *motives* of communist belief and endeavor. Again and again, *Pilgrims* contrasts lyrical evocations of benign nature and unpossessive love with sharp, ironic accounts of mundane corruption and viciousness, and the alternations deny facile retreats into private tranquility. The sympathetic reader of *Pilgrims of Hope* and Morris's other socialist romances is caught again and again in renewed cycles of communal effort, and suspension or failure of each cycle suggests the need once again to redeem past experience within another. In *Pilgrims of Hope,* as in all of Morris's most serious art, this balance of interior vision and historical reality provides evidence that struggle and resistance within these cycles may yet achieve some of our deepest human purposes.

CAROLE G. SILVER
Joseph Riggs Dunlap
Pilgrim of Hope

The story of Joseph Riggs Dunlap is, in effect, the story of the birth and growth of the William Morris Society in America. For, to suggest that Joe (as most people call him) almost single-handedly fostered Morris studies in the United States is only slightly hyperbolic. While his tangible contributions to scholarship, though extensive, may be chronicled and even bibliographed, the spirit in which he lives and works—his commitment to the ideas and values espoused by Morris—is less easily catalogued. For this reason, it seems appropriate to dedicate a volume of intangibles—thought, hopes, perceptions—to him.

Born in 1913 in China, where his father served as a medical doctor, Joe lived in the Orient until he was almost fifteen. Even his childhood reading led him to Morris. Such books as *The Boy's King Arthur,* with its illustrations by Howard Pyle, created an interest in what he then thought was medievalism (and later learned was Victorian medievalism). His high school career was interrupted by tuberculosis, but he entered the College of Wooster (Ohio) in 1932. He does not remember whether his undergraduate years included the study of William Morris, but the groundwork for his later interest was laid by his recognition of how large a role Victorian medievalism played in Victorian art, architecture, literature, ecclesiastical decoration, and political life.

It was in a course on books and printing at the Columbia University Library School that Joe first learned about Morris's contributions to the book arts— essentially negative contributions, according to the instructor. And, it was in the late 1930s, while working at the library of City College, that he saw and began to browse in the twenty-four-volume *Collected Works.* His real involvement with Morris commenced after the Second World War when, with the help of the G.I. Bill, he began coursework toward the Ph.D. at Columbia. Interested in the history of printing, he wrote an initial paper on Morris's views on book and print design. At about the same time, his reading of Mackail's *Life* and of Morris's early and late prose romances cemented his interest in a figure he found both multifaceted and fascinating. He began to collect Kelmscott Press books and other samples of Morris's craftsmanship, purchasing *A Dream of John Ball,* for example, for some twenty-five dollars. And, he decided to concentrate on that aspect of Morris which most intrigued him, Morris as a printer and maker of books.

A six-month sabbatical spent in England in the winter and spring of 1957 was a watershed in his career, for Joseph Riggs Dunlap became the second American member of the newly formed William Morris Society. He met the aged and infirm Sydney Cockerell (Morris's friend and personal secretary), and he began to locate the important Morris materials he was later to use and to share with others. He became eastern secretary of the William Morris Society (a position he was to hold until 1983) and thus, one of the founders of the Morris Society in America.

Later trips to England brought further and fuller acquaintance with others interested in and informed about Morris. Joe had a second visit with Cockerell in response to a message from Sir Sydney that read: "If you have any more questions you'd better come to England and you'd better come soon." He began the arduous process of tracking down the descendants of Harold Peirce, a Philadelphia lawyer who had collected materials associated with William Morris. Because of Margaret and Mary Peirce and Joe's efforts on their behalf, the Berg Collection of the New York Public Library and the City College Library gained a rich trove of letters and memorabilia. Joe also began his own collection of the trial sheets for the Kelmscott Press, many of them bearing decorated borders that showed the process of Morris's brain and hands at work.

By the mid–1960s, Joe had become one of the major resource people in America on all aspects of Morris. Almost single-handedly, he created, organized, and administered William Morris Society activities on the East Coast. He invited speakers, created seminars, organized celebrations, and wrote and circulated an American newsletter, "News from Anywhere." His energy and enthusiasm were major factors in creating the revival of American interest in Morris in the 1960s. He aided everyone—from designers and graduate students (myself among them) to renowned literary historians—in searches and researches. In addition, he began to produce his own important scholarship on Morris and the book arts—commentaries on Morris's calligraphy and manuscript illumination as well as on his work in printed books before the Kelmscott Press.

Beginning with *William Caxton and William Morris: Comparisons and Contrasts* (1964), a study of the similarities and differences between the two great printers, Joe published a series of essays on Morris as a printer; part of his doctoral dissertation on the subject (he received his Ph.D. from Columbia University in 1975) was included in the *Victorian Poetry* Special Issue on William Morris (vol. 13, nos. 3–4, Fall–Winter 1975); he contributed "William Morris: Calligrapher" to *William Morris and the Art of the Book,* ed. Charles

Ryskamp (New York: Pierpont Morgan Library, 1976), and he wrote his favorite essay, "On the Heritage of William Morris: Some Considerations, Typographic, and Otherwise," for the New York Typophiles in 1976. In the early 1970s, as well, he put together May Morris's important introductions to the *Collected Works* in an accessible two-volume edition (New York: Oriole Editions, 1973). His book on the scheme that never materialized, the collaboration between Morris and Edward Burne-Jones to create a beautiful edition of *The Earthly Paradise, The Book That Never Was,* was published by Oriole Editions in 1971. Throughout the 1970s, Joe continued to work, spending much time in editing and arranging the publication of volumes of scholarly papers for the William Morris Society in America. He contributed richly to such volumes as *Studies in the Late Romances of William Morris* (WMS, 1975), *The After-Summer Seed: Recon-siderations of . . . Sigurd the Volsung,* (1978), and most recently, Florence Boos's edition of *The Juvenilia of William Morris* (1983).

But his contributions to Morris studies far transcend his contributions as a writer, editor, and collector. His generosity in lending what he owns, from fabric and wallpaper samples to rare editions, is remarkable. The same gener-osity makes him the reader, formal or informal, of the work of others on Morris. He is the person one telephones or writes to for the date of something, the name of a minor figure Morris knew, the location of a stained glass window. If he does not know the answer, he will find it, using a combination of his skills as a librarian and what can only be described as second-sight. It is he, as well, who connects other Morris enthusiasts, serving as a conduit between scholars who need each other and between people who might enjoy each other.

It is no surprise that Joseph Riggs Dunlap's favorite work by William Morris is *News from Nowhere,* for he lives by its parting adage. He has followed the injunction to: "Go on living while you may, striving, with whatsoever pain and labor needs must be, to build up little by little the new day of fellowship, and rest, and happiness." He has helped to make others see a "vision rather than a dream." Because the true spirit of fellowship informs all he does, we dedicate this volume to him.

SUGGESTED FURTHER READING

ANDERSON, PERRY. "Utopias." In *Arguments within English Marxism,* 157–75. London: New Left Books, 1980.

BAX, E. B., and WILLIAM MORRIS. *Socialism: Its Growth and Outcome.* London: Swan Sonnenschein, 1893.

BERNERI, MARIE LOUISE. "William Morris: Nowhere." In *Journey through Utopia.* London: Routledge and Kegan Paul, 1950.

BONO, BARBARA. "The Prose Fictions of William Morris: A Study in the Literary Aesthetic of a Victorian Social Reformer." *Victorian Poetry* 13 (1975): 43–59.

BOOS, FLORENCE S. "Morris' German Romances as Socialist History." *Victorian Studies* 27 (1984): 321–42.

BRANTLINGER, PATRICK. "*Nowhere:* William Morris's Socialist Anti-Novel." *Victorian Studies* 19 (1975): 35–49.

FRYE, NORTHROP. "Varieties of Literary Utopias." *Daedalus* 94 (1965): 323–47.

GOODE, JOHN. "William Morris and the Dream of Revolution." In *Literature and Politics of the Nineteenth Century,* edited by John Lucas, 221–80. London: Methuen, 1971.

GRENNAN, MARGARET R. *William Morris: Medievalist and Revolutionary.* New York: King's Crown Press, 1945.

HOLZMAN, MICHAEL. "Propaganda, Passion and Literary Art in William Morris' *Pilgrims.*" *Texas Studies in Literature and Language* 24 (1982): 372–93.

LE MIRE, EUGENE. *Unpublished Lectures of William Morris.* Detroit: Wayne State University Press, 1969.

MACDONALD, J. ALEX. "The Revision of *Nowhere.*" *Journal of the William Morris Society* 3, no. 3 (Summer 1976): 8–15.

MEIER, PAUL. *William Morris: The Marxist Dreamer.* Translated by Frank Gubb. Atlantic Highlands, N.J.: Harvester, 1978.

MORRIS, MAY. *William Morris: Artist Writer Socialist.* 2 vols. Oxford: Basil Blackwell, 1936.

MORRIS, WILLIAM. *The Collected Works of William Morris.* Edited by May Morris. 24 vols. London: Longmans, 1910–1915.

———. *The Socialist Diary of William Morris.* Edited by Florence Boos. London: Journeyman Press, 1985.

MORRIS, WILLIAM, et al., eds. *The Commonweal,* 1885–1889. In *Commonweal* Morris published: "Socialism from the Root Up," coauthored with Ernest Belfort Bax, May 1886–May 1888; "The Pilgrims of Hope," April 1885–June 1886; "A

Dream of John Ball," November 1886–January 1887; "News from Nowhere," January–October 1890.

MORTON, A. L. Introduction to *The Political Writings of William Morris*. New York: International, 1973.

MORTON, A. L., ed. Introduction to *Three Works by William Morris*. New York: International, 1968.

NAIRNE, SANDY, TERESA NEWMAN, IAN TOD, and RAY WATKINSON, eds. *William Morris Today*. London: Institute for Contemporary Arts, 1984.

REDMOND, JAMES, ed. *News from Nowhere*. London: Routledge and Kegan Paul, 1972.

SILVER, CAROLE. "Eden and Apocalypse: William Morris's Marxist Vision in the 1880's." *University of Hartford Studies in Literature* 13 (1981): 62–77.

———. *The Romance of William Morris*. Athens: Ohio University Press, 1981.

SPEAR, JEFFREY L. "Political Questing: Ruskin, William Morris, and Romance." In *New Approaches to Ruskin: Thirteen Essays,* edited by Robert Hewison, 175–93. London: Routledge and Kegan Paul, 1981.

THOMPSON, E. P. *William Morris: Romantic to Revolutionary.* 2d ed. New York: Pantheon, 1978.

WILDING, MICHAEL. *Political Fictions.* London: Routledge and Kegan Paul, 1980.

ABOUT THE CONTRIBUTORS_____

FLORENCE BOOS is Professor of English at the University of Iowa and former chairperson of the governing committee of the William Morris Society in the United States. She has edited Morris's *Juvenilia* (1982) and *Socialist Diary* (1982; reprinted in 1985); assembled and edited *Bibliography of Women and Literature* (1989); and written *The Poetry of Dante G. Rossetti* (1976) and *The Design of 'The Earthly Paradise'* (1989).

LAURA DONALDSON has taught English and Women's Studies and published widely in the area of feminist and critical theory. Her book *The Miranda Complex: Colonialism and the Question of Feminist Reading* will be published by the University of North Carolina Press.

MICHAEL HOLZMAN is a consultant for the New York State public school system. He is the author of *Lukács Road to God: The Early Criticism against the Pre-Marxist Background* (1985) and co-author with Marilyn Cooper of *Writing as a Social Action* (1988).

LARRY D. LUTCHMANSINGH is associate professor of art history at Bowdoin College. He works in the area of modern and Victorian art and is currently engaged in a study of the Arts and Crafts Movement.

ALEX MACDONALD is associate professor of English at Campion College, University of Regina. He teaches Victorian literature as well as Utopian literature and thought.

LYMAN TOWER SARGENT is professor of political science at the University of Missouri–St. Louis. He is the editor of *Consent: Concept, Capacity, Conditions, and Constraints,* Papers from the Sixth Conference of Amintayshi (1979), and the author of *Contemporary Political Ideologies: A Comparative Analysis* (1969), *New Left Thought: An Introduction* (1972,) and *British and American Utopian Literature, 1516–1975: An Annotated Bibliography* (1979).

CAROLE SILVER is professor of English at Stern College, Yeshiva University and chairperson of the University's Division of Humanities. She is the author and editor of many articles and several books on William Morris, most notably *The Romance of William Morris* (1982) and *The Golden Chain: Essays on Willliam Morris and Pre-Raphaelitism* (1982). She has recently completed a revised edition of *Kind Words: A*

Thesaurus of Euphemisms, coauthored with Judith Neaman, and is presently finishing a book on the Victorian fascination with fairylore.

DARKO SUVIN is professor of English and Comparative Literature at McGill University. He is the author of *Metamorphoses of Science Fiction* (1979), *Victorian Science Fiction in the United Kingdom* (1983), and *Positions and Presuppositons in Science Fiction* (1988). He is also the author of other books and articles on theater and the theory of culture and of a book of verse, *The Long March* (1987).

NORMAN TALBOT has been a specialist in William Morris since reading the prose romances in 1968. He is associate professor at the University of Newcastle, New South Wales, Australia, and has published widely on literature of the last two centuries, especially on Keats, Dickens, and Morris. His special interest in narratology has recently focused on a year as visiting fellow at Linacre College, Oxford, studying the myriad versions and variations of the story of the Temptress. He has also published many volumes of poetry.

CHRIS WATERS has taught at Harvard and Stanford universities and for the Open University in Britain. Interested in the history of popular culture and socialist theory, he has recently completed a book, *British Socialists and the Politics of Popular Culture, 1884-1918.* He is currently an assistant professor of history at Williams College.

INDEX